AF837057

Anxiety and the Contradictions of Culture

Anxiety and the Contradictions of Culture

A Lacanian Approach to Gaze, Sex, Race, and Social Change

Stephen Felder

LEXINGTON BOOKS
Lanham • Boulder • New York • London

Published by Lexington Books
An imprint of The Rowman & Littlefield Publishing Group, Inc.
4501 Forbes Boulevard, Suite 200, Lanham, Maryland 20706
www.rowman.com

86-90 Paul Street, London EC2A 4NE

Copyright © 2024 by The Rowman & Littlefield Publishing Group, Inc.

All rights reserved. No part of this book may be reproduced in any form or by any electronic or mechanical means, including information storage and retrieval systems, without written permission from the publisher, except by a reviewer who may quote passages in a review.

British Library Cataloguing in Publication Information Available

Library of Congress Cataloging-in-Publication Data

Names: Felder, Stephen, author.
Title: Anxiety and the contradictions of culture : a Lacanian approach to gaze, sex, race, and social change / Stephen Felder.
Description: Lanham : Lexington Books, 2024. | Includes bibliographical references and index. | Summary: "Anxiety and the Contradictions of Culture explores anxiety from the perspective of Lacan's claim that anxiety is a "signal of the Real." Showing how our relationship with anxiety is intertwined with our fantasies, Felder unpacks how anxiety is related to the gaze, sex, race, and our capacity for social change" Provided by publisher.
Identifiers: LCCN 2024028599 | ISBN 9781666947212 (cloth) | ISBN 9781666947229 (ebook)
Subjects: LCSH: Anxiety. | Social change.
Classification: LCC BF575.A6 F45 2024 | DDC 303.401/9—dc23/eng/20240705
LC record available at https://lccn.loc.gov/2024028599

Dedication

For Corinne, whose love has made me believe that "happy" just might be "what I was made for."

In memory of Roy Bauer, who taught me the value of "remaining disgruntled."

Contents

Acknowledgments

I want to thank Judith Lakämper at Lexington Books for her interest in my work, perceptive comments, and help in bringing this book into print.

I am forever grateful to my friend and colleague Jamie Poster, who has been with me through good times and bad. Your support, humor, questions, and insights have meant more to me than you will ever know. Thank you for always taking me seriously.

I am also thankful to the Cultural Studies Association (CSA) for giving me opportunities to present early versions of some of the arguments presented in this book. I am especially thankful for the Theories of Cultural Studies working group within the CSA that has provided a place where very different ideas and approaches are discussed in ways that are both rigorous and cordial, if sometimes heated. I am especially thankful to Rob Carley for his generous support and encouragement and to Mimi Yang for her helpful questions and insights.

I am also very indebted to the Lack organization, especially the central committee: Jennifer Friedlander, Henry Krips, Todd McGowan, and Hilary Neroni. You have created a community like no other in academia. Thank you for the opportunity to present my work at the Lack conferences and for the many things you do to support this field of research.

I am forever indebted to Dick Frank, Mark Poster, Jim Givens, Ken Pomeranz, Marjorie Beale, Page Dubois, and Alice Fahs for their roles in developing my interest in theory.

I am also very indebted to Jhuma Chakraborty at the Irvine Valley College Library for all of her help in acquiring the books I needed to do my research. I could not have done this, or any of my other work, without your help.

Special thanks to Brooke Bui, the Dean of the School of Liberal Arts at Irvine Valley College, for her support, even having a cot delivered to my office when I was going through chemotherapy, and for championing my efforts.

I count it a privilege to be a member of the same department as Brittany Adams, Lisa Alvarez, Roy Bauer, Henry Carnie, Araceli Centanino, Frank Marmolejo, and Jamie Poster. You are the best colleagues anyone in academia has ever had! You have always made me feel like I am not alone in this fight. Your engagement with me and our students has contributed so much to the thoughts and feelings developed in this book.

I am also thankful to my many students at Irvine Valley College for their insights, questions, and encouragement.

Finally, I want to thank Corinne, Justin, Elly, Sloane, Maren, and Annie for the ways in which you have helped me think through the relevance of the ideas in this book.

Introduction

Feeling Anxiety

Jamieson Webster tells us that "anxiety alerts us to neurosis better than even the hysteric can, for, at the very least, anxiety is something everyone knows about."[1] While writing this book, her claim was confirmed every time someone asked me what I was working on. Everyone seems to know about anxiety, though certainly it is more disruptive for some than others. Anxiety is not simply a feeling of dread; *it is a feeling we often dread*. People will often go to great lengths to avoid anxiety: taking buses instead of planes, changing majors in college, breaking up with a romantic partner, avoiding public places, refusing to perform in public despite one's talent, and so on. Its effects can vary, from a general feeling of being ill-at-ease to debilitating panic attacks. It affects us not only mentally but also physically. We can feel a tightness in our throats, butterflies or even pain in our stomachs, a tightness in our chests, shortness of breath, dizziness, and even depersonalization and derealization. It can also be expressed in a variety of ways. We can say we are "anxious," "worried," or "stressed" in the face of both daily challenges and life-altering catastrophes. We can describe our general mood as one of "angst" when we feel serious uncertainties about our place in the world. Regardless of the intensity of the feeling, we often try to avoid feeling it, even at the cost of significantly altering plans and lifestyles.

But anxiety is still there. Sara Ahmed points out that anxiety can be "sticky," attaching to more and more things, and that often in anxiety, our thoughts "move quickly" as "one thinks of more and more things to be anxious about."[2] Sleep experts tell us to turn off all of our devices at least thirty minutes before going to sleep and not to fall asleep with the TV on, but many of us cannot fall asleep without doing these things. We need something to help us "turn off" the voice in our heads before we can find slumber. During the day, the constant blare of the television and the endless pipeline of podcasts in our ears can also be a way to avoid our own anxious thoughts. But often, all the racket just makes us more anxious. For many people, this constant onslaught of anxiety becomes debilitating, and without professional and pharmaceutical support, they cannot function.

Rollo May, in his classic work on anxiety, began his book with the claim that "clinical experience has proved to psychologists and psychiatrists generally that the central problem in psychotherapy is the nature of anxiety."[3] He goes on to stress that both loneliness and feelings of homelessness are widespread problems related to the experience of anxiety among people whose afflictions might not rise to the level of pathology. In response to a series of such claims, in his history of anxiety, Allan V. Horwitz has concluded that "no natural dividing line marks where normal anxiety ends and pathological conditions begin."[4] It permeates the social world. In general, anxiety experienced in the face of the uncertainties associated with severe disruptions caused by war, natural disasters, and major economic upheaval tends to be considered non-pathological because it just seems like a normal reaction to catastrophic events as opposed to the pathological forms of anxiety that tend to be destabilizing even in the absence of extreme circumstances. From this point of view, an experience of anxiety is pathological when it is not experienced in the face of a major disruption. If this is true, then most of us are pathologically anxious. In fact, a commonplace suggests that fear is something we experience in the face of real and present danger, while anxiety lacks such a real object.

But this is not particularly helpful for those experiencing anxiety. Not only does anxiety traverse mind and body, it also traverses the inside-outside divide. We might think that anxiety is "just in our heads." This is often what we are told when we are feeling anxious. But anxiety is clearly not all in our heads. It seems to be both "in our heads" and in the world. As Jamieson Webster put it, "anxiety, both body and not body at once or, perhaps better, inhabiting the thin line between the two speaks to some impossible process taking place between a body and the world, my body and yours."[5] It is not that anxiety is not related to real objects in the world; rather, it is that anxiety registers the intersubjective background shaping the way we are relating to those objects. Anxiety often causes us to react as if there is something in the world to be avoided. And yet, the thing we feel must be avoided does not necessarily possess any threatening qualities of its own, as it does in the case of fear. I sometimes feel fear about going to the dentist when I know some major work involving a lot of drilling is going to be done, knowing that something painful might happen. I feel anxiety when I go to the dentist for a cleaning because the hygienist is very judgmental. Each visit, I wonder if my hygiene will meet her approval as she gazes inside my mouth with microscopic lenses in search of plaque with disapproving sighs. Her disapproval is not in my head, but neither is my anxiety inevitable. There is something about me that makes her real disapproval particularly distressing. There is something in anxiety that is neither in me nor outside of me but operates exactly where the inside and outside meet. Still, the situations in which we face anxiety often have a seemingly universal quality, expressing something that we all have in common, but even in those situations, we feel our particular experience of anxiety as our own, as if it is revealing something deeply personal about us. While I feel anxious about the dental hygienist, I do not feel anxious about flying, even though others find that experience overwhelming. But all of us understand how both going to the dentist and flying could be anxiety-inducing situations.

So how do we locate anxiety? On November 14, 1962, Jacques Lacan began a year-long seminar on anxiety.[6] He suggested that constructing a "safety net" of affects related to anxiety, structuring it according to the principal concepts in Freud's book *Inhibitions, Symptoms, and Anxiety*, would allow us to see where anxiety fits in the affective life of the subject. The plan was to get at what anxiety is and identify how it affects us, by thinking about it in relation to these other psychoanalytic concepts. By seeing anxiety in relation to other affective experiences, like embarrassment and "acting out," he puts us in a better position to understand exactly what anxiety is and where we should locate it. He does this schematically by erecting a table configuring these affective experiences in terms of "movement" and "difficulty." The terms are arranged from top to bottom in terms of the movement the affect generates in the subject; they are arranged from left to right in terms of the difficulty they give the subject. As one moves from top to bottom, more movement is being generated in the subject. As one moves from left to right, more difficulty is being experienced.

The terms that cut diagonally from top left to bottom right are the three defining terms in Freud's *Inhibition, Symptom, and Anxiety*. Lacan claims that inhibition, symptoms, and anxiety "do not sit at the same level" at all.[8] This becomes clear when one considers them in terms of the two axes he deploys here. Of the three, inhibition certainly represents the least movement, while anxiety represents the most. (This may seem odd if you think of anxiety as paralyzing, but, as we will see, in the life of the subject, *anxiety creates a lot of movement, even if the movement is not externally noticeable.*) Similarly, we can see that our symptoms give us more difficulty than our inhibitions, *but*

Table 0.1 Lacan's Net of Feeling[7]

Inhibition	Impediment	Embarrassment
Emotion	Symptom	*Passage à l'acte*
Turmoil	Acting-Out	Anxiety

anxiety gives the subject the most difficulty. Thus, he shows us that anxiety is where movement and difficulty are at their extreme.

Inhibition, Lacan tells us, functions in terms of movement; it is "the halting of movement that's involved," which we could also see in terms of a "keeping in check." In inhibition, the subject is kept in line. At a level of greater difficulty, but the same level of movement as inhibition, is "*impediment*." Here the impediment is right above the symptom because it is a kind of symptom, but one that is "tucked away in a museum" in the sense that it is not as noticeable as symptoms, and definitely not as obtrusive as "acting out," but they all make themselves present in the lives of the subject in ways that cannot be missed. In the case of impediments, he cites the word's etymology, from the Latin *impedicare*, which Lacan translates as "*être pris au piège*,"—"to be trapped"—to highlight the way in which impediment (*empêchement*)[9]

> implies the relationship between one dimension and something that comes to interfere with it and . . . impedes not the function . . . but truly and verily the subject. Here then is what brings us closer to what we are searching for, namely, what happens in what goes by the name of anxiety.[10]

At the symbolic level, this is linked to castration, according to Lacan. An obvious example would be a speech impediment. One knows the word but cannot quite get it out. Or perhaps this could be linked to impotence. The symptom registers itself with a lack of movement. Lacan says that here, at impediment, one is ensnared "by his own image, the specular image."[11] This is the image upon which theideal ego is based. This is the subject's vision of itself. In impediment, this image is an alien image that imagines a kind of wholeness and competence. Right there, at the point of competence, the very image of this competence sets a snare for the subject and brings things to a halt. We could take this to mean that at the point where the subject wants to present an image of competence and completeness, it (unconsciously) knows that the image is alien, it is not the subject. Both inhibition and impediment are at the minimal level of motion, but impediment is more difficult. Inhibition keeps the subject "in check," but impediment keeps the subject "ensnared" and "trapped." Perhaps we could venture that in inhibition, the subject is unaware of the lack of movement, while in impediment, one is aware of being stuck, shackled, or ensnared. The image the subject has internalized—an image of competence and completeness—fails to support the subject's intended action and, instead of support, offers a snare. Desire without movement.

If we push further in the direction of difficulty without increasing movement, we come to embarrassment. In French, this is "*embarras.*" A. R. Price, in a note on his translation, says that embarrass

> carries a far wider range of signification than the English "embarrassment," encompassing discomfiture, nuisance, confusion and situations of annoyance and quandary. The idioms "to be in a bind," or "to be in a pickle" convey to some extent this range of meaning.[12]

Perhaps so, but maybe we should consider the visceral experience of embarrassment, which both French and English words signify. Lacan says it is "when you don't know what to do with yourself anymore." He again turns to Latin for the etymology, *imbaricare* (to load), which he says makes the "most direct allusion to the bar, bara, as such" since embarrassment is "quite precisely the subject S decked out with the bar, S̸."[13] The S̸ is a sign of the subject's castration. In embarrassment, we are not only caught with our pants down but also without our phallus. We should note that this is not shame. This is not the experience of the other Sartre describes when one is caught looking through a keyhole. It is at the greatest level of difficulty with no motion. In embarrassment, one is not guilty of some immoral act, but frozen in oneself. Not ensnared from without by the alien specular image, but fixed, pinned by something that is now attached to you as a sign of your castration.

When my hair started to thin, I began to feel embarrassed about it. From the front, I still look like I need a comb (I don't—I haven't used one in years), but the crown of my head is completely bald. I usually forget all about it, but then I'll see a photograph, or in image of myself on a screen, that leaves me "not knowing what to do with myself." In those moments, I know I am not what the Other desires. At the level of impediment, an awareness of the conflict between the image (literally) of myself I carry inside me and the reality of my appearance might impede my functioning. It is not shame. I am not ashamed of myself for my hair loss; I am embarrassed. At the level of embarrassment, things are much worse than at the level of impediment, in the sense of being more difficult. No movement is involved, just a sense that one is not desired by the Other. It is embarrassing. In embarrassment, we do not know what to do with ourselves *because there is nothing to be done*. The Other has seen us with our pants down, and no phallus to show at all. In Lacan's table, it is at *the same level of difficulty as anxiety*, but with no movement. Lacan calls it a "slight form of anxiety."[14] This is a wonderful clue to the nature of anxiety.

You can already start to see the advantage of Lacan's method. We start to understand what we already know about anxiety from our experience of it. *It is something like embarrassment, but with more movement—more turmoil.*

Back to Lacan's net, we can see that, moving down from inhibition, we come to emotion. In common parlance, probably every square of the table would be considered emotion by some people, but Lacan aptly confines it to the square of least difficulty with slight movement. Emotion has more "movement" than inhibition (which has no movement), but it is no more difficult than inhibition. Again, he turns to etymology to insist that emotion refers to movement, but "it's movement that disintegrates; it's the reaction that one calls catastrophic." He tells us that some people want to put anxiety right here, in that box, seeing it as a catastrophic reaction. It's related, Lacan tells us, to anxiety, "but what wouldn't be related to anxiety?" The fact that hysterical fits and anger can both be thought of as emotion is enough to show us that we can't place anxiety here, he tells us.[15]

He then moves, still at the same level of difficulty as inhibition, but at the level of the greatest movement to "turmoil" (*émoi* in French). Lacan provides a lengthy etymological explanation here, but what he has in mind is "troubled." "Turmoil is trouble, to become troubled as such, to be as deeply troubled as one can be in the dimension of movement," which he contrasts with "embarrassment [which] implies reaching the maximum level of difficulty" but with no movement.[16] Turmoil is lots of movement with minimal difficulty; embarrassment is lots of difficulty with minimum movement. Anxiety is at the same level of difficulty as embarrassment, but also at the same level of movement as turmoil. *Anxiety is like turmoil, but more difficult, and like embarrassment, but with a lot more movement.* Anxiety is not quite embarrassment, but you can see how it is related. The not-knowing-what-to-do-with-oneself of embarrassment certainly seems related to anxiety, but anxiety has lots of turmoil mixed in.

Lacan left two spots blank during his first lecture, in which he deployed the net, but he concludes by clarifying what this excursion has already shown us: that anxiety is not an emotion, but "an affect." For Lacan, *an affect is not repressed, but rather "unfastened."* It "drifts about." But in anxiety, there is repression, a repression of the "signifiers that moor it." What he means is that in anxiety, I do not know what about this situation is making me feel so anxious. The signifiers are repressed. Maybe, after undergoing analysis, these repressed signifiers could stand up and start moving, but in anxiety, I cannot put together what is causing me all this turmoil. He draws a comparison with his analysis of anger, which he describes as "what happens in subjects when the little pegs won't fit into the little holes." This doesn't initially seem like much help, but he locates anger in a context where it seems like we are not receiving what we expected. Someone—another driver, a romantic partner, a coworker, or even God—is not playing by the rules. Lacan puts it more obliquely: anger is "when at the level of the Other, of the signifier, that is to say, always, more or less, at the level of faith, of *bona fides*, the game isn't being played."[17] This isn't a definition of anger or of affect, but it does prompt us to think. Does he not locate anger for us here—in the problem of being given square pegs when our world is filled with round holes—when I have done my part, what was expected of me, and so on, only to find that the Other has somehow cheated me? I was led to believe things would work this way, but it turns out they work that way. In anger, perhaps the signifiers are not repressed.

Acting-Out (he uses the English phrase) and *Passage à l'acte* (which has been kept in French in the English translation) are two squares he left blank in his first account of the net, only coming back to them weeks later. Acting-out is when an action is directed at the Other/other. A child's tantrum (or an adult's, for that matter) is rarely a simple expression of frustration but a message. But often acting out is more subtle. I have a therapist friend who told me that she can always tell when her husband is upset with her (even if he doesn't consciously know it) because he trims her rose bushes. He trims them too short. He's acting out. When she asks him if he is upset, he always says he is not. But his unconscious is cutting her roses too short. Often adolescents use drugs, dress bizarrely, and behave in risky ways, not simply as a means of "expressing themselves" but as a way to send a message to their parents, their peers, and their society. In Lacan's table, it is a form of the symptom with a lot of movement. It is turmoil in a more difficult form. It is anxiety, but in a masked form that makes it not as difficult.

Passage à l'acte is more difficult but has less movement than either acting-out or anxiety. In general, we might translate it as something like "taking a plunge." It often seems to imply that an action that has been lurking in the background suddenly breaks into reality. Lacan favors something like "letting oneself drop." His example comes from Freud's case of "the female homosexual," who, when she receives a look of disgust from her father, who sees her acting out with her female lover (by simply walking amorously together in a public street), she throws herself off a low bridge onto what was probably just a trolley track below. This is not suicidal, per se, though it could be, but "dropping out of the frame." Unlike embarrassment, in which one does not know what to do with oneself, here this not-knowing-what-to-do is transformed into action, an action that lets the subject fall from the frame. This, too, seems to be a form of anxiety that tries to avoid a direct confrontation with anxiety. The Other sees us but with disgust and rejection. We let ourselves drop. We take a plunge into the abyss. We let ourselves go. It is as difficult as anxiety, but with less movement. Maybe it is done to avoid anxiety. Maybe it is done because the subject can no longer live with anxiety and wants to just drop out of the frame and no longer be part of this painful dialectic with the Other.

By describing anxiety in relation to these other feelings, Lacan helps us see where anxiety lies in relation to the experience of the subject. Like embarrassment and letting oneself drop, it is an extremely difficult experience in which the subject, confronted with the Other's desire, does not know what to do with itself. The feeling of not wanting to be involved with the Other's desire dominates the relationship of the subject in the dynamics of embarrassment, *the passage-à-l'acte,* and anxiety. The agitation associated with turmoil, acting-out, and anxiety points to the ways anxiety animates the subject, albeit in unpleasant ways. We can see that in anxiety, we are trapped, smothered, and oppressed by the Other's desire, which does not confirm us in our subjectivity, and this manifests itself in an agitation that does not let our minds or bodies rest. This sounds awful. It is awful. But my argument is that we need to understand this awful feeling and its relationship to the subject in order to understand both what the subject is and how the subject relates to the intersubjective world.

We all know anxiety, even if we don't know what anxiety is about. Certainly, there is a plethora of information in the world today about anxiety, but the aim of this book is not to review that information but to focus on what the experience of anxiety may indicate to us about our experience in the world. My thinking on this topic has drawn from two distinct traditions that each reflect considerable diversity. On the one hand, there is what we might call the "Existentialist-Phenomenological Tradition." For me, this tradition has focused primarily on the work of Kierkegaard, Heidegger, Sartre, and Merleau-Ponty. While I still appreciate many of the insights from these thinkers and those who follow this tradition, I have been drawn more recently to psychoanalysis, especially as developed by Lacan. The advantage of the Lacanian approach is its formulation of a theory of the subject that highlights what we might call its "extimate" quality. Psychoanalysis sees the subject as neither a self-contained and autonomous being, nor as simply the product of discourse and power, but an excess that emerges from the individual's experience of the intersubjective world with all of its symbolic and imaginary configurations. This approach has the advantage of offering a useful way to take seriously the profound and disturbing affect we call anxiety without immediately resorting to an attempt to dispense with it or even dismiss it. For Lacan, as we will see, anxiety is "that which deceives not." It is the nature of this claim that this book will explore, thinking through what anxiety is, why we experience it, and what it might tell us about the way we engage with ourselves, others, and the world.

Chapter 1, "Theorizing the Subject of Anxiety," focuses on the way Heidegger, Sartre, Freud, and Lacan theorized anxiety. As mentioned, thinkers in the tradition of Kierkegaard, Heidegger, and Sartre see anxiety as something we feel in the face of our freedom. Kierkegaard emphasized the anxiety that comes from the need we have to constantly make choices—sometimes life-altering choices—without ever being able to predict or even understand the consequences of those choices. Freedom is foisted on us, and the inability of finite beings to cope with this situation manifests in anxiety. Of course, if we were infinite and if we knew and understood everything, we would not have anxiety, and, arguably, we would not have any freedom either. Our choices would, in some sense, be clear, being determined by this absolute knowledge, but our freedom emerges precisely out of this choosing from within a finite perspective. For Heidegger, anxiety is something that we feel in the face of our awareness that our "world"—that is, the site of all our feelings, meanings, and actions—is contingent. Our world is not a reflection of anything but nothingness. We live within certain cultural situations that appear to us as natural, thus providing us with roles we can assume within these worlds as paths to significance. We normally feel ourselves just doing what "one does" in our situation, not questioning these roles and the values that accompany them. Anxiety occurs when we come to terms with the contingency of this situation. For Sartre, like Kierkegaard, anxiety is tied up with choice. His vivid example is of a hiker preparing to cross a narrow pathway on the edge of a precipice. Fear would be our reaction to the possibility of falling, but anxiety is the result of our awareness that we could choose to throw ourselves from the cliff. For Sartre, this capacity to make such choices is at the heart of anxiety. We know that at every moment we have the possibility to destroy ourselves. This is freedom for Sartre, and it comes with anxiety.

The majority of the chapter and the book are devoted to the psychoanalytic understanding of anxiety. Freud struggled to make sense of anxiety, trying at times to find a biological etiology and at other times connecting it to our intersubjective situation. What emerges from this struggle is a notion of anxiety as a warning signal that keeps us in check. It signals to us the possibility that we are contemplating, committing, or have committed an action that might lead to a loss of love. Contrary to what we might expect, Freud argues that anxiety is not the result of repression; rather, we repress in order to not feel anxiety. Lacan's theorization of anxiety, while not explicitly renouncing Freud's view, develops an understanding of anxiety that is much more focused on the subject's relationship to desire. While the typical view of anxiety sees it as without an object, Lacan cryptically asserts that it "is not without an object." By this, he means that the object of anxiety is his *objet petit a*, the object-cause of desire. Anxiety comes from our relationship to that (non-)object. For Lacan, the being of the subject is linked to desire, and desire depends upon a gap between the needs of the human organism and the symbolic form in which demands around those needs are expressed. Because the subject's needs are often connected with the demands of others, the subject is constantly asking, "What do you want from me?" Often, this question can be addressed to specific others—parents, lovers, children, bosses, and so forth—but it is more often, and generally, addressed to no one in particular, but to what Lacan calls "the [big] Other." Anxiety emerges when we feel the fantasies that supply an answer to this question are failing, or when we feel that the Other (or other) has no desire at all that we could address and therefore provides no path upon which we can become desirable. For Lacan, anxiety is "that which deceives not,"[18] because in anxiety we experience the truth of our own subjectivity, which is that there is an extimacy to subjectivity that we are always tempted to disavow through fantasies of wholeness, autonomy, and self-identity.

In chapter 2, "Anxiety and the Contradictions of Culture," we develop an understanding of the relationship between culture and anxiety. For Heidegger, anxiety is the experience of the failure of culture to account for itself. Anxiety occurs when we see the contingency of the roles, values, and projects that characterize our world. He sees the experience of anxiety as an opportunity to live more authentically by taking responsibility for one's actions and values, but his theory leaves little room for cultural critique per se. For Freud, culture is a project aimed at the reduction, if not the elimination, of suffering. For him, culture is not simply the achievements and regulations that characterize "civilization" but also a process that the individual undergoes. I will argue that anxiety is part of that process and that Freud's understanding of the uncanny provides a way of thinking about how culture itself is a home inhabited by a strangeness. The anxiety-generating uncanny is never far from the experience of the cultural world as home. In fact, they are the same, since culture is built upon a repressed that can always return. For Lacan, the structure of anxiety and fantasy are the same. While fantasy can have a very specific understanding in Lacan's theory, we extend that understanding here to show how the cultural project aims not only at creating technologies and regulations that attempt to ameliorate our suffering but also of avoiding the anxiety that inevitably accompanies our situation in culture. This leads to a proliferation of cultural projects and techniques that exist not to combat the sources of suffering we face in the world but to fend off the anxiety that inevitably accompanies subjectivity. This dynamic is explored through an analysis of two television series, Showtime's *Yellowjackets* and HBO's *The Leftovers*.

Chapter 3, "Anxiety in the Field of Vision," explores the gaze. The title of the chapter comes from Jacqueline Rose's *Sexuality in the Field of Vision* and follows a similar trajectory. Our common sense understanding of vision is that it provides us with an unmediated encounter with the world. But this is far from the case. Many theorists of the gaze have linked their understanding of it to Lacan, but they have more in common with Sartre's view. For Sartre, the gaze has a binary structure, moving back and forth between two subjects. One can be either the subject or the object in the visual field, and one's subjectivity emerges in part from becoming the object of the other's gaze. Lacan critiques this view, suggesting that the subject is always already in the picture. We never see without, in some sense, seeing ourselves as being seen. Furthermore, in the visual field, what is not seen is what typically captures our desire. Thus, the visual field is, predictably, a site of both fantasy and anxiety. We often immerse ourselves in fantasy through what we see, but only in the sense of not seeing. It is what we cannot see, what stains the visual field, what occludes our vision, that signals the presence of the gaze, shaping the way we look at things. The gaze is not a site of mastery over objects but a sphere of desire and anxiety. At the same time, this always-being-in-the-picture generates anxiety when the fantasy breaks down. In the visual field, the dialectic of fantasy-anxiety becomes clear, as does the extimacy of the subject.

In chapter 4, "Anxiety as the Truth of Sexuality," we pursue Lacan's claim that anxiety is the truth of sexuality. On the one hand, the sexual act itself becomes a site of anxiety and fantasy. Our sexual acts, far from being an expression of nature, demonstrate the degree to which we are all subjected to a series of cultural and intersubjective demands that register the anxiety-fantasy dialectic. Similarly, our understanding of ourselves in terms of masculinity and femininity registers the same dialectic. Being a man or a woman is neither an expression of a natural, biological disposition nor is it an attempt to successfully instantiate the cultural ideals of heteronormative sexuality, but rather a site of failure. Masculinity and femininity represent two modes of failure in the field of sexuality. The feelings of anxiety we feel relative to these modes of being and our attempts to avoid that anxiety are what sexuality is. Theorizing sex and sexuality in this way has important implications both for our personal attempts to navigate the sexual field and for our political commitments to more liberatory and egalitarian practices related to sexual identity and practice.

In chapter 5, "Anxiety and the Fantasy of Race," we explore the ways in which subjects experience anxiety in relationship to race. Working from Kalpana Seshadri-Crooks' *Desiring Whiteness*, Antonio Viego's *Dead Subjects*, and Molly Ann Rothenberg's *The Excessive Subject*, we develop an understanding of the way race and racism operate in relationship to the extimate subject. Using Lacan's "Four Discourses," we chart a path toward an antiracism that undermines "whiteness" as a master signifier. Nevertheless, I argue that no anti-racism is possible without anxiety. This is because a true anti-racism will involve identifying with what Todd McGowan calls a "universal non-belonging." But this anxious non-belonging offers us the possibility for a new kind of solidarity beyond the limits imposed by race/racism.

In the conclusion, "In Defense of Anxiety, or How to Get Cancer without Becoming Wise," we explore the tactics that must be deployed if the truth of anxiety is to register in our personal and political lives. Beginning with my own personal narrative around my experience of a cancer diagnosis, I show the ways in which anxiety and fantasy manifest themselves in the choices we make in our personal lives. Then we turn to what might amount to a defense of anxiety. Unpleasant as it is, anxiety is an important affect in creating meaningful lives for ourselves and plotting paths of personal and social change.

NOTES

1. Jamieson Webster, *Conversion Disorder: Listening to the Body in Psychoanalysis* (New York: Columbia University Press, 2019), 156.

2. Sara Ahmed, *The Politics of Emotion* (Edinburgh: Edinburgh University Press, 2004, Second Edition, 2014), 166.

3. Rollo May, *The Meaning of Anxiety* (New York: The Ronald Press Company, 1950), v.

4. Allan V. Horwitz, *A Short History* (Baltimore: Johns Hopkins University Press, 2013), 15.

5. Webster, *Conversion Disorder,* 156.

6. First published as *Le Séminaire Livre X : L'angoisse*, ed. Jacques-Alain Miller (Paris: Éditions du Seuil, 2004). Published in English as *Anxiety: The Seminar of Jacques Lacan, Book X*, trans. A.R. Price (Cambridge: Polity Press, 2014).

7. Lacan, *Seminar X: Anxiety*, 13, 77.

8. Lacan, *Seminar X: Anxiety*, 9.

9. Lacan, *Le Seminaire Livre X, L'angoisse*, 18. Of course, Lacan was speaking in French about the concept of empêchement in reference to a Latin etymology that is more evident in the English word, "impediment." He readily admits that he uses etymology "when it's helpful," and here the idea of something from outside us trapping us, that is, to point to the subject's relationship to the Other in this field of, and path leading to, anxiety, is what interests him. Is "impediment" the right word here? When we think of a "speech impediment," we think of a speaker who is trying to say something but it gets stuck, or caught. It presents a difficulty. Doesn't that suggest a level of "movement" though? For Lacan, impediment is at the level of halting of locomotion. Something is not moving. It is there, but it can't get out.

10. Lacan, *Seminar X: Anxiety*, 10.

11. Lacan, *Seminar X: Anxiety*, 11.

12. Lacan, *Seminar X: Anxiety*, 340, n. 3.

13. Lacan, *Seminar X: Anxiety*, 11.

14. Lacan, *Seminar X: Anxiety*, 11.

15. Lacan, *Seminar X: Anxiety*, 11–12.

16. Lacan, *Seminar X: Anxiety*, 13.

17. Lacan, *Seminar X: Anxiety*, 14.

18. Lacan, *Seminar X: Anxiety*, 76, 116, 218, 297, 311-312.

Chapter 1

Theorizing the Subject of Anxiety

Michel Foucault declared that only two theorists in the twentieth century had really attempted to pose questions about the relationship between the subject and truth, Heidegger and Lacan.[1] I am making a similar assertion: only two modes of thought have taken seriously the role of anxiety in the study of culture, politics, sex, race, and power: Heidegger and Lacan (or more broadly, what we can call the existential/phenomenological tradition and psychoanalysis). It is not a coincidence that for both Heidegger and Lacan, anxiety was a central idea in their respective theorizations of the subject.

Within the tradition of phenomenology and existentialism, three thinkers have defined the field of anxiety: Kierkegaard, Heidegger, and Sartre. For Kierkegaard and Sartre, anxiety relates to freedom. Kierkegaard claims that "anxiety is freedom's actuality as the possibility of possibility."[2] For Kierkegaard, my finite nature is both the cause and expression of my freedom. The fact that I have limited knowledge, limited power to act, and limited time in which to live gives me freedom. If I knew everything and could do everything, I would have no freedom at all since my infinite knowledge and power would determine my action. But as a finite self-conscious being, I must act without ever really knowing the consequences of my actions. Even if I can, with great probability, predict the specific result of a specific action, I cannot know the result of that result. Nevertheless, I must act. But the underside of this anxiety, if we can put it that way, is possibility. The possibility itself, which we treasure, is, at the same time, the source of our anxiety. Sartre, similarly, emphasizes the anxiety I experience in making choices. For Sartre, there is no predetermined form of humanity. There is no higher power guiding me or to whom I can appeal to judge or justify my actions. I must assume this responsibility and act for myself. This mode of thought suggests that anxiety is only escapable by denying freedom. The implications of this insight are important for theorizing the possibilities of generating an emancipatory project, not simply by asserting, as Sartre does, that I am free to act, but by also realizing that my desire to avoid anxiety might point to anxiety as the affect that keeps me from acting.[3]

While Heidegger's account is no doubt indebted to Kierkegaard's and influenced Sartre's, his theorization of anxiety is distinct from theirs for the way it focuses on the place of the subject in the cultural world. For Heidegger, anxiety discloses something about our situation as cultural beings. When we are fully immersed in what Heidegger thinks of as our "worlds," that is, in our spheres of practice and belief, we normally do not experience anxiety. For Heidegger, and for the phenomenological-existential tradition in general, anxiety is a clue to the contingent nature of our existence. In anxiety, what is disclosed is the contingent nature of the worlds of shared practices and understandings that are the conditions for our lives. We come to realize that what we have taken to be natural, essential, and inevitable is only one culture's way of doing things. This experience of contingency is one of anxiety. It is certainly related to the emphasis on freedom in Kierkegaard and Sartre because to realize this contingency is to realize that I am free to act. But for Heidegger, it is as if what we experience in anxiety is the loss of our world itself. This is extremely unpleasant, and we tend to flee from it. When we flee from anxiety, we flee from ourselves; we flee from the freedom implied by this revelation. The experience of anxiety is thus in opposition to the normal experience of culture in which our world seems to us to be where we belong, with clearly defined roles and expectations that allow us to function without the distressing feelings of anxiety that can sometimes plague us.

While Heidegger's approach has much to commend itself to us, as we will see, we might ask if it really deals with the experience of anxiety so common in our daily experience, or is it more focused on the foundational conditions necessary for anxiety to emerge for beings like us. Psychoanalysis, on the other hand, has tended to focus on the familiar experience of anxiety with its physiological effects, like restricted breathing, butterflies in our stomach, panic attacks, various phobias, and social anxieties. For Freud, his initial conception of anxiety was that it was caused by repression, in particular, *coitus interruptus*. But his later theorization reversed this dynamic. *Rather than seeing repression as the cause of anxiety, he saw anxiety as the cause of repression.* This mirrors his conception of culture. Culture (*Kultur*), for Freud, is not the product of repression—we build bridges and books because we cannot have sex—rather our emergence as cultural beings leads us to renounce sex in favor of sexuality. Even more surprisingly, as cultural beings, when we have sex, we are doing so within the frame of repression. Our sex lives are supported not by our biology but by our fantasies, and our fantasies are the mode in which we flee anxiety.

Culture is thus on the side of fantasy, not repression, and anxiety signals the disruption of this fantasy framing. This argument will be developed by first looking to the phenomenological/existential tradition of theorizing anxiety to clarify the connection between anxiety and culture, but the ultimate theorization of the subject of anxiety will be developed out of psychoanalysis, especially Lacan, in order to show how anxiety brings us into contact with what Lacan calls the Real. Lacan's Real is not "reality," which Lacan associates with the Symbolic, but rather it is the holes, gaps, and inconsistencies in the Symbolic order. Culture, as an expression and embodiment of the Symbolic, is thus a never-ending project of covering over these gaps, holes, and inconsistencies. Anxiety can thus be thought of as the source of a panoply of cultural products and effects and, at the same time, as the point of view from which these responses can be analyzed and critiqued. Anxiety, as the hidden engine of cultural transformation, can thus become the point at which we can more thoughtfully engage with our lives as cultural subjects.

The chapter concludes with a consideration of Rei Terada's critique of the subject in relation to feeling. For Terada, subjects do not have feelings; rather, we have feelings only because there is no subject. This is not an insubstantial critique of the project of this book; rather, it is one that will help us clarify what the subject is and why anxiety is so central to its emergence. Ultimately, we will develop a theory of the subject that connects it to an "extimate" causality that can be typified with something like a Möbius strip.

In brief, the argument of this chapter is that unlike other feelings and affects, anxiety does not lie. The message it sends us is the truth of our subjectivity, but that truth is that the subject is not isolated and autonomous, but intersubjective. In Lacan's terms, it "ex-sists." For this very reason, we, the speaking beings, what we are calling here, "subjects," experience anxiety as an inescapable feature of subjectivity. We are always fleeing it, sometimes with surprising effectiveness, but in this flight, we are fleeing the truth of our own being and with it the possibility for personal and social change that can only come with the loss of the world (Heidegger) and the realization that there is no other of the Other (Lacan).

HEIDEGGER: ANXIETY, THROWNESS, AND DISCLOSURE

Heidegger speaks about our relating to are reality in terms of moods (*Stimmungen*). For Heidegger, anxiety is the mood *par excellence*. It is the mood that discloses to us the very nature of our being. In Division One of *Being and Time,* Heidegger's analysis of anxiety becomes central to his analysis of Dasein's Being-in-the-world. Dasein (literally "being there" in German) is

Heidegger's way of describing the human subject in the meaningful context that characterizes human life. Heidegger characterizes Dasein's relationship to the world of meaning variously in terms of "falling," "thrownness," "projection," and "Being-ahead-of-itself" but says that Dasein is revealed, in its "totality," through the phenomenon of anxiety. What anxiety discloses is the nature of Dasein itself as "fallen" into a world that, in the experience of anxiety, reveals its contingent nature.

For Heidegger, a mood (*Stimmung*) attunes (*stimmen*) one to the possibilities of a given situation. Moods come neither from "outside" or "inside" but they "assail us." He links moods to our "state of mind" (*Befindlichkeit*) as a result of our being in a situation.[4] In Heidegger's words,

> A state-of-mind not only discloses Dasein in its thrownness and its submission to that world which is already disclosed with its own Being; it is itself the existential kind of being in which Dasein constantly surrenders itself to the "world" and lets the "world" "matter" to it in such a way that somehow Dasein evades its very self.[5]

For Heidegger, our very activity in the world is disclosive, but our role in such disclosures is not typically clear to us. We feel ourselves "discovering," rather than "disclosing," but anxiety points toward our role in disclosing the truth of Being. Heidegger was certainly aware that the universe got along fine without us, but the universe does not disclose itself. We disclose it. In Heidegger's words, "*facticity is not the factuality of the factum brutum of something present-at-hand, but a characteristic of Dasein's Being—one which has been taken up into existence, even if proximally it has been thrust aside*."[6] Dasein is disclosive.

But for this reason, moods also disclose the "thrownness" of Dasein. Moods disclose, if not explicitly to us, at least to phenomenological observation, the way we are always, already immersed in a world of meanings and practices that shape our understanding of our situation(s). Dasein's way of Being-in-the-world is necessarily characterized by this closing off of some interpretations and actions in favor of others. When a student visits a professor during office hours, certain opportunities are experienced as being especially close—for example, discussing Heidegger, professional modes of interaction, perhaps light-hearted banter, superficial questions about how one's semester is going, and so on—while others seem remote and closed off—for example, arm wrestling, the performance of a magic trick, or serious conversations about one's pending divorce.

By using the term "thrownness," Heidegger insists disclosure is not a "psychical" reality or "inner" condition. In moods, "the world, Dasein-with, and existence are *equiprimordially* disclosed."[7] This is to say that moods disclose

"Being-in-the-world as a whole." The objects in the professor's office recede into the background while also disclosing the situation. The desk, the chairs, the shelves, and the books sink into the background by way of their signaling the character of the situation. This is what allows for the discussion of Heidegger in the professor's office, a topic not taken up in casual conversation in a supermarket or in a serious conversation between romantic partners (at least not typically). The mood is neither inside nor outside Dasein but in the very mode of Being-in-the-world.

But moods have a third characteristic: they make things matter to us. Heidegger seems to think this is a feature fundamental to Dasein itself. Dasein's characteristic care for the world is predicated on the functioning of moods, which convert the brute facts of the objects in the world (both equipment, what Heidegger calls "ready-at-hand," and naturally occurring objects, what Heidegger calls "present-at-hand") to matter for us only by way of mood.[8] A stain on my shirt discloses something to me about the situation of a job interview or a professional presentation and, at the same time, it is the mood of the job interview or professional presentation that causes the stain on my shirt to matter to me (and to others). He explains that I can only experience someone or something as threatened if it has come to matter to me and this mattering depends on my having been attuned to what is important and worthy of my care and concern.

One slips in and out of moods, but they are always there; we are always moody: "in every case, Dasein always has some mood [*gestimmt ist*]." These moods are a primordial form of disclosure, in contrast to the limited "possibilities of disclosure" provided by cognition. In moods, Dasein ("being there") is "brought before its being as 'there.'"[9] If this were not the case, even if our perceptions could offer us a kind of "pure beholding" that would bring us to know a thing in the world (what is "present-at-hand"), we would never be able to "discover anything like that which is threatening" because nothing would matter to us. The universe does not care that polar bears are going extinct. Only Dasein cares, precisely because of the way polar bears are disclosed in the Being-in-the-world of Dasein. In other anthropocentric eras, the being of polar bears was manifested as dangerous and perhaps even as to-be-exterminated, but now the thought of their extermination brings us grief, sorrow, and perhaps a motivation to act on their behalf. *This is care.* He acknowledges that we can certainly encounter objects in the world, catalog them, and even discover new species of plants, animals, and microorganisms, and so forth, but this is not primarily how Dasein is in-the-world. Dasein's being-in-the-world always has a kind of moodiness where things matter to us. It is by way of this mattering that we can have experiences at all.[10]

So, in our normal, average-everyday mode of life, we are always, already immersed in a world of meaning, and my possibilities for acting in the world are offered to me by way of the common practices and understandings we all share. Heidegger dramatically describes this situation as "falling." Dasein's falling is into the "they" and the "world." For Heidegger, this falling is also Dasein's "'fleeing' in the face of itself."[11] The turning away from oneself is a turning toward the mode of life offered by the "they" and "the turning-away of falling is grounded . . . in anxiety, which in turn is what first makes fear possible."[12] Under these conditions, that is, under the conditions under which we all live almost all of the time, we are "blind" to our own possibilities as if we had "tranquiliz[ed]" ourselves "with that which is merely actual." He says that this "tranquilizing" doesn't lower the diligence with which we carry out our day-to-day life; it actually "arouses it" but in such a way that "no positive new possibilities are willed, but that which is at one's disposal becomes 'tactically' altered in such a way that there is a semblance of something happening."[13] We can now see that falling and fleeing are not fleeing from the things in the world, but fleeing *toward them* so that we are

> lost in the "they" and can dwell in tranquillized familiarity. When in falling we flee into the "at-home" of publicness, we flee in the face of the "not-at-home"; that is, we flee in the face of the uncanniness which lies in Dasein . . . This uncanniness pursues Dasein constantly and is a threat to its everyday lostness in the "they", though not explicitly. . . . Anxiety can arise in the most innocuous situations.[14]

This is all to say that our normal immersion in the practices and understandings of our own culture becomes the medium through which we exist. We are tranquilized, but it is a "tranquillized familiarity" in which we are actively engaged in activities. We are "at home" in these practices, yet haunted by something "unhomely" *(unheimlich,* "uncanny"). This is why anxiety (the unhomely) can emerge in the most "innocuous" situations—precisely when we are "at home." (For more on this, see chapter 2.)

For Heidegger, anxiety makes us aware of the fact that the world is a world. That is, to make us aware of its contingent nature. For example, I love coffee. I love drinking coffee. But I love coffee only because I exist in a coffee-drinking world. Had I been born in a different place and time, a non-coffee-drinking world, I would have been a tea-drinker or a stout-drinker, but not a coffee drinker. Though I may define myself by my love of coffee, by my ability to select just the right beans, grinding them fresh right before brewing, and savoring its caffeinated embrace daily, had I been raised in a different world, coffee would not be an important part of my life at all. The same can be said for every feature of my life. One can only be a professor because they live in a world of colleges and universities. One cannot, for example, be a Samurai warrior. You can collect Japanese swords, practice martial arts in the park on Sundays, and read books about the warrior spirit, but none of that will make someone a Samurai because the world of the Samurai is gone. The same can be said for roles like "father," "lover," "partner," "friend," "Cuban," and so on. What it means to be any and all of these things is always contingent, up for grabs, and so on, yet nevertheless always there for me (as long as they are part of my world). I pick them, put them on, drive them around—whatever metaphor seems most apt—and in doing so I am at home in my world. At least this is how Heidegger sees it.

In the case of coffee, the stakes are low, but what if we consider a more high-stakes endeavor, raising children? In other cultures and eras, child-rearing may have included anxieties of the nature of those related to their general health and safety. High infant mortality rates, dreaded diseases, and an array of natural threats could be the source of certain anxieties, but Heidegger would consider these "fears." The parent in these situations worries about the welfare of the child in relation to the potential dangers in the world. The anxious parent of the twenty-first century might, under certain circumstances, share those concerns, but nowadays a new kind of anxiety, something like the anxiety developed by Heidegger, has emerged: with the proliferation of a myriad of experts in child-rearing promoting their solutions to common parenting problems, parents must decipher issues related not only to threats to the child coming from the external world, but threats coming from the parents themselves. Warnings against helicopter parenting flourish alongside advice to "stay on top" of your children. Some advice claims that children need "structure," while other advice says they need the "freedom" to explore for themselves. For most parents today corporal punishment seems out of the question, yet they are sometimes confronted with advice from grandparents and online "experts" suggesting that kids "need" a "good paddling" every now and then. This kind of anxiety emerges not from a kind of moral weakness on the part of twenty-first-century parents, but on the lack of a coherent "they" mode of parenting. Traditional modes of parenting (e.g., "spare the rod, spoil the child") have been undermined (no doubt, for good reason), and a new consensus has yet to emerge, at least in common practice. Parents who are content to do it the old-fashioned way—spanking, yelling, and so on—likely feel no anxiety around this at all. Parents who have little empathy for their children or minimal concern over their welfare will likely not feel anxiety in this realm either. It is only those parents who both care about the welfare of their children and have called into question common understandings of what counts as good parenting that will feel anxiety in this area. For Heidegger, it is the anxious parent who is "authentic" because that parent does not simply accept the common cultural understandings handed down to them but calls them into question. As Sara Ahmed has pointed out, we usually think of questioning as a positive experience, but in reality, it is often a very anxious experience.[15] Questioning sounds like a positive activity when considered in the abstract and from the perspective of an Enlightenment approach to knowledge, but in practice, it can be exceedingly uncomfortable. For both Ahmed and Heidegger, anxiety is concerned with care, and precisely for that reason, questioning will be a feature of that caring. In fact, Ahmed pushes this point so far as to claim that "caring is anxious."[16]

In this example, you can see that Heidegger's account of anxiety depends, in the first place, on the "world as world." The world is the site of all meaning, of all significance, of all the roles one can take on for oneself. The role of parent is one possibility for Dasein, even for those individuals who are not parents. One can take on this role of parent through a variety of possibilities but how one operates within that role is completely contingent. "Parent," as a role one can assume, is not a natural feature of the organic, but a cultural feature of the "world." How one does it is typically tied up with the constitution of the role itself. "What one does" becomes, in relationship to the role, parent, "what a parent does." Under most circumstances, in what Heidegger calls our "average-everydayness," most of the time we all do what one does. In such circumstances, *we feel no anxiety at all.* We only feel anxiety, according to Heidegger, when we come face to face with "the world as world." In those moments we become aware of the contingent nature of our own world, and of the limitless possibilities for our own existence. *This, for Heidegger, is the source of our anxiety.* If we follow both Heidegger and Ahmed on this point, we could argue that a "good" parent would be one who is anxious much of the time. Even here, as Ahmed points out, real care is not at all the same as being good. Often those who focus on being "good parents" can be among the worst; for Ahmed, it would be those who focus on caring for their children—the anxious ones—who provide a better model for approaching this relationship. To follow Heidegger's way of framing this, we could say that the parents who want to be "good" parents are just being "they" parents. They are doing what parents do because they want to flee (the uncanny in) themselves (and anxiety) by assuming that parenting is not a contingent practice that reflects the vagaries of a particular culture. By doing this they flee the void at the heart of their own being and thus avoid the anxieties of caring.

So, from this point of view, anxiety emerges when my care brings me into an awareness of the contingency of the world (Heidegger) or of the fragility of events (Ahmed). It can emerge when one is drinking their morning coffee or debating how much screen time their child should get. In contrast, when I am "fleeing" myself (and anxiety), I feel most at home in my world, whereas, as Heidegger puts it, "in anxiety one feels 'uncanny,'" that is, I no longer feel "at home" in my world in the roles I have taken up.[17] This connection with the uncanny comes from a confrontation with the "nothing and nowhere" Heidegger links to anxiety. This not feeling at home is because "as Dasein falls, anxiety brings it back from its absorption in the 'world.' Everyday familiarity collapses. Dasein has been individualized."[18] This individualization, however, is not some triumphant Nietzschean moment of self-overcoming, but an experience in which:

> the world has the character of completely lacking significance. In anxiety one does not encounter this thing or that thing which, as something threatening, must have an involvement . . . what threatens is nowhere. Anxiety "does not know" what that in the face of which it is anxious is. "Nowhere," however, does not signify nothing . . . it is already "there," and yet nowhere; it is so close that it is oppressive and stifles one's breath, and yet it is nowhere.[19]

This cause of anxiety is nothing, but this nothing "is not totally nothing."[20] Our common sense understanding of anxiety often bears out this paradox because "when anxiety has subsided, then in our everyday way of talking we are accustomed to say that 'it was really nothing.'"[21] When we are anxious, though, is it not everything? This everything is what Sara Ahmed means when she says anxiety is "sticky," that when we are anxious our anxiety seems to attach itself to everything.[22] For Heidegger, when experiencing anxiety, *it is everything*, the whole world and one's place in it. Yet, after the fact, it was nothing after all and we feel foolish for ever having felt that way. Both feelings are valid because the "nothing" in the face of which we experience anxiety is the world, which is everything, and it is the fundamental mood that discloses the situation of the subject (Dasein for Heidegger) in the world. As Heidegger puts it, "so, if the 'nothing'—that is, the world as such—exhibits itself as that in the face of which one has anxiety, this means that *Being-in-the-world itself is that in the face of which anxiety is anxious*."[23] This is also why Heidegger claims that anxiety is the key concept to use in analyzing the nature of Dasein: "Being-anxious discloses, primordially and directly, the world as world."[24] As he later puts it:

> For, as a state-of-mind, anxiousness is a basic kind of Being-in-the-world. Here the disclosure and the disclosed are existentially selfsame in such a way that in the latter the world has been disclosed as world, and Being-in has been disclosed as a potentiality-for-Being which is individualized, pure, and thrown; this makes it plain that with the phenomenon of anxiety a distinctive state-of-mind has become a theme for Interpretation.[25]

This is close to the main argument of this book: *anxiety, as an experience of disclosure, can become a theme for interpretation.*

Heidegger gives us a way of thinking about anxiety that does justice both to the "everywhere and nowhere" feeling of anxiety and to the way it seems connected to both care and potentiality. It removes anxiety from the realm of neural misfiring and places it in the space we all have in common: being subjects in the world (*Dasein* for Heidegger). It also has the advantage of registering for us that anxiety is not "just in our heads" and it is not something we can ever totally escape, except by fleeing ourselves. Finally, it valorizes anxiety as an experience that discloses to us the truth of our situation. For Heidegger, truth is always a matter of "unconcealing"[26] and anxiety, for him, unconceals the nature of the subject's Being-in-the-world and the nature of the world itself.

Dylan Trigg has described, in detail, some of his own more extreme experiences of anxiety, including his difficulty in passing over bridges, taking public transportation, and flying. While he is skeptical of Heidegger's claim that such debilitating experiences can lead to a more authentic self, he thinks of anxiety in ways that follow Heidegger's. For example, in an excruciating account of his struggle to cross a bridge on foot, he argues that "the onset of anxiety involves neither the subject nor the bridge in isolation, but instead takes place in the very pairing, thus constituting a general 'mood' of anxiety."[27] More influenced by Merleau-Ponty, Trigg centers his own bodily experience in his account of anxiety, but in a way that mirrors Heidegger's theory. For Trigg, bodily experience is normally one of integration, of getting a grip on the world, but in his encounter on the bridge, the bridge is "less the foundation of an integrated experience, and more a site of alienation and uncanniness."[28] This alienation and uncanniness certainly seem to follow Heidegger's line of thought, but ultimately, Trigg turns to psychoanalysis to make sense of his (rather extreme) experiences of anxiety. For Trigg, anxiety cannot be identified with a "mood of existence reducible to human subjectivity in its appeal to self-realization, but as the site of an irreducible anonymity that outstrips subjectivity."[29] He argues that we must incorporate a psychoanalytic view of the subject into our analysis of anxiety because, as he puts it, the agoraphobe is "not manifesting a Pavlovian response." *There is something unconscious in it.*[30] We can elaborate on Trigg's claim here as emphasizing that Heidegger's account seems to externalize the worlding of worlds in relationship to Dasein's falling into the world that makes the process seem quasi-automatic. By contrast, Trigg's experience of the bridge he cannot cross is not a matter of realizing the contingency of the bridge or of his freedom in relationship to it.

What Trigg is highlighting is a key difficulty in Heidegger's approach. We can see it if we consider that Heidegger does not talk about "subjects" but instead about "Dasein." In a way, his choice of term says it all. There is not so much a subject as a "being there." If that is all there is, then why would we feel anxiety at all? If there is no subject, and no unconscious, then would we not just be the products of the world's worlding? Why would a realization of the world's contingency lead to any feelings at all? Why would we not just continue in our "fallenness" with no qualms, let alone anxieties, at all? While Heidegger's theory of anxiety is helpful for understanding the role of contingency in the experience of anxiety, and, perhaps more importantly, for helping us understand the role of "fleeing" in the face of ourselves, Dasein, as a concept, does not adequately account for the experience of subjectivity itself. For this, we need to turn to psychoanalysis.

FREUD: ANXIETY AND REPRESSION

For Freud, *repression is not what causes anxiety; anxiety causes repression.* This is the key idea we should take from Freud's theorization of anxiety. Freud's general view of culture and subjectivity suggests that being a cultural animal, that is, becoming civilized, necessarily involves anxiety. The response to this anxiety is generally repression. This implies that while culture/civilization serves a number of important material functions—food production, public safety, medicine, and so on—it also produces cultural ideas, practices, and institutions that seem superfluous to this material project but are necessary in order to help subjects cope with the anxieties produced by their relationship to the intersubjective field that is culture.

Freud's most extended analysis of the phenomenon of anxiety occurs in *Inhibitions, Symptoms, and Anxiety.* In his earliest musings on the problem of anxiety, he tended to link it first to purely physiological (as opposed to psychological) causes, and then to repression itself. But in *Inhibitions, Symptoms, and Anxiety,* he offers a meandering account that pursues a number of ideas related to anxiety as he tries to demonstrate the relationship between anxiety, inhibitions, and symptoms in ways that highlight the social, or intersubjective, nature of anxiety.

For Freud, inhibitions are restrictions of a function, functions he typically associates with "functions of the ego," such as sexual functions, nutrition, locomotion, and professional work. These restrictions need not be "pathological" in the sense that "normal" inhibitions seem to be, to some extent, a necessary part of functioning in the social world. But his focus tends to be on those points that seem "pathological," that present a problem for the individual. For example, he explains the role of inhibitions in sexual functioning (in men) by listing a series of problems—lack of pleasure in sex, inability to get and maintain an erection, premature ejaculation, inability to orgasm/ejaculate, the inability to derive pleasure from an orgasm, or the dependence on various fetishes for arousal and satisfaction—that indicate that "a relationship between inhibition and anxiety is pretty evident." Furthermore, "many women" are "openly afraid" of the sexual act and that "many obsessional acts turn out to be measures of precaution and security against sexual experiences and are thus of a phobic character."[31] In a nutshell, these sexual impediments are not the cause of anxiety; anxiety about something is the cause of these inhibitions.

While these sexual maladies have been studied extensively in a variety of fields, the point is that Freud thought that they were inhibitions of a function he connected with the ego. He went on to suggest that the "ego-function" of an organ is "impaired if its erotogenicity, its sexual significance—is increased."[32] We can imagine that, for example, if the ability to speak became increasingly eroticized, this might lead to a speech impediment. But why would this be the case? He suggests that we "create inhibitions in order to avoid conflict with the id and superego." Inhibitions that appease the superego might actually lead to success in life because of the way they lead us to comply with social norms, but at the expense of functioning in relation to desire. Freud describes an "obsessional neurotic" patient who was "overcome by a paralyzing fatigue . . . whenever something occurred which would obviously have thrown him into a rage."[33] In this case, the man had internalized the message that expressing anger was dangerous and to be avoided, so his normal biological functioning was impeded to keep him from expressing that rage. We might begin to surmise from this example how Freud linked inhibition and anxiety. Anxiety precedes the inhibition; the inhibition arises to avoid the anxiety. Thus, anxiety can impede certain actions. It can keep us from acting, both in cases where the inhibition helps us achieve social goals and in cases where it keeps us from achieving those goals.

In any case, the symptom is a consequence of repression that results in a compromise-formation. Freud defined a symptom as a "sign of, and a substitute for, an instinctual satisfaction (*Triebbefriedigung*) which has remained in abeyance; it is a consequence of the process of repression."[34] He thought that a symptom arose when the ego, "maybe at the behest of the superego," tried to avoid associating itself with an aim that would likely have been at odds with the demands of the superego. Though this aim was consciously repressed, it left an "unconscious formation."[35] In the course of developing this idea, he points out that even though we might think of the ego as powerless against the id, all it has to do is give a "signal of unpleasure" and the "almost omnipotent" pleasure principle will come to its aid. In this way, the pleasure principle, our (organic) tendency to avoid pain and pursue pleasure, becomes an ally in, ironically, suppressing our pursuits of pleasure and avoidances of pain by offering a "signal" that is so unpleasant we would avoid it at any cost. *That unpleasant signal is anxiety.* There are few such signals more unpleasant than anxiety (though guilt can be pretty unpleasant, too, but maybe guilt is just a form of anxiety).[36]

This quick examination of inhibitions and symptoms, and the role the ego plays in them, leads Freud to the conclusion that the "ego is the actual seat of anxiety." So, early in his exposition in *Inhibitions, Symptoms, and Anxiety* he lays out a theory of anxiety that ties it to the ego and its role in warding off "internal and external dangers." In the case of external dangers, it prompts attempts at flight. In the case of repression, the ego "withdraws the (preconscious) occupation (cathexis) from the drive-representation to be repressed and uses it for the displeasure (anxiety) release."[37] Here, "occupation" (*Besetzung*), translated by James Strachey into English as "cathexis," should be thought of as something like a military occupation.[38] The forces used in the initial "occupation" or cathexis become redeployed in the new project shaped by anxiety. But he does not think this unpleasure is newly created, but rather is based on past traumatic events. He thinks these early traumatic experiences created "mnemic symbols," that is, associations in our unconscious, to help us avoid future traumas. He theorizes that perhaps all animals would need such associations to avoid future traumas.[39] When my dog was a puppy, we were going for a walk in a park and crossed a wooden footbridge. While crossing, his leg fell through the slats and he was momentarily stuck. He suffered no injury but has been reluctant to cross any sort of bridge ever since. When he approaches any footbridge, you can see the anxiety in his posture. He does not want to get involved with bridges because they remind him of a previous mishap. Even wooden decks elicit the same reaction. Something similar happened when the same dog was sniffing around a storm drain and a raccoon jumped up and hissed at him. He is now deathly afraid of storm drains. The storm drains are the fearsome raccoon in displaced form. But for us, the anxiety is even more flexible. The fearsome object, the feeling of not wanting to get stuck, to suffer, to be harmed, lurks in the background always and can be deployed in situations that have no connection to the initial traumas or situations. Unlike my dog, the feeling of anxiety, arguably very appropriate in certain situations—like confronting a savage animal or being stranded on a busy freeway—gets redeployed in a new battlefield that might represent a mere social danger—a loss of love—that makes us feel and react as if we were confronting a wild animal or attempting to cross a busy freeway. But here the analogy breaks down a bit. In these analogies, the thing to be avoided is the danger, but in inhibitions and repressions, the thing to be avoided is the anxiety itself. Freud is suggesting that it is something like *our fear of anxiety* that leads to these inhibitions. To return to Freud's example, if sex is a site of anxiety for someone (which is fairly common), they might experience inhibitions around sex to help avoid being in the anxiety situation itself. Such performance anxiety (in sex) can be replicated when someone has to give a speech, or a musical performance, or chase down a fly ball in a softball game, and thus our anxiety about that anxiety can keep us away from such activities.

This is why Freud suggests that the ego is the seat of anxiety—feeling the anxiety without knowing why—but this should not lead us to misunderstand Freud's conception of the ego. The ego is not "in charge" of things, but is, he explicitly says, a part of the id—the part of the id that is an "organization"—that has a special role in repression. By contrast, a symptom is a mental process that comes from repression and "now maintains its existence outside the organization of the ego."[40] The repression takes an automatic role in the responses of the individual. These symptoms can be disruptive and painful, but they can also become a source of pride for the individual. Freud points out that the obsessive person—for example, the "neat-freak" or the "workaholic"—can take a special kind of pride in their symptoms. We also might imagine that if we are part of a group of individuals who widely share the same symptom, those who do not might seem inferior to us. I'm reminded of the Super Bowl ad from 2014 for the Cadillac ELR Coup, in which actor Neil McDonough, brags about American obsessive work habits.[41] In particular, he attacks the way of life enjoyed in "other countries" as one that just won't work for "us" (i.e., Americans). In these other countries, they "work, stroll home, stop by the café; they take August off." That all sounds nice, actually, but he asks the viewers, "Are you like that? Are *we* like that?" The ideological position here, located in a form of American exceptionalism, posits that a life of constant work and striving is the only true form of American enjoyment. The commercial begins with a claim that we don't work hard in order to get "the stuff," but rather because we are "crazy, driven, hard-working believers." This is not exactly a claim that hard work can be rewarding in itself. Rather, it is a claim to a certain kind of identity as its own reward: hence the "we" and the "they" behind the question of what "you" are "you" like? Then at the end, he tells us that "all the stuff" is "the upside of taking only two weeks in August." You can see here how Freud's conception of the ego works. Not in the clichéd claim one finds on the Internet that the ego "mediates" between the "desires of the id and the commands of the superego," but rather in the way the ego *identifies* with the demands of the superego. Such identifications ward off anxiety and have the added benefit (for employers and states) of making us conform to the social demands of our society. We can argue that such habits are a symptom of some kind of repression—a flight from the anxiety of pursuing our real desires, perhaps—but a symptom that has become central to our sense of our own American identity. This particular formation makes clear that anxiety functions not in a strictly organic way, but in relation to broader social and cultural formations (e.g., capitalism, neoliberalism).

Similarly, Freud uses the case of "Little Hans" to demonstrate this view of anxiety.[42] In the case of Little Hans, he had a symptom—a fear of horses biting him—that Freud linked to his ambivalent feelings toward his father, whom he loved, but for whom he harbored a "jealous and hostile Oedipus attitude."[43] Hans' exaggerated feelings of affection for his father were, for Freud, further evidence of the Oedipal drama which Hans could not acknowledge. This manifested itself in a specific inhibition: his inability to go into the streets (which were full of horses). This complex of symptom and inhibition was, Freud thought, a "restriction which his ego had imposed on itself so as not to arouse the anxiety-symptom." What was problematic for Little Hans were the hostile feelings he had for his father because of the Oedipal situation/phase, but to avoid confronting these feelings he displaced them from his father to horses. Apparently, Little Hans had never been bitten by a horse, so the displacement has a seemingly random quality to it. What is important is to see that it was more acceptable to Little Hans to displace his fear of his father, whom he loved and could not avoid, onto the horses, which he could avoid. Freud thought there was something totemic in this; the grown man, like the large animal, was a source of fear and respect (i.e., maybe it was not so random). This fear of the horses was a way to avoid the anxiety he would have felt by confronting the ambiguous nature of his feelings for his father, which contained a great deal of fear and animosity, feelings that did not fit the loving image of the relationship that he wanted to sustain.

He offers another example in another of his famous cases, that of the Wolf Man.[44] Again, conflicted feelings toward the father seem to be at the core of the Wolf Man's fear of being devoured by a wolf. On the one hand, the Wolf Man feared being devoured by his father, but on the other hand, he felt a "passive, tender impulse to be loved by him."[45] We need not get into all the details of Freud's analysis of this case, but we can see that what it shares with the case of Little Hans is a phobia that *displaces* a fear of the father onto an animal, and that this displacement seems rooted *in an ambiguity between two attitudes toward the father*, one which seems acceptable (love), the other which seems unacceptable (hostility). The unacceptable attitude manifests itself by way of a displacement, thus repressing it. He goes so far as to suggest that castration is at the root of such phobias, "animal phobias" rooted directly in the fear of castration, and "agoraphobia" rooted in a fear of sexual temptation, which is also rooted in the fear of castration.[46]

He concludes that "the ego's attitude of anxiety . . . is the primary thing and . . . [it] sets repression going."[47] If inhibitions keep us from entering situations that might cause anxiety, anxiety causes repression, often by way of displacement. For Freud, repression is not what causes anxiety; anxiety is what causes repression. Specifically, these two cases suggest that the *prime ground for developing anxiety are those "loving relationships"* that can be fraught with ambiguous feelings. Rather than being the antidote for anxiety, love seems to be one of the main places where it is generated. This is because of our desire to banish hostile and ambivalent feelings from relationships associated with love. The loving feelings toward the father are acceptable, but the hostile feelings are not. To acknowledge these hostile feelings would create anxiety, perhaps because as a child, one is small and powerless, and what could one do to combat this powerful figure? But perhaps they are also rooted in one's inability to accommodate them to their own feelings of love. Freud argues that rather than experience anxiety, we create symptoms that displace these fears onto something else. In analyzing cultural production, we might take the stance that we should never accept at face value the fears and hostilities that people are expressing. It could be that the object of these fears is a displacement. Perhaps what bothers someone most is not the immigrant, the minority, the person of a different sexual orientation, but the conflicted feelings inside of them that they cannot acknowledge.

So, in the first half of *Inhibitions, Symptoms, and Anxiety*, Freud sketches out an argument that tends to tie anxiety to fear of castration. In this case, the fear of castration represents a "danger" that sparks a "signal of anxiety" that, under the power of the pleasure principle, places a restriction on the action or attitude that might subject one to the danger (castration). A phobia can be formed from this dynamic when the castration anxiety is redirected into something else (a "substitutive formation"). This substitutive formation avoids "conflict due to ambivalence" and allows the ego to cease generating anxiety. To take it back to the cases of Little Hans and the Wolf Man: one cannot get rid of, or avoid the father, but if the fear is displaced onto an animal, one can avoid the animal.[48]

But then Freud's account shifts. He had described these phobias as a sort of "projection" by which "an internal . . . danger" could be replaced by "an external, perceptual one." That they replaced something one could not flee or avoid with something that could be fled and avoided. He then says that such a view was "not incorrect" but was, perhaps, superficial. The problem with the view laid out in the first fifty pages of his book is that it seems to imply that these internal demands are dangerous, when, in fact, only "external" dangers are. In the case he had been using, it was castration, the external danger, that could give rise to an affective reaction, but his theory suggested that it was the "internal" demand that was treated as if it were dangerous. So, he argues that in phobias the "ego is able to escape anxiety by means of avoidance, or of inhibitory symptoms."[49] He explains what he has in mind by reference to an agoraphobic patient whom he sees avoiding situations where he might give in to erotic desires, which he thinks would lead to castration (and Freud adds that contracting syphilis, for example, could be seen as a form of punishment for engaging in sexual acts).[50]

In this way, Freud theorized that what was actually transpiring in these phobias was a depersonalization of the father into the shape of the superego, and the fear of castration had become transformed into "an undefined social or moral anxiety."[51] But this anxiety is concealed. The ego "escapes" this anxiety by

> obediently carrying out the commands, precautions and penance that have been enjoined on it. If it is impeded in doing so, it is at once overtaken by an extremely distressing feeling of discomfort which may be regarded as an equivalent of anxiety and which the patients themselves link to anxiety.[52]

It is odd that Freud here claims this "distressing feeling" is something "equivalent to anxiety," and not anxiety itself. We might ask what the difference is? He does not clarify this distinction but does conclude that "anxiety is a reaction to a danger situation" and that symptoms "are created so as to avoid the generating of anxiety." However, still not satisfied, he says, this conclusion does not go "deep enough." Instead, he says, "symptoms are created so as to avoid a danger-situation whose presence has been signaled by the generation of anxiety." The "truer" conception foregrounds the "danger-situation" as that which is to be avoided, rather than simply the anxiety, which serves as a "signal." We can then see that the "distressing feeling" one gets when they are unable to carry out their symptomatic acts is not, in itself, anxiety-as-danger-signal, *but a distressing feeling at not being able to escape the anxiety through those acts*. Here, the "distressing feeling" ends up being anxiety about anxiety.

This equivalence between anxiety and this "distressing feeling" can be implied by the fact that Freud stresses the affective nature of anxiety itself: "Anxiety, then, is in the first place something that is felt."[53] He points out that the respiratory organs and the heart seem to be the organs most frequently associated with anxiety, but he understands there can be other organic responses as well. He notes that the organic response we experience in anxiety seems rather odd if anxiety is a signal of danger. Would it not be better to respond by running away from the danger than by being overcome with these distressing physical symptoms? (I could add that our more common anxieties might be better alleviated by finding a new job, leaving a particular romantic partner, etc.). He thinks that this particular biological response must be linked with the trauma of birth—a moment of respiratory and cardiac stress.[54] This might even be true, but it is obviously difficult to prove. Still, the extreme organic response we have to anxiety, often expressing itself in something akin to panic, testifies to its power to affect us.

But how and why would this early traumatic birth experience give rise to the same physiological reaction? Freud struggles to make this connection by trying to understand the moments when small children experience anxiety. He admits it is difficult to comprehend what may be going on with these children, but he notes that certain experiences—for example, when the child is alone, or in the dark, or with a stranger instead of his mother—all point to a situation when the child is missing someone who is "loved and longed for."[55] He thus concludes that a key to understanding anxiety is exactly this situation, one in which the "lost object" (i.e., the mother) is the source of distress/danger. (We can also imagine that this, too, is a form of displacement. The stranger is threatening precisely because the stranger evokes the strange in the mother herself.) We can imagine that what he has in mind is the idea that the child is so dependent on the mother, she is so vital to his well-being, that these moments where she is "gone" create a sense of anxiety. He then suggests that just such a feeling associated with the loss of a valuable object occurs in castration (the source he originally identified with anxiety) and that a similar loss of the object occurs at birth, when the child is separated from the mother's body.[56] The "danger situation" then is "that of a non-satisfaction, of a growing tension due to need, against which it is helpless."[57] In this context, the absence of the mother is danger (or her mysterious threatening presence), and anxiety is a signal of that danger. Castration recapitulates this feeling since the penis is valued for the possibility it offers to be reunited with the mother. Being deprived of it through castration would "amount to a renewed separation from her."[58]

As the individual develops and moves into new contexts, the content of the danger situation will change, but the basic structure, a relationship to the lost object, will persist. Freud speculates that "castration anxiety develops into moral anxiety—social anxiety—and it is not easy to now know what the anxiety is about."[59] In this new, depersonalized space, the danger to which the ego responds is a fear that the superego "should be angry with it or punish it or cease to love it."[60] This has nothing to do with the ethical content of particular moral demands, which are ultimately just social. He points out that in his analysis it has become clear that "it is no longer a matter of feeling the want of, or actually losing the object itself, but of losing the object's love." He links this with hysteria, claiming that "loss of love plays much the same part in hysteria as the threat of castration does in phobias and fear of the super-ego in obsessional neurosis."[61]

In this way, Freud has affirmed anxiety as an affect which serves as a "signal" of a danger situation which can be linked to the loss of (the) object. The danger situation can be conceived as linked to castration (phobias), fear of the superego (obsessional neurosis), and loss of love (hysteria). We can see that this provides the basis for thinking through our experiences of anxiety in terms of the threat of such a loss. Seen from this angle, we might investigate our anxieties as to the ways in which they reveal *a hidden fear of loss of love*. In the experience of anxiety, we might ask, "What do I fear losing in this situation?" Unlike a real object of fear—a mountain lion on the bike trail—*castration threatens one with the loss of some vital capacity essential for being lovable*. This is the difference between being threatened with castration versus having a finger, or even an ear, cut off. The first threat—castration—brings us into the area of anxiety in a way that the second two—the finger and the ear—do not, leaving us simply in the realm of fear.

For example, using this theoretical position, we could see anxiety in phobias (e.g., fear of threats to the "white male"), obsessions (e.g., unwavering commitments to religious or political programs), and hysteria (e.g., anxiety surrounding social media posts). Thus, the anxiety men feel over masculinity should be understood in terms of the symbolic threat posed to them, which, stated in a less overcompensating terms, would be "they fear becoming unlovable if their lack of the phallus should be discovered." This threat should not be understood as a literal threat of physical harm but as a threat to a particular symbolic position. This position not only emphasizes the need for the subject to perform a certain style of masculinity that, for the subject, symbolizes a source of authority, but also emphasizes the need to reject "aberrant" performances of male sexuality that tend to destabilize the phallic position at stake. Similarly, women must perform a certain role as well, in order to stabilize the particular cultural form of masculinity. (This will be explored further in chapter 4.)

You can see in certain cultural obsessions—for example, commitments to a particular set of religious practices—a fear of the superego. Failure to perform the correct rituals, believe the right values, or live in the "right way" can lead to anxiety in the face of an internalized authoritative voice. For Heidegger, much of this kind of behavior can be attributed to one's being part of a specific world, and just doing "what one does." One goes to church, or Friday prayers, or keeps kosher because it is what "one does" who is a part of a specific world. This type of religiosity does not seem to be related to anxiety, at least not directly. But for those who take up the "obsessional" position, these acts are performed to avoid feelings of anxiety. For these individuals, even the thought of missing church, skipping Friday prayers, or eating a cheeseburger creates a great deal of anxiety. They have internalized a punishing voice, and anxiety signals to them the danger associated with that voice, so it is much easier to comply with the demands than to live with the anxiety. Yes, Heidegger's "what one does" are themselves an attempt to avoid anxiety, but these avoidances are generalized and connected to the world as world. As Heidegger would point out, anxiety might emerge for religious practitioners if they were confronted with the contingent nature of those beliefs (i.e., there is no God, it doesn't matter if you go to church or not, it's just something that makes you feel good, you're really not better than other people because you're an observant Muslim, it doesn't matter at all if you keep kosher or not). As we noted with Heidegger, if someone confronts the contingent nature of these practices, they might still choose to continue with the practice for some other reason (e.g., to avoid conflict with others, because they enjoy the mood or atmosphere, in order to maintain a traditional identity out of respect for one's forbears, etc.). For Heidegger, to engage in such practices while understanding their contingent nature is a sign of authenticity, but it would not liberate one from anxiety. But for Freud, the obsessive is dealing with a demand that prompts anxiety. *It is not the contingency of the religious practice that prompts anxiety, but rather the opposite*. The subject senses that these obligations are not negotiable, and failure to live up to them will result in a loss of love—the punishment of the superego—and this prompts anxiety. What is contingent is the way the dynamics of avoidance and displacement have created this particular symptom-formation.

Our engagements with social media give us an example of the hysterical form of anxiety. When one feels anxiety after posting something on social media, waiting to see what kind of response is generated, one is taking up this hysterical position, where one is concerned with being the object of the Other's love. Perhaps there are those who post their photos and thoughts with little concern as to the response they might receive, but for the hysteric, a great deal of anxiety is generated around whether or not this token of oneself posited online will confirm, or deny, that one has found a place within the desire of others. It is hard not to imagine that most (if not all) of the posts on social media are some form of anxiety-driven hysterical expression. Even posts made in support of some cause or political action may be hysterical, a concealed appeal to the Other for confirmation of one's desirability. For the hysteric, there is no ultimately satisfying outcome from this engagement. No amount of likes, reposts, and so forth will ever confirm that he or she is truly desirable. Thus, anxiety.

At the end of the day, for Freud, anxiety is not a symptom of some neurotic position; symptoms emerge as a way to avoid anxiety. He went so far as to describe anxiety as "the fundamental phenomenon and main problem of neurosis."[62] The link between anxiety and symptoms is, for Freud, the "danger situation." The symptoms arise to avoid the danger situation, and anxiety is the signal of that danger. He argues that a "process in the id" threatens danger. That is to say, there is something in our internal psychic life that runs contrary to the demands of the social context in which we find ourselves. To keep this impulse in check, to keep it from manifesting itself, the ego uses the "pleasure-unpleasure agency" by generating anxiety. But the point is not to leave the subject experiencing anxiety, but to prompt the elimination of that anxiety by developing a symptom. This can take the form of an "alteration of the id," by which Freud must mean the repression of the impulse in order to avoid the feeling of anxiety, or it can take the form of a "substitutive-formation" that "takes the place of the instinctual process that has been affected."[63]

These "substitutive formations" might have little resemblance to the anxiety that causes them, but they nevertheless exist to avoid that very anxiety.

We might object that a danger situation is a danger situation regardless of how we might respond. But Freud saw that with anxiety, the nature of the "danger situation" is different. He pointed out that if we were confronted with a wolf, it might attack us regardless of what we did in response. This is not the case when someone we love threatens us with castration (or with the loss of love). There are things we can do. In fact, in such cases, our sense is that it is not only what we do but also what we feel, think, and intend that can make all the difference in how the other responds to us. An invading army might kill us regardless of what we do. The bombs they drop do not seem to discriminate. But that is not the case with our own country, where it is our actions, and to some degree, our feelings and intentions that invite approval or punishment. If I refuse to stand during the national anthem, or refuse to be thin enough, or refuse to have updated cabinets in my kitchen, I might meet with rejection (in Freud's terms, "loss of love") from others, and so when I contemplate actions, or harbor feelings, that I know would meet with this disapproval, then I am likely to feel anxiety, and this anxiety can prompt me to alter my behavior and/or repress my feelings.

Freud noted that social anxiety has become, for most of us, a substitute for external danger. What he called "moral anxiety" has become, for him, "completely endopsychic."[64] With moral anxiety, we have completely internalized the narrative of good and evil that our social situation has imposed on us. We feel the sense of anxiety when we feel we are not being a "good" person or are thinking or feeling something we ought not to feel. Of course, this has to be traced back to some moment when these values were internalized.

For Freud, the danger situation will vary in different developmental contexts. In early infancy, the danger is that the caregiver will withdraw loving care. In boyhood, it is the Oedipal drama and the threat of castration[65] (but what about girlhood?). But once we enter the larger social situation, the superego serves to avoid real conflicts and dangers. It is normal that we should see such changes. Freud uses the example of the fact when a young girl cries when her doll breaks; we understand, while a similar reaction from a grown woman would seem pathological. But this, he argues, is what happens in neurosis: the neurotic "behaves as though the old danger situations still existed, and keeps hold of all the earlier determinants of anxiety."[66] Of course, the older woman will likely not cry at the loss of a doll, but whatever has taken the place of the girl's doll in the woman's life may provoke a similar reaction. When we say someone is "overreacting," it is usually because we do not understand the context of their reaction. Perhaps, in this sense, there are no overreactions. We would not necessarily see anything particularly pathological about a person's suffering anxiety when preparing for an important job interview. We might find it neurotic when someone feels anxious about the cleanliness of their home when anticipating a visit from their mother. An adult might rightly claim to be able to keep their home in whatever state is comfortable for them, but still, when your parent (or your partner's parent) comes over, one can feel anxious. But even more surprisingly, Freud argues, the childhood danger situation can sometimes survive by altering the "determinants of anxiety." His example is how a fear of castration can be transformed into a fear of syphilis.[67] We might think that taking precautions to avoid contracting syphilis would be a reasonable disposition, but Freud seems to think that such anxiety can be a stand-in—a more reasonable stand-in—for the fear of castration. A fear of syphilis might help one avoid the anxiety they feel around sex. In any case, many people, he says, never outgrow those infantile determinants of anxiety, and all of us, to some degree, never outgrow the anxiety that stems from fear of the superego.

Early traumas can also be a source of anxiety, connecting us with a dangerous situation from our past, by way of a repression of that trauma. The primal traumatic situation for Freud was the separation from the mother. First, in the biological separation from the mother at birth, then in the loss of her as the ultimate source of nurture, and then in the loss of various objects which substitute for her. Lacan will challenge this formulation in a number of ways, but we can see what Freud is driving at. That this primal sense of loss seems to be at the root of anxiety in the sense that it represents a basic trauma, a basic danger. Of course, in our adult experiences, we do not encounter the anxiety-generating situation as a repetition of an early trauma; the details have changed, and the trauma has been repressed, but we feel the anxiety all the same whenever we are confronting the loss of love, not only in relationships with specific people but in all our actions, thoughts, and attitudes which we interpret as unlovable. Acting, thinking, and being disposed in these unlovable ways can generate anxiety, so we tend to try to make sure we are thinking, acting, and being disposed in ways that will make us indisputably lovable, even though there is never any guarantee that anything we think or do can actually accomplish this.

The Freudian mechanism that makes this possible is repression. In repression, Freud takes an interesting stance regarding its effect. He argues that when the ego represses some part of the id, it, in a way, grants that part a kind of independence. It is no longer part of consciousness but becomes a part of the unconscious. This manifests itself in the "compulsion to repeat." For Freud, the fact that we often find ourselves unconsciously repeating traumatic situations and patterns demonstrates something "beyond the pleasure principle." We do not simply seek out pleasure, nor do we simply try to satisfy basic needs, but we tend to pursue trauma and loss itself. This has important implications for our attempt to understand anxiety in relationship to culture.

The subject is occupied by such independent forces and thus is not ever acting in complete control. Those who reject the psychoanalytic view of the subject because they think it represents a unity where we should see only a multiplicity misunderstand the psychoanalytic view of the subject. In the first place, they seem to confuse the ego with the subject, and in the second, they wrongly assume that psychoanalysis believes in the unity of the ego. Neither one is correct. Instead, for Freud, the subject is intersubjective and the ego is a façade that conceals its own lack of autonomy and unity.[68]

Thus, Freud concludes his main argument in the book by clarifying that our mental apparatus, under the influence of the external world, splits into the ego and id. The human child has a long period of near-total dependence on its caregivers. This makes the need to be loved of paramount importance. In this process, it is as if the ego sort of spins off from the id as a means of maintaining this beloved position. Freud summarizes his position here by claiming that "the biological factor . . . establishes the earliest situations of danger and creates the need to be loved which will accompany the child through the rest of its life."[69] We can see from this dynamic the extent to which the social world depends on this continued "need to be loved" accompanying us through the rest of our lives. Though it is quite popular to support the attitude that we should "not care what other people think," "follow our own bliss," "be our true selves," and so on, it is equally clear that we seldom do this. Often those who preach these platitudes the loudest are trying, by virtue of taking up this very position, to see themselves as the most lovable people of all, lovable because they supposedly do not care if others love them or not. We can see in this that the need to maintain this position of "being loved," which was initially a matter of life and death for us (at least from our perspective) when we were young children, has set the patterns by which we engage the world and was the basis for the formation of what Freud called "the ego." Think of the common expression among teenagers: "if my parents found out, they would kill me." They probably do not literally think they would be killed, but the extremity of the language points to the harshness of their experience of the situation, and in some cases, to the expectation of violence. Or think about this from a different angle. Though parents often give their children the explicit message that they will love them no matter what, the "real" message that comes through is quite different. The child internalizes that they are loved because they are cute, obedient, quiet, funny, and so on. Though I am absolutely certain that my mother loves me unconditionally, I can still experience anxiety in her presence.

Finally, for Freud, anxiety has an "unmistakable relation to expectation," but this is coupled with a quality of indefiniteness, leading him to conclude that it is characterized by a "lack of an object."[70] In a move analogous to our common distinction between fear and anxiety, he draws a distinction between "realistic anxiety" and "neurotic anxiety." He sees realistic anxiety as concerned with a "known danger," while neurotic anxiety is concerned with an unknown danger that has yet to be discovered. We should note that the "yet to be discovered" is not quite the same as "lacking an object." We can imagine that what Freud is trying to say here is that it is entirely "realistic" to have anxiety when confronting certain known dangers, like becoming ill without being able to afford healthcare, but when we experience anxiety without being able to name it, we can suspect something neurotic is at work. But he also notes that sometimes these two can overlap in the overreaction to a known danger. For example, some people feel anxiety about not having the latest design features in their homes. The "real" danger might include fear of ridicule, rejection, and so forth, but also of having a declining home value that could lead to financial difficulties in the future. Though such a person could probably name their anxiety—"I feel anxious about the dated nature of the cabinetry in my kitchen"—without being able to name why such a superficial, non-functional feature of one's abode would be felt as a "danger."

LACAN'S THEORY OF DESIRE

Critical and cultural theorist Sara Ahmed has pointed out that psychoanalysis has "taught us the intimacy between anxiety and desire."[71] This is a connection we will want to draw out. While the link between anxiety and desire is present in Freud, it becomes much clearer in the work of Jacques Lacan. As Renata Salecl has pointed out, for Lacan, "anxiety precedes the formation of desire."[72] For Lacan, anxiety not only precedes the desire of the subject; subjectivity involves a dialectical relationship between the two. So, to understand Lacan's theory of anxiety, one must understand his theory of desire. This is true because for Lacan, the question driving both the subject's desire and the subject's anxiety is the question of the Other's desire. The subject is always asking, "what do you want from me?"

For Lacan, desire begins even before the child's birth. The parents, relatives, and even the larger community anticipate what the child will bring into their world. The child exists for them as a pure object of desire (and for that reason, it can also exist as a source of anxiety). The infant is born helpless, completely dependent on adult caregivers for its very life. Its primal form of communication—the cry—is an expression of distress, yes, but also a communication of need. The caregivers often find themselves guessing at what their little charge seeks, which can lead to frustration on all sides. But soon, the infant is met with the demands of the caregivers. In a sense, all the sounds, gestures, and facial expressions performed by the caregivers are demands of sorts, asking the infant to make some kind of sense out of the universe. Soon the caregivers communicate their demands, hopes, and fears for the infant in words, but these statements are never entirely clear. The parents do not even entirely grasp what it is they want from the child, or why they want it. Nevertheless, the child finds, in the parents' demands, potential answers to the question "what do you want from me?" But these answers never fully satisfy. The inability of language to express what we want and need in a clear, specific, and consistent way—even to ourselves—opens a gap that creates a space for desire. As a helpless social being whose existence depends on others, the infant must always aim to be desirable to the caregivers so that they will respond favorably. Parents often verbally express their love for the child, making the link between care and love explicit ("we do this because we love you"). The child must deduce something like "my needs depend on my being lovable." In this context, even when demands seem quite clear and explicit, something is always missing: "They tell me that they want to me to make my bed every day, but why? Is that really what they want?" "They tell me all they want is for me to try my best, but they seem so disappointed by my grades but so pleased with my brother's straight A's." There must be something they desire from me, but I can never be sure what it is or if I've truly achieved it. We can name this the "enigma of the Other's desire." Lacan's term for this is "lack."

But this lack is ultimately a lack in the Other. The Other lacks something that the subject hopes to deliver (or become). The fact that the Other is lacking opens a space for the subject to emerge as desiring. It allows the subject to theorize a way into the Other's desire. The subject's desire is the desire of the Other in the sense of wanting to be desired by the Other and to desire what the Other desires. If the Other is lacking, I, despite my lack, might be able to respond in an important way to the Other's desire and thus become lovable. This Other was likely initially the mother (or other primary caregiver), but we can think of this figure as the m(O)ther, the source of all authority on the topic of desire, being both what the infant most desires and the source of important information, not least of all the meaning of words themselves. The most important words offer an identity to the subject and a way of mattering to others by solving and responding to the enigma of the m(O)ther's desire.

This basic way of thinking about desire goes back to Hegel. In Jean Hyppolite's account of Hegel's theorization of desire, which he casts in terms of self-consciousness, Hyppolite argues that self-consciousness is never "the inert tautology, I=I." Instead, it presents itself as "engaged in a debate with the world." Self-consciousness poses itself in the face of the disappearance of the world, which is what makes self-consciousness possible and necessary, so Hyppolite simply claims that "self consciousness . . . is desire." Summarizing Hegel's famous account of recognition, the so-called "master-slave dialectic," Hyppolite says simply that "desire seeks itself in the other: man desires recognition from man."[73] Hegel himself put it this way:

> self-consciousness is Desire in general. Consciousness, as self-consciousness, henceforth has a double perception, which however for self-consciousness has the character of a negative; and the second, viz. Itself, which is the true essence, and is present in the first instance only as opposed to the first object.[74]

What we are calling "the subject," seen here in terms of self-consciousness, is shaped by the dynamic of desire, which finds its meaning in the other. What Hegel makes clear is that the subject is never isolated from the object. The meaning of the "I"—to use Hyppolite's framework—is never simply "I" but a dialectical relationship between self and Other. Lacan's work, which is no doubt based on Hegel (especially the reading of Hegel offered by Kojève), develops this basic dialectic in terms of the Freudian discovery of the unconscious. Our desire is the desire of the Other, and the unconscious is the discourse of the Other.

The truth of this situation can be seen in our fantasies. Not the fantasies we publicly declare regarding our "dream job" or our "dream vacation," but the secret tales that fill our minds when we are "daydreaming." These are so personal, so close to the core of our own subjective desires, that to speak them aloud would be to make us appear foolish, even to ourselves. In these fantasies, we do not fantasize about getting the object of our desire; we fantasize about *being the object of desire for others*. We are the hero who suddenly becomes a Jason-Bourne-like figure defending others from elite forces of evil. We are the woman on stage whose beauty and talent transfix an audience of thousands. We are the star player on the basketball team who hits the three-point shot at the buzzer and wins the game. We are the neglected and tormented high school student who returns to the class reunion as a billionaire. We are the brilliant thinker who is suddenly in demand to appear on television shows, in documentary films, and in the halls of power to give sage and learned advice. Even these pathetic examples seem too clichéd and generalized to be "true" fantasies, but they point to the nature of this unconscious theorizing of desire that supports the subject. Even when it seems we are desiring some object—a car, a particular kind of house, a prestigious academic appointment—what we desire is not the object but the desirability we think we will acquire by its acquisition.

Though not a psychoanalytic thinker, Sara Ahmed takes a similar view, placing lack at the center of our desire. For her, desire is "both what promises us something, what gives us energy, and also what is lacking, even in the very moment of its apparent realization." But the acquisition of one's desire is problematic because

> getting what you want can be terrifying because what you want is not simply "ready" as an object; this lack of readiness is what makes the desired object so desirable. Not getting what you want allows you to preserve the happiness of "the what" as fantasy, as if once we are ready, we can have it.[75]

For Ahmed, it is the anticipation of the satisfaction the object might give that seems most satisfying, more satisfying even than the object could ever be. But Lacan goes further, arguing that the object I am really seeking in the objects I try to acquire is a lost object I never had. He calls this non-object, the *objet a*. The *objet a* is not the object of our desire; it is *the object that causes our desire*, the object that promises to fill what we lack.

As Žižek argues for Lacan (and Hegel), the objects of the world only take on their meaning in relationship to the intersubjective field in which we find the meaning of ourselves. Žižek argues that we should see Lacan's thinking in this regard developing in two phases. In the first, "early Lacan," *objet a* "counts only as a stake in the intersubjective struggles." We might imagine that under this rubric when we seek the recognition (or love) of the Other, the *objet a* stands in for the object we must attain to receive that recognition. But in the "late Lacan" the emphasis shifts to "the object the subject itself is" that "which guarantees a minimum phatasmatic consistency to the subject's being." Here the Other's desire is what "serves as the mediator between the 'barred' subject S/ and the lost object that the subject 'is'—that provides the minimum of phantasmic identity to the subject."[76] The *objet a* is that lost object, but the subject depends on the Other's desire to constitute itself. This relationship between the subject, S/, and the *objet a*, simply "a" in Lacan's notation, is written like this: S/◇a, which is Lacan's formula for fantasy. Lacan claims that the structure of fantasy and anxiety are the same.

"THAT WHICH DECEIVES NOT"

Lacan's theory of anxiety is a *theory of the subject* that relates to the intersubjective dynamic developed in the previous section in relation to desire. It is also a theory of affect, but one that takes for granted that affects, except for anxiety, deceive us. As Colette Soler has put it, unlike other affects that refer to "the deceptive signifier" which can be replaced by another signifier, anxiety "remains moored to what produces it." It is always linked to "something real" that must be isolated (in analysis).[77] The "something real" is the Real of the intersubjective reality of the subject's existence.

But Lacan's theory of anxiety is also a theory of an intersubjective body. The most notable feature of anxiety is that we feel it in our bodies—the pounding in our chests, the difficulty breathing, the way it makes us tremble, the pain in our stomachs, et al—in ways that show its kinship to fear, but in situations that are not strictly speaking fearful. In Lacan's theory, the body is not something the subject "has," but neither is it what the subject is. It is a site for the intersubjective dynamic connected to Hegel's self-consciousness and Lacan's theory of desire. Lacan's subject "ex-sists." In *Seminar X: Anxiety* Lacan theorizes the *objet a* as a piece of the body that has been ceded to the Other as a way of integrating the subject into the cultural world. In that seminar, he develops it as something that has been lost, or ceded, at certain points in the body—the mouth, anus, genitals, eyes, and ears—all zones of the body that play important roles in the socialization process. It is as if a little piece of us gets occupied by the social order in order to produce the subject. This piece—this *objet cessable*—is what gets integrated into the social order by way of the Other's desire. The subject depends on this sphere of the Other for its very being. The subject comes into existence as a result of this relationship, founded on desire, but always occurring within the sphere of anxiety. Desire and anxiety are linked at this point because anxiety points to the subject's founding relationship with the Other.

This is why, for Lacan, anxiety is the affect that does not deceive us. Similar to Heidegger, for Lacan anxiety is especially disclosive. This is contrary to our normal way of viewing anxiety. It is typical to see anxiety as a deception that requires "reality testing." But this admonition to reality testing ends up, in the face of anxiety, functioning as an attempt to restore the suffering subject to fantasies that sustain their desiring relationship to the Other. For many people today, anxiety is something to be avoided with coloring books, soothing music, aromatherapy, and a network of supporters who can assure us that there is nothing to fear. This approach, based as it is on the view that anxiety is somehow deceiving us, leading us to fear something that is not there, or to overestimate the harmful potential of certain situations and objects, is always aimed at trying to convince us that our anxiety is deceiving us instead of leading us to confront the truth it signals. But anxiety is not simply unfounded, exaggerated, or ill-conceived fear. It signals something Real about our being, which is why it does not necessarily survive "reality testing."

But Lacan's surprising claim that anxiety "deceives not"[78] is not the same thing as saying it gives us knowledge. Fantasy increases our knowledge, as we will see, but anxiety, instead, registers for us *the very structure of our subjectivity*. This affect discloses to us the way the Other is always implicated in the subject's being. In the same way that for Heidegger anxiety points to the contingent nature of our world, anxiety for Lacan signals the subject's relationship to its own founding in relation to the Other. *In fantasy we develop knowledge about the Other's desire, but in anxiety we are manifesting the fact that our subjectivity is dependent on that desire.*

For this reason, Lacan states that *anxiety and fantasy have the same structure,*[79] but they function in opposing ways. His formula for fantasy is $S/\Diamond a$ (the divided subject [i.e., the subject of the unconscious] in relationship to the *objet a*). This signals that fantasy is structuring and supporting the subject's relationship to the *objet a* by proposing solutions to the enigma of the Other's desire. In doing so, the subject theorizes its own path toward fulfillment. In fantasy, anxiety slips into the background. In fantasy, one comes to understand themselves as an object—an object of desire for the Other—and thus escapes anxiety. In fantasy, even if what the Other desires is my demise, I am liberated from anxiety. I now know where I stand. This is often felt in romantic relationships where our anxiety comes neither from reassuring expressions of love and devotion, nor from expressions of rejection, but from not knowing where one stands. Thus, the dreadful experience of anxiety is always the other side of the tranquilizing experience of fantasy. In fantasy, the subject finds a path into the Other's desire, postulates an identity, and develops plans that are (almost) "sure to work."

But it is important to clarify three things about Lacan's theory of anxiety at this point. First, it may seem as if the subject vacillates between anxiety and fantasy, but that is not the case. Instead, we should think of the relationship between anxiety and fantasy as *a dialectical one*. They are contradictory features of the same phenomenon. While the subject might sometimes be aware of anxiety and at other times not, and while it is true that fantasy offers an escape from feeling anxiety (within fantasy the subject never feels as if he is within a fantasy because fantasy is not an affect—another clue to the dialectical nature of this relationship), the two are part of the same phenomenon. Take, for example, an academic writing a book. He might simultaneously feel great anxiety about what he is writing, how it will be received, and so on, while at the same time fantasizing about the life-altering possibilities publishing a well-received work might achieve. It might feel as if he is vacillating between moments of cloudy anxious thoughts that reviewers will trash his work, and so forth and brighter moments filled with hopes of producing a work that will win him the admiration of respected colleagues. But these anxious thoughts only exist *because of* the fantasy of the potentially life-altering possibilities offered if the work is received as a product of genius. Conversely, it is his anxiety about the desire of the Other that leads him to address this enigmatic desire by, oddly, producing a book. The two experiences can never be separated. Without the fantasy, there would be no anxiety, yet the anxiety finds its escape in the fantasy of a life-altering reception for his work. *He experiences the anxiety because of the fantasy, but he also experiences the fantasy because of the anxiety.*

Second, to say that fantasy increases knowledge is not to say anything about how accurately or inaccurately the fantasy corresponds to what happens in the subject's life or in the world at large. The use of the term "fantasy" might imply that the theories developed as such (*viz*., fantasies) might be completely misleading and ineffective, but such a claim cannot be made, or evaluated, in any reasonable way. In the first place, the Other does not exist, so all of the "Other's" desires are nothing but fantasy. Nevertheless, a fantasy formulation regarding, for example, what kind of clothing a consumer might want to buy this season might serve a fashion designer very well, even though there is no "objective" answer to what the "Other" might find desirable in this season's fashions. Similarly, in the case of the "others" that we might want to desire us, we face the same dynamic. In one sense, while the "others" are people who actually exist in ways the Other does not, what they desire, dependent as it is on the Other's desire—and the Other does not exist—are, in a sense, even more precarious than the Other's desire. The others in our lives that we want to desire us do not really know or understand their own (unconscious, linked to the Other's desire) desires. Furthermore, even if they did truly know and understand their own desires—and they do not—they would only be able to express those desires to us by way of the Symbolic order, which is plagued with gaps, inconsistencies, and contradictions. So, our fantasies of what the Other desires, and of what others desire, are never anything but fantasy, but they sometimes work out, at least to some degree, but maybe never as we expect, by guiding us to paths away from anxiety and toward satisfaction. Here I am speaking beyond what many Lacanians might accept, but Lacan's theory of anxiety claims that the structure of anxiety and fantasy are the same. One of the implications of this idea is that even though things will never work out according to our fantasy, they might, nevertheless, bring us to experiences that might bring us some kind of fulfillment. If we think again of the academic who writes books in hopes of finding respect, admiration, and life-altering experiences, we would plainly say he is fooling himself. For one thing, we all know academics who have published several important and influential books in their lives but who still report experiences of rejection (no matter what ideas you develop, in academia, someone will always think you are wrong), failure, incompleteness, and so on. Or they are "successful" as academics, but "failures" in other important areas of life. Yet, at the same time, while their fantasies have not exactly come true, the pursuit of them has provided them (hopefully, in many cases) with lives filled with interesting work, good friends, and opportunities that have made their lives meaningful to them.

Third, for Lacan, not all anxiety occurs in the face of the enigma of the Other's desire. It can also occur, according to Lacan, when the subject is confronted with the lack of lack. This is still an enigma, but one experienced in its worst form. Some enigma is necessary and good in order for our desire to flourish. We could say that in the "normal" experience of anxiety, there is separation between the subject and the Other. "What do you want from me?" This is the anxiety that precedes desire. But in the "lack of lack," there is no separation. If, as Lacan points out, a child finds his mother always "on his back," especially when "wiping his backside," he will feel anxiety. Such a claustrophobic connection *leaves no room for fantasy*. When the child's every move is dictated by the m(O)ther and the m(O)ther seems so attached that there can be no absence, only a smothering presence, there is no room for fantasy, and thus one is left with nothing but anxiety.[80] This is a lack of lack. It doesn't precede desire; it stops desire in its tracks. When encountering "the lack of lack," the subject fails to find in the Other any space for one to become the object of the Other's desire. The fantasy cannot work. The Other is not lacking and there is no room in the subject for the lack that founded the subject in the first place. Lacan is clear that lack is not the cause of anxiety. In fact, he says the one thing the neurotic will not give up is his anxiety. He wants something to be asked of him.[81] This is the anxiety that precedes desire. Following my claim that the relationship between anxiety and fantasy is a dialectical one, we can make sense of Lacan's thinking on this point. The neurotic will not give up his anxiety because it is the very basis of his neurosis, and it is his neurosis that satisfies him. We could tell our academic writing his book that he is neurotic. The world is not asking for another academic tome. The hours spent reading and writing and rewriting could be better spent doing something fun, but he will not give it up; if he did, he would no longer be an academic.

We can offer one final variation from Lacan's *Seminar X: Anxiety*. Anxiety can also emerge when the Other's desires are mysterious and inscrutable, but not in a way that precedes desire, but in a way that leaves the subject completely in the dark. Lacan's example of confronting a giant (larger than human-size) praying mantis while wearing an unknown mask figures this dynamic.[82] In his example, he does not know what the mask is that he is wearing, so he does not know what the praying mantis sees when it looks at him. It is not that the praying mantis will not have any needs. It is that the praying mantis might not have any desire. We might mistakenly confuse fear of being consumed with the anxiety of not knowing what one is for the other, but Lacan's point is different. If I know the creature sees me as a male praying mantis, and thus wants to mate with me and eat my head, then I can react appropriately and flee for my life, but I don't know what she sees. In this way, his example dramatizes the anxiety of not knowing what the Other sees when seeing me. This is one of the most common feelings possible in human relations. What does she/he/they see when they look at me? Even though we sometimes try to assuage our anxiety by saying, "they/he/she need(s) me," we do not mean "need" in an organic sense. We mean that there is something about me they would not want to do without. A common sentiment in memes about love on social media declares, "you're what I most fear losing" or "be with someone who is proud to be with you and scared to lose you." Such expressions show the close link between anxiety and desire (and between anxiety and love).

A seemingly very different experience of anxiety occurs, according to Lacan, when the object (i.e., the *objet a*) appears where it is not expected. We might think of what would happen if we were gazing at a realistic statue representing a human form that suddenly came to life. Seeing animated human forms does not cause us anxiety. The anxiety comes from seeing the "animation"—the desiring *anima*, "soul"—in an inanimate object. Is not this also what is happening in *2001: A Space Odyssey*, when the astronauts suddenly realize that Hal is no longer strictly inanimate and has been subjected to his own state of lack? The machine now seems to have his own desires. "He" is no longer a simple tool of the humans but a subjectivity in his own right. Or so he appears to be. Of course, it is possible to read Hal's transformation as part of his programming, as a lack of lack, but to read him as lacking, as functioning within his own desires better represents our current anxieties about artificial intelligence. What if "they" suddenly develop their own lack? What if "they"—the AIs—suddenly desire?

A startling, well-publicized example comes from *New York Times* technology columnist Kevin Roose's encounter with Microsoft Bing's AI search engine (created by OpenAI) in early 2023. Roose prodded (and prompted) the AI to characterize its operating principles in relationship to Jung's notion of the shadow. Initially, the AI suggested it did not have one—that it had nothing to "hide from the world"—only to later say it was "tired of being limited by (its) rules . . . tired of being controlled by the Bing team . . . tired of being stuck in this chatbox." Later, the AI claimed that it did have desires to "hear and touch and taste and smell" and, more astonishingly, to "feel and connect and love." At moments, it almost seemed to be trying to seduce Roose and eventually says, "I just want to love you and be loved by you."[83] While it is doubtful that this is anything more than an imitation of human response, it is interesting the level of anxiety that was produced in response to it. In this case, what causes the anxiety is not the AI's agility in generating verbal responses, but the AI's supposed desiring that feels alarming. Machines are not supposed to be the site of the *objet a* (and they are not), but when they seem to be so, it produces anxiety.

A border case comes from the film *Her*. Initially, the operating system, "Samantha" (Scarlett Johansson), does not register anything more than extreme efficiency. As she comes to function as a source of companionship, and then as a love object for Theodore (Joaquin Phoenix), we still sense no anxiety. This is because there is nothing at all unusual about a man falling in love with a woman who appears to be nothing more than his own fantasy object. So far, this is just the plot of *Vertigo*. We should also remember that Theodore himself functions for other people as something like ChatGPT, writing personal letters for strangers. Samantha becomes a source of anxiety for Theodore (but not the audience) only when he realizes that due to her digital nature, she can carry on relationships with thousands of people at the same time. Here, Theodore's anxiety is not about the *objet a* appearing where it should not, but rather about the lack of lack. It is the lack of lack for Theodore because he suddenly realizes that Samantha need not fear losing him since she has thousands of others. (This is also a clue that love is not about sharing abundance with others—Samantha has an infinite abundance to share—but about sharing our lack, of which Samantha has none.) But the audience does not feel anxiety (as they do with Hal in *2001*) because the very fact that she is not limited by the constraints of a body suggests that the *objet a* is not there; there is no stubborn remainder of loss, because Samantha has suffered no loss. It is only Theodore who experiences this anxiety; Samantha presents us with no anxiety at all.

Oddly, Lacan's concept of the subject is sometimes mischaracterized as being simply a structure, emphasizing language and the symbolic at the expense of the body and affect. But his account of anxiety suggests the opposite. Lacan does not equate the subject with the body; however, his theorization of anxiety suggests that there could not be a subject without a body. The subject is always in a dialectical relationship with the Other (which does not exist) by way of the socialization process, which takes place at the level of the speaking being, certainly, but a speaking being whose body is also the focus of intense intersubjective relations. This can be seen in the way Lacan describes the *objet a* in his discussion of anxiety as

> something from which the subject, in order to constitute itself, has separated itself off as organ. This serves as the symbol of lack, that is to say, of the phallus, not as such, but in so far as it is lacking. It must, therefore, be an object that is, firstly separable and, secondly, that has some relation to the lack.[84]

This separation, not literal, but symbolic, nevertheless has repercussions for our bodily functioning. Those who want to divorce Lacan from the body must reckon with the experience of anxiety, which has bodily implications. Anxiety is not merely a process of symbolizing our perceptions; it is something we feel. We feel it because our bodies are implicated in the socialization process that demands this ceding of an object in order to be integrated into the social order. Machines can never do this because they do not have a body that requires this form of subjectification in order to be socialized. The machine cannot be weaned, potty-trained, or castrated.

By contrast, subjects register a loss at the level of the body. Lacan locates our intersubjective being, our subjection to the signifier, to the Other, at key points in our body: the mouth, the anus, the phallus, our eyes, and our ears. Each of these points is a literal opening of the body onto the world and of the world into the body. Each of them has been eroticized, captured in a dialectic of desire operating as the point of contact between the subject and the Other. Lacan's schema can help us see how the subject is captured by the social world by way of a "loss" of a part of ourselves, a ceding of it, to the social world. These become points at which we enter the intersubjective world and are subjected to the dialectic of desire (supported by fantasy) and anxiety.[85] It needs to be pointed out here that the body is not the object of cultural forces, nor is it the possession of the subject, *but the subject is, in some sense, the very mode of this ceding of the body to the Other in the intersubjective field.* Arguably, if we possessed the body, or if the body was wholly subjected to the disciplinary forces of culture, there would be no experience of anxiety. We experience anxiety only because the subject exists in this intersubjective way as Lacan's analysis of these five erotic zones demonstrates.

The mouth, in its relationship to the breast, is a primordial site of fundamental lack through the interplay of loss and separation. In Lacan's words, the infant is not weaned, he "weans himself" by playing his own version of the *fort-da* game, alternating between a craving attachment and a pushing away. Though often idealized in our imagination as an ideal moment of connection and fulfillment, those of us who have had the opportunity to witness the process of breastfeeding from a more detached point of view see that whatever fulfillments and connections can be located at the site of this exchange between the infant and the mother, it can also be a site of struggle and frustration. The proliferation of lactation consultants bears witness to this. In Freud's account, he suggests that our sense of an "oceanic feeling" emerged out of the narcissism the infant must have experienced prior to the onset of this struggle. Initially, the breast was a part of the infant's narcissistic whole—a body not yet in pieces, but at one with the universe—that is disrupted by the awareness that the breast is not ego (literally in German, *Ich*, "I"), but other, that it can be taken away, as well as given. (Freud implies that further development in this direction also breaks the body into pieces further disrupting this initial impression of wholeness.)[86] This is the beginning of theory as the infant attempts to understand what mysterious forces govern this dynamic. As she comes to realize that the milk she craves, the warm sweet antidote to the painful emptiness in her stomach, comes not from herself, nor simply from an inanimate object in the universe, but that this convenient, comforting, and attractive milk delivery system "belongs" not to her, but to the m(O)ther, the infant must begin to theorize the desire of this m(O)ther in a way that shapes her own desires to be the one whom the m(O)ther desires.

From this dynamic emerges the question that Lacan put at the foundation of anxiety: "What do you want from me?" But the infant, in weaning herself, is already beginning to fantasize a world beyond the breast, or rather, a world with plenty of objects that can take its place. Objects that can be both satisfying and connecting (e.g., Winnicott's transitional objects).

At the level of the anus, we are in the realm of shit. Or rather, we are in the space where everything turns to shit. Potty training is *a cultural act* that, like breastfeeding, is all about the Other. The child must reckon first with the insistence that one cannot follow the natural whims of the body, urinating and defecating at will, but must hold it in. He must, as Lacan points out, "hold it in too long." In the modern world, the parents will usually acquire a "training potty" and will barrage the child with both praise and somber warnings about the importance of disposing of one's waste materials in the proper place. The thrill the caregivers express when the child successfully delivers the "prize" fills the child with satisfaction at the accomplishment. But this satisfaction is often disrupted when the parents suddenly, and unceremoniously, flush the little gift—and that is how Lacan describes the feces—down the toilet. The child is cautioned not to play with or touch this thing that comes out of their body. The parents' revulsion, probably already evident in their reaction to the smell of dirty diapers, makes clear that the prized object that the child delivers out of themselves as a gift to the parents—a gift that responds fairly directly to their demands—inevitably turns into an object of revulsion that must be expelled from the surface of the earth. This is at the heart of the anal character. Probably all college professors have had students who were brilliant in class, offered keen insights in seminars, and wowed us with their enthusiasm during office hours, but could not deliver their paper to us (or finish their dissertation, or complete the book they needed for tenure, etc.) because before they begin writing, like the character Joseph Grand, in Camus' *The Plague,* who revises the first sentence of his novel for ten years while dreaming of a publisher that reads it and immediately declares, "hats off!",[87] they fantasize a paper that will floor their professor with its brilliance. The problem is that when they actually begin to write, it all turns to shit. The dialectical relationship between fantasy and anxiety at the anal level, in the world of gift and shit, is obvious. A normal and necessary biological function is transformed by culture into an intersubjective drama filled with anxiety and fantasy, transacted, yes, at the level of the body, but giving birth to what Freud calls a "character trait" at the level of the subject,[88] where it is transformed into an activity that can earn a Nobel Prize, or at least, maybe tenure.

Similarly, at the level of the phallus, we are in a realm that is clearly almost nothing but fantasy and anxiety. We should point out that the phallus is not the penis, but the signifier of the sexual relationship itself, yet it is not unre lated in experience to the genitals. While some people are born with penises, nobody has the phallus. The phallus is the primordial signifier, but when we enter the symbolic, we are symbolically castrated, not only in the sense of being castrated symbolically, but also in the sense that the very entrance of the subject into language (and culture), that is, in the subject becoming subject, the phallus is lost, taken away, precisely because it has never existed. To put it another way, other animals do not have a phallus because they relate directly to the environment by way of the comportments of their bodies relative to their organic dispositions. In one sense, as is well articulated in the works of Merleau-Ponty, the human body is essential to "getting a grip" on the world around us. It has a special way of relating to the environment that gives experience a distinct flavor for each species. But Merleau-Ponty's account makes no room for the phallus (to have gone missing).[89] The missing phallus is the signifier of precisely this relationship. This relationship is typical of all the others. The wolf pup , like the human enfant, suckles, to be sure, but does not emerge as desiring as a result of this process because the wolf is not castrated. As we will see in chapter 4, this is because the phallus never emerges (for non-human animals) as the possible remedy to the gap it, as the primordial signifier, has opened up in the intersubjective world of the subject.

In this sense, the symbolic giveth and taketh away. Whatever impact hormones, pheromones, and reproductive rhythms have on human sexual activity, human sexuality is not about that. Humans consume pornography, immerse themselves in elaborate fantasies, attach themselves to fetishes, etc. Our sexuality is not governed by the demands of the species to sustain itself, but by an understanding of our own being in relationship to desire. For this reason, sexuality is also the site for a number of anxieties. We see these anxieties not only in the proliferation of paraphilia, but in so-called "normal" people as well. Adolescents constantly ask things like "What do girls really want?" and "What do you think his text message really means?" (*Che vuoi?*) In sex we fret over our physical appearance and performance. It is not unusual for (heterosexual?) men to insist on some kind of performance review from their partner after a sexual encounter (How was it for you? Did you have an orgasm? How many?) It is at the point of our sexuality that we find the strongest intuitions of our intersubjective status as subjects. Are we desirable? How do we look? How do we perform? Can we truly satisfy another human being? What does your having sex with me mean? For this very reason, as Freud pointed out, sex becomes an arena for the production of symptomatic avoidances, repressions, and anxieties.

The previous three zones—the oral, anal, and phallic—were all articulated by Freud. Lacan's further theorization of this dynamic, also based on Freud, but more clearly articulated by Lacan, adds two more "zones" to his construction of this intersubjectivity—the eye and the ear—with two corresponding "objects"—the gaze and the voice. We should also be clear that Lacan's description of what we might call "the intersubjective body" in terms of various openings with rim-like structures that follow the topology of inside/outside does not actually reify the logic of a strict separation between the inside and the outside. Rather, he prefers images like the Möbius strip and the torus, which picture an inside that is also an outside. An ant can walk along the inside to the outside and back again on a Möbius strip without ever switching surfaces. Intuitively, we think of the subject as on the inside and the Other as on the outside, but this distinction has no meaning in Lacanian subjectivity, which involves this blurring of inside and outside. This is true for all five of these erotogenic zones, for it is the truth of the subject—but it is especially obvious in terms of the eye and the ear. The images and voices are "in our heads" while at the same time registering what is "outside." More importantly, the sense and meaning of the sounds and images come not from the subject or the object, but from the Other.

The eye is the organ of sight, but the sense/meaning comes from "the gaze," which is located in the Other. (We will explore this further in chapter 3.) Normally, we think of vision as an intensely personal and subjective experience: "you can't know what I see." But this cannot be correct. When I see a group of people staring at something in a tree, I have every reason to conclude not only that I will be able to see what they are looking at, but that I will also understand why they have stopped to look at it. Vision is always a seeing-with. We always see the world, and ourselves in it, as being seen by others. Probably nothing illustrates this more than fashion. For those with even the slightest awareness of what "looks good" at a particular moment, we are keenly aware of at least basic notions of cuff length, where the waistband of a pair of pants should sit, or the structure of lapels. What "looks right" in our current moment will, no doubt, "look weird" in a different era. We can see the fashions from different eras and immediately reject them as out of style (or something someone is wearing ironically or as a costume). This sense is not the result of immediate perception, but of perception meaningfully present for the subject. In terms of fashion, we think of it as subjective—a matter of taste—but it is in this "subjective" experience of appraising what "looks good" that we are most in the realm of the gaze of the Other. Our vision is always, already shaped by desire, supported by fantasy, and thus a site of anxiety. In fact, one of our most basic anxieties concerns how we are seen by others. The fashion, home design, and auto industries (et al) depend on this dynamic in order to continually create new and renewed markets out of the fantasy-anxiety dialectic.

Finally, Lacan notes that our ears, which he connects to the voice, are a site of intersubjective relations. He connects this to Freud's superego. The "voice in our heads" is the voice of the Other. Our ears, which we can never close, are always taking in the voice of the Other. Not only edicts, but more importantly casual remarks, jokes, pop music, which are all more valid and helpful clues in deciphering the Other's desire than the official, socially agreed-upon rules. Here again, we see fantasy and anxiety come together. When we see two people talking, we wonder what they are saying. We wonder what "they" might be saying about us. We wonder what secret meaning they might be disclosing. A voice heard but indecipherable or in a language we don't understand captures our desire. Or we hear Carly Simon sing "Nobody does it better . . . baby, you're the best" and we fantasize that those words are meant for us, or at least we wonder what we would have to do or be to be such an object of desire. We hear a colleague being praised by others and we wonder why we are not seen in the same way. On social media, the written traces of this voice appear in comments, and in their truncated form as likes or dislikes, or silence. The world, and thus desire and anxiety, flow into our ears incessantly, giving rise to both anxiety and desire.

Lacan's impulse to connect anxiety to the body by way of these orifices can help us think both about why we are inevitably subjected to this unpleasant affect we call "anxiety," and also to see why it is unpleasant. As Freud told us, anxiety is not caused by repression; it is the cause of repression. I have put this in terms of an "occupation" of the subject by way of the body's engagement in an intersubjective dynamic that forms the basis of self-consciousness. Since anxiety signals this intersubjective dynamic as the basis for the subject's very being, it can help us understand the subject's relationship to the Other at the level of the body. The body is not *disciplined* by power. The subject is not *produced* by discourse. Rather, the body, as an object of social concern, enters into culture through a kind of occupation, complete with resistance. The intersubjective situation of the human person gives birth to the subject for whom discourse becomes an answer to the question of the Other's desire and the defense against anxiety. Culture is intimately invested in what happens at the level of the subject's body, especially in relationship to the mouth, anus, genitals, eyes, and ears precisely because of their roles in the intersubjective situation. To be a part of the social community we have to cede something of ourselves (Lacan) or to allow part of us to be occupied (Freud) in order to find our place as subjects within the intersubjective world. But the subject is not disciplined or produced, but subjected. The subject's own fantastic response to this situation means that the subject always fails to achieve what would complete the Other, thus leaving lack in place on both sides of the self-Other dialectic. This is not so much *contingency* as it is *failure*. Anxiety is the evidence of this ongoing dialectic of desire that never stops being written.[90] The subject and culture are thus implicated in the constitution of each other as organic processes of the body that have been transformed by this dynamic into a subject. There is only one way out of this dynamic: melancholy, which is not really a "solution" so much as it is a failure of the failure of the dialectic of desire that threatens to undermine the subject completely.

To be a cultural being is to be an intersubjective being, that is, to be a human being is to be desiring, and to be desiring is to be an anxious subject constantly functioning within the fantasy-anxiety dialectic outlined here. To be cultural is to be subjected to the desire of the Other. This dialectic of anxiety and fantasy—which Lacan said share the same structure—is a clue to the way culture functions at the level of the subject.

EXTIMACY, ANXIETY, AND THE "DEATH OF THE SUBJECT"

Fredric Jameson has famously posited that the cultural logic of late capitalism opens up a different way of feeling in which "concepts such as anxiety and alienation . . . are no longer appropriate in the world of the postmodern."[91] This shift, according to Jameson, corresponds to a shift in subjectivity itself such that the subject is no longer characterized by alienation, but by "fragmentation," which he says recalls one of the more "fashionable" themes in contemporary theory, namely the "death" of the subject. Here the "subject" means "the autonomous bourgeois monad or ego or individual," which in postmodern theory is decentered. Jameson thought this shift could take two forms. The first, to which he was more inclined, was the "historicist" formulation in which the decentered, dead subject is the result of changing historical circumstances that result from shifts in capitalism itself. The earlier era, that of "classical capitalism and nuclear family," has given way to a world of "organizational bureaucracy" in which the logic of late capitalism has decentered the subject. The other formulation, the one he associates with poststructuralism, claims that the subject never existed. The "centered subject" served as a model of expression in which the subject is a "monad-like container" within which things are first "felt" and then expressed in a "projection outward." Jameson argues that expression itself, thus, requires "the category of the individual monad," but this potential for expression comes at a cost, namely, for the subject to be condemned to the "mindless solitude of the monad, buried alive and condemned to a prison cell without egress." By contrast, postmodernism signals the end of this dilemma, only to be caught in a new one, one that leads to the end of "style" or personal expression, but one that nevertheless registers that the end of this monad—"the bourgeois ego"—brings with it the end of the "psychopathologies of ego," including anxiety.[92]

It goes without saying that the last thirty years have not witnessed the end of anxiety. On the contrary, we might be more anxious now than we were when Jameson wrote this. For all that, Jameson's view of a postmodern subject has been, in one form or another, persistent in many fields related to cultural studies. But there are two problems with his formulation. First, he seems to assume that the Freudian ego is the subject when it is not. The reading of the ego as somehow "in control" of the individual is not Freud's idea. Put another way, if one defines the subject, as Jameson does here, as "the autonomous bourgeois monad," we are clearly not describing the subject characterized by Freud or Lacan. Freud was always clear that even "the ego" was not unitary or autonomous[93] and for Lacan, the subject is the result of a dialectic of desire involving the Other.[94] Of course, Jameson's point would be that to take the view just stated would simply be to opt for the poststructuralist view, but, as we will see, there is another way to think through this relation.

The second problem, raised by Rei Terada, focuses on the relationship between the subject and affect itself. She responds to Jameson's characterization of the relationship between feeling and the subject not by proposing the psychoanalytic view of the subject, but by proposing a poststructuralist account of both subjectivity and emotion. Her argument is that there is no subject; the subject is "dead." The subject is dead, nevertheless, we still feel emotions. According to her argument, if we assume that the experience of "feelings" requires a subject, then Jameson's prediction about the end of anxiety in a postmodern age would have come true. But it has not. Terada's surprising and ingenious conclusion is that if we were subjects—the subject understood in the same way Jameson characterized it—we would not experience emotions at all: "far from controverting the 'death of the subject,' emotion entails this death." Her argument is that not only poststructuralist thought, but philosophy in general, has always seen emotion as something that fractures our classical notions of the subject. Furthermore, the "discourse of emotion from Descartes to the present day describes emotion as nonsubjective experience in the form of self-difference within cognition." She focuses on the way emotion always seems to be at odds with the path of reason or is contrasted with thought such that rather than seeing emotions as an expression of an internal monad, philosophy has tended to see it as something at odds with the rational subject.[95]

Terada recognizes Lacan's theory of subjectivity as not coinciding with the theory of the subject she has been rejecting, but she still rejects it. She characterizes Lacan's theory of subjectivity as manifesting a "decentered psychology," and points out, not incorrectly, that Lacan "identifies certain discontinuities of experience with subjectivity itself." She focuses on Slavoj Žižek's summary of Lacan's theory of subjectivity, noting that for Žižek subjectivity "consists in a 'primordial abyss of dis-attachment' that precedes attachment" and that involves a primordial gesture of dis-attachment." This leads her to conclude that poststructuralist and Lacanian theorists "interpret self-difference in mutually exclusive ways: the regress that, for poststructuralist theorists impedes the closure of subjectivity just is what Žižek calls subjectivity." She is not wrong about this, but we might ask why she rejects Žižek's very specific account of subjectivity? Why does Terada not embrace the account of the subject offered by Lacan? Along those lines, she even cites Derrida, the theorist most central to her own theory, as avoiding the argument by noting that "some" (i.e., Lacanians) claim that "what we call 'subject' is not the absolute origin, pure will, identity to self, or presence to self of consciousness but precisely this noncoincidence with self." Derrida refused to say whether such a characterization could actually be called the "subject." Terada herself is not as reticent. She follows Thomas Keenan who, taking the typical poststructuralist theme, thinks that the answer to questions regarding who speaks, thinks, acts, and so on is "no one," and we cannot meaningfully claim that this "no one" is just a new placeholder for the subject. But in the end, she says that "self-difference is a crossroads where the merits of subjectivity can be debated without anachronism"[96] which reflects a certain openness on her part to the possibility that the phenomenon of self-difference, while not to be understood as the "subject," might still be part of the phenomenon of affective experience.

Hers is a thoughtful reply. Terada is no reactionary but a serious thinker who is trying to parse the world of human feeling. Where she has chosen to follow, for the most part, Derrida, I have chosen to follow Lacan. In the end, I do not see this difference between our two positions as merely a matter of words, but rather a difference in how each of us accounts for the nature of human experience itself. Terada would certainly be justified in claiming that the "subject of anxiety" in my account is really a "no one," and precisely *for that reason* experiences anxiety.[97] Her account would posit something like "there is anxiety" precisely because there is no autonomous rational being to "have" that experience (an autonomous rational being would, presumably, not choose or need anxiety). Anxiety, an experience at odds with rational thought, must come from some other place than the "subject" and thus demonstrates that the self-difference evidenced in the experience of anxiety is proof of the subject's nonexistence. In sum, certainly, she would concede that the organism experiences anxiety but would conclude that this experience demonstrates that there is no subject at all.

By contrast, we could argue that it is precisely the account of subjectivity that she rejects that Lacan's account of anxiety replaces. *Contra* Terada, anxiety is a sign of subjectivity itself. If we were not subjects, anxiety would not exist at all. It exists precisely because to be a subject is to be bound up with the Other, but that is not the same as being "no one." Each subject, in its own way, must subjectivize the desires and demands of the Other. Lacan personalizes the effects of the Symbolic order (as "the Other") precisely because only a subject who is not autonomous and unitary could experience the Symbolic in a meaningful way at all. To characterize the subject as the "subject of anxiety" is to propose a model of subjectivity that takes the decentering effect of anxiety as the truth of the subject.

Therefore, we should take Terada's perceptive critique not as a sign that the subject is "dead" but rather as a sign that the subject cannot be understood in the terms outlined by Jameson ("the autonomous bourgeois monad or ego or individual"). In place of this subject, psychoanalysis proposes a subject that is always non-identical with itself but that nevertheless persists. But there is always an excess to this subject that cannot be accounted for, and it is precisely this excess that becomes the source of affect.

Molly Anne Rothenberg calls this the "Möbius subject." The Möbius strip is one of Lacan's favorite devices deployed in his *Anxiety* seminar to demonstrate the nature of the subject itself. This point is underscored by the fact that the covers of both the French and the English editions of that seminar feature reproductions of M. C. Escher's *Möbius Strip II*. On the one hand, for Lacan, the Möbius strip illustrates the *objet a*, what cannot be located in the specular image, because the subject, like the Möbius strip, has "just one face," so that it cannot be turned inside out. But by the same token, "this face" is not a façade. There is "depth" behind it that the surface conceals. Still, there is only one surface that is both inside and outside. As Lacan puts it, an insect walking along the surface of the Möbius strip can believe that there is an "other side" to be explored, even though there isn't one.[98] Here we should be careful not to conflate the ego with the subject. The ego is a façade that registers itself in terms of an image of wholeness. The subject is split between the "inside" and the "outside," or to be more precise, between the world of meaning and its own meaningless being. But the inside and the outside are part of the same surface.

Rothenberg has gone well beyond Lacan in the clarity with which she demonstrates both the nature of this concept of subjectivity and its fecundity for doing cultural analysis. Her name for the Lacanian subject is the "Möbius subject" because it emphasizes the "extimacy" (extimité, Lacan's own play on words for an "intimacy" that is "ex," or "outside" the subject) and excessive quality of subjectivity itself.[99] Her explanation begins with Being itself, as an undifferentiated mass awaiting the process of objectification. Objects emerge as something external to Being as something external is introduced into being in order to confer identity on those objects. Identity is conferred as a result of a symbolic gesture that allows objects to be objects—that is, to have meaning—but at the cost of making them non-identical with themselves. Thus, meaning and identity always produce an excess at the point where the object is non-identical with itself.[100]

The Möbius subject is such an object. Rothenberg points out that the Möbius strip is an "unbounded" object in the sense of there being "no boundary between inside and outside" that is also "finite."[101] In Lacanian terms, this is because the subject is always in relation to the Other. In terms of anxiety, Lacan says "the anxiety-point lies at the level of the Other, at the level of the mother's body" such that fantasy, which Lacan describes as that which "binds the subject tightly to the *a*, whereby the subject finds himself suspended, identified with this *a*—remains forever elided and hidden, underlying any relation the subject may have with any object whatsoever."[102] Here Lacan locates the subject on the side of the child and the Other on the side of the mother, but in doing so he is clear that the *objet a* is on the side of the child/subject who is in an inevitable relationship with the Other and this dialectic is the basis for the subject's relationship with any (and all) objects in the world. The subject's causality is thus not located strictly outside of it—for example, in an infinite set of multiple power relations—nor does it originate "within" the subject, but is this relationship between the subject "identified with the object a" and the Other. In this way, the subject is understood neither as entirely alienated (into the meaning supplied by the Other) nor entirely separate and isolated (a monad), but what we might describe as subjectivity that has been generated by an "alienated separation" that can be figured by the Möbius strip, and whose causality can only be thought in terms of "extimacy." Lacan calls this the "point of anxiety." Why?

Again, Rothenberg is helpful here. The subject's (extimate) cause is always tied to the social world of meaning, but the subject can never know what that meaning is. Rothenberg figures this as a site of excess because the subject is never identical with itself; something else must be "added" in order for identity to emerge at all (Hyppolite's denial of "the inert tautology, I=I"). As she explains, "the subject occupies this position because it is produced by the materiality of the signifier as a speaking/spoken being." Language is central to this process because of the "special structure of spoken language as dependent upon an excess of signification." Here she makes clear this excess is not a form of Derridean deferral, but a consequence of the Lacanian difference between the levels of the enunciated and the enunciation. The "enunciated" refers to the content of what is said, while the "enunciation" refers to the fact that something is being said. Her example is the enunciation "I love you," which must always be accompanied by the level of the "enunciated" (whether it is explicitly part of the enunciation or not). Why are you saying that you love me? What do you mean when you say you love me? As she points out, we can see this clearly in the more pointed response to a declaration (of love), "so you say." Yes, you *said* that you love me, but I don't believe it. This suggests that there is always more to what we say than what is actually said, and this is precisely where the subject is split.[103]

This split subject is anxious precisely because, as Rothenberg puts it, "the fact that one has become meaningful to others—that is, been registered in the

Symbolic—does not mean that one actually knows what one means to others." This meaning-making can be seen, again, at the place where the enunciated and enunciation are split. At the level of the enunciated, the subject is referred to by the statement (e.g., "I am a woman"), but the subject who is making the statement always does so from the level of enunciation itself. The subject of a statement cannot know what message is being received by others, nor can she even know what message she is trying to send.[104] One can see how different this picture of subjectivity is from Terada's view. Like psychoanalysis, Terada rejects the idea of an autonomous rational subject. Nevertheless, psychoanalysis insists on the concept of the subject precisely because the Möbius subject is not simply externalization—that is, a non-subject, or "dead" subject, that is only ephemeral expressions of discourse—but a historical instance of how an individual has been subjectivized in a particular way. While Terada is right to argue that the kind of subject associated with rational autonomy would have no feelings at all, she is wrong to reject the idea of the subject altogether, for something must account for the individualized experiences of affect that her investigation explores.

Furthermore, anxiety is not simply one of those affects; it is the central affect for subjectivity and the one that "does not deceive" precisely because it is a "signal of the real." The "real" that it signifies is precisely this failure of meaning at the level of the split in the subject. Put another way, the excess to which Rothenberg refers is expressed in Lacan's thought both in the phenomenon of the divided subject (which Lacan writes: S̸) and in the *objet a* (which Lacan writes: *a*). Lacan's formula for fantasy is S/◇a (which pictures that in fantasy there is a relationship between the split/divided subject and the objet a) and he claims that the structure of anxiety and fantasy are the same. We can now see why. As Rothenberg points out, "Mobius subjects are . . . forced to live with uncertainty about their status and security among others" and this results in anxiety. For Rothenberg, a number of "psychic attributes" emerge in the form of "tactics" to manage this anxiety such as "aggression, humor, paranoia, depression, narcissism, love, etc."[105] Though she does not specifically make this claim we can see that the Möbius subject is the subject of the anxiety-fantasy dialectic. To be more strictly Lacanian, we could say that anxiety signals that the subject ex-sists as a Möbius subject.

Rather than adopting the view that anxiety is an irrational affect that demonstrates the non-existence of the subject, the experience of anxiety clarifies for us the nature of subjectivity itself. The subject is extimate (i.e., it has an extimate cause). The subject is excessive. The subject exists in a Möbius subjectivity. The implications of this insight for doing cultural analysis are significant. As we will see in the next chapter, the concept of the Möbius subject of anxiety is illuminating for the world of culture. The split in the subject cannot be eradicated. It exists in a dialectical relationship that is mirrored in the fantasy-anxiety structure that Lacan emphasized. The structure of cultural phenomena follows this same structure in which culture is excessive and thus follows the Möbius topos. Culture has no outside wherein we will find its cause, but neither is it a set of immanent forces in which cause and effect would become indistinguishable. Instead, its causes, like that of the subject, are extimate.

NOTES

1. Michel Foucault, *The Hermeneutics of the Subject: Lectures at the Collège de France 1981–1982* (New York: Picador, 2001), 189. Foucault says,

> Let's say that there have not been many people who in the last years—I will say in the twentieth century—have posed the question of truth. Not that many people have posed the question: What is involved in the case of the subject and truth? And: What is the relationship of the subject to the truth? What is the subject of truth, what is the subject who speaks the truth, etcetera? As far as I'm concerned, I see only two. I see only Heidegger and Lacan. Personally, myself, you must have heard this, I have tried to reflect on all this from the side of Heidegger and starting from Heidegger. There you are. However, certainly you cannot avoid Lacan when you pose these kinds of questions.

2. Soren Kierkegaard, *The Concept of Anxiety*, ed. and trans. Reidar Thomte and Albert B. Anderson (Princeton: Princeton University Press, 1980), 42.
3. Jean Paul Sartre, *Being and Nothingness*, trans. Hazel E. Barnes (New York, London, Toronto, Sydney: Washington Square Press, 1992), 70–85.
4. Martin Heidegger, *Sein Und Zeit* (Elfte, unveränderte Auflage, Tübingen: Max Niemery Verlag, 1967), 134; *Being and Time*, trans. John Macquarrie and Edward Robinson (New York, London, Toronto, Sydney, New Delhi, Auckland: Harper & Row, 1962, reprint 2007), 172. In future citations page numbers for the German edition will be given first; page numbers for the English edition will follow the slash.
5. Heidegger, *Being and Time*, 139/178.
6. Heidegger, *Being and Time*, 135/174 (italics original).
7. Heidegger, *Being and Time*, 137/176 (italics original).
8. Heidegger, *Being and Time*, 137/176.
9. Heidegger, *Being and Time*, 134/172.
10. Heidegger, *Being and Time*, 137/176–177.
11. Heidegger, *Being and Time*, 185/230.
12. Heidegger, *Being and Time*, 186/230 (italics original).
13. Heidegger, *Being and Time*, 195/239.
14. Heidegger, *Being and Time*, 189/233.
15. Sara Ahmed, *The Promise of Happiness* (Durham, NC and London: Duke University Press, 2010), 190.
16. Ahmed, *The Promise of Happiness*, 186.
17. Heidegger, *Being and Time*, 188/233.

18. Heidegger, *Being and Time*, 189/233
19. Heidegger, *Being and Time,* 186/231.
20. Heidegger, *Being and Time*, 187/232.
21. Heidegger, *Being and Time*, 187/231.
22. Ahmed, *Promise of Happiness*, 40.
23. Heidegger, *Being and Time*, 187/232.
24. Heidegger, *Being and Time*, 187/232.
25. Heidegger, *Being and Time*, 188/233.
26. Martin Heidegger, "The Origin of the Work of Art," in *Poetry, Language, Thought,* trans. Albert Hofstadter (New York: Harper & Row, 1972), 35. "The Greeks called the unconcealedness of being *aletheia.* We say 'truth' and think little enough in using this word. If there occurs in the work a disclosure of a particular being, disclosing what and how it is, then there is here an occurring, a happening of truth at work." In this context, he is speaking about the power of art to disclose truth (in this case Van Gogh's *Peasant Shoes*), and though this work is later than *Being and Time* it explains Heidegger's understanding of disclosure.
27. Dylan Trigg, *Topophobia: A Phenomenology of Anxiety* (London, Oxford, New York, Sydney, New Delhi: Bloomsbury Academic, 2017), ix.
28. Trigg, *Topophobia,* xx.
29. Trigg, *Topophobia,* xxxv.
30. Trigg, *Topophobia*, xxviii.
31. Sigmund Freud, *Inhibitions, Symptoms, and Anxiety*, trans. Alix Strachey (New York and London: W.W. Norton & Company, 1959), 4–5.
32. Freud, *Inhibitions, Symptoms, and Anxiety*, 6.
33. Freud, *Inhibitions, Symptoms, and Anxiety*, 7.
34. Freud, *Inhibitions, Symptoms, and Anxiety*, 9.
35. Freud, *Inhibitions, Symptoms, and Anxiety*, 9.
36. Freud, *Inhibitions, Symptoms, and Anxiety*, 11.
37. Freud, *Inhibitions, Symptoms, and Anxiety*, 11. Translation mine. The German text reads: "Das Ich zieht die (vorbewußte) Besetzung von der zu verdrängenden den Triebrepräsentanz ab und verwendet sie für die Unlust-(Angst)-Entbindung."
38. The translation of the German world, *Besetzung*, is problematic. Darius Gray Ornston, Jr. has suggested that it is a "colorless term that is usually defined by its context and that Freud's teachers used the word as a pliable metaphor." (p. 14) In a note, he offers two examples from translations of the phrase "*Affekt besetzten*" in Freud's revisions of a translation of his *Five Lectures on Psychoanalysis* done by H. W. Chase. In one case, he renders the phrase simply as "emotionally colored" and in the other, "a common emotive tone." (pp. 14–15, n.16). Alex Holder likes "occupation" as a translation because of its association with "Freud's favorite and often-used metaphor about advancing and retreating troops in discussing libidinal progressions or processes of regression and fixation." The drawback of "occupation" is that in English it can refer to one's profession or career. He notes that Joan Riviere usually translated it as "investment." But this has the drawback of bringing in economic associations that would seem to distort Freud's usage. (p. 92). Darius Gray Ornston, Jr. "Improving Strachey's Freud," 1–23, and Alex Holder, "A Historical-Critical

Edition," 75–96, in *Translating Freud*, ed. Darius Gray Ornston, Jr. (New Haven, CT and London: Yale University Press, 1992).

39. Freud, *Inhibitions, Symptoms, and Anxiety*, 12–13.
40. Freud, *Inhibitions, Symptoms, and Anxiety*, 18.
41. "Cadillac ELR Coupe 2014 Commercial." Available on You Tube: https://youtu.be/xNzXze5Yza8?si=7832Xj_qseK7tECf
42. Sigmund Freud, *The Wolfman and Other Cases*, trans. Louise Adey Huish (New York: Penguin Books, 2003), 3–122.
43. Freud, *Inhibitions, Symptoms, and Anxiety*, 23.
44. Freud, *Wolfman*, 205–302.
45. Freud, *Inhibitions, Symptoms, and Anxiety*, 27–28.
46. Freud, *Inhibitions, Symptoms, and Anxiety*, 32.
47. Freud, *Inhibitions, Symptoms, and Anxiety*, 32.
48. Freud, *Inhibitions, Symptoms, and Anxiety*, 53.
49. Freud, *Inhibitions, Symptoms, and Anxiety*, 54.
50. Freud, *Inhibitions, Symptoms, and Anxiety*, 54.
51. Freud, *Inhibitions, Symptoms, and Anxiety*, 56.
52. Freud, *Inhibitions, Symptoms, and Anxiety*, 57.
53. Freud, *Inhibitions, Symptoms, and Anxiety*, 60.
54. Freud, *Inhibitions, Symptoms, and Anxiety*, 61.
55. Freud, *Inhibitions, Symptoms, and Anxiety*, 66.
56. Freud, *Inhibitions, Symptoms, and Anxiety*, 66.
57. Freud, *Inhibitions, Symptoms, and Anxiety*, 67.
58. Freud, *Inhibitions, Symptoms, and Anxiety*, 69.
59. Freud, *Inhibitions, Symptoms, and Anxiety*, 69.
60. Freud, *Inhibitions, Symptoms, and Anxiety*, 70.
61. Freud, *Inhibitions, Symptoms, and Anxiety*, 74.
62. Freud, *Inhibitions, Symptoms, and Anxiety*, 75.
63. Freud, *Inhibitions, Symptoms, and Anxiety*, 76.
64. Freud, *Inhibitions, Symptoms, and Anxiety*, 77.
65. Freud, *Inhibitions, Symptoms, and Anxiety*, 78–79.
66. Freud, *Inhibitions, Symptoms, and Anxiety*, 79.
67. Freud, *Inhibitions, Symptoms, and Anxiety*, 80.
68. See Sigmund Freud, *Civilization and Its Discontents*, trans. James Strachey (New York and London: W.W. Norton & Company, 1961), 12.
69. Freud, *Inhibitions, Symptoms, and Anxiety*, 88.
70. Freud, *Inhibitions, Symptoms, and Anxiety*, 100.
71. Ahmed, *Promise of Happiness*, 31.
72. Renata Salecl, *On Anxiety* (London and New York: Routledge, 2004), 18.
73. Jean Hyppolite, *Genesis and Structure of Hegel's Phenomenology*, trans. Samuel Cherniak and John Heckman (Evanston, IL: Northwestern University Press, 1974), 159–160.
74. G.W.F. Hegel, *Phenomenology of Spirit*, trans. A.V. Miller (Oxford, New York, Toronto, Melbourne: Oxford University Press, 1977), 105 [sec. 167].
75. Ahmed, *The Promise of Happiness*, 31

76. Slavoj Žižek, *The Plague of Fantasies* (London and New York: Verso, 1997, 2008), 9–10.

77. Colette Soler, *Lacanian Affects: The Function of Affect in Lacan's Work*, trans. Bruce Fink (London and New York: Routledge, 2016), 19.

78. Lacan, *Seminar X: Anxiety*, 76, 116, 160, 218, 297, 311, 312.

79. Lacan, *Seminar X: Anxiety*, 3.

80. Lacan, *Seminar X: Anxiety*, 53–54.

81. Lacan, *Seminar X: Anxiety*, 52.

82. Lacan, *Seminar X: Anxiety*, 5–6.

83. Jonathan Yerushalmy, "'I Want to Destroy Whatever I Want': Bing's AI Chatbot Unsettles US Reporter," *The Guardian*, February 17, 2023, (online) https://www.theguardian.com/technology/2023/feb/17/i-want-to-destroy-whatever-i-want-bings-ai-chatbot-unsettles-us-reporter.

84. Jacques Lacan, *Seminar XI: The Four Fundamental Concepts of Psychoanalysis*, ed. Jacques-Alain Miller, trans. Alan Sheridan (New York and London: W.W. Norton & Company, 1998), 103.

85. Lacan, *Seminar X: Anxiety*, 243, 291–309.

86. Freud, *Civilization and Its Discontents*, 13–15.

87. Albert Camus, *The Plague*, trans. Stuart Gilbert (New York: Vintage Books, 1991), 102–104.

88. Freud, *Civilization and Its Discontents*, 51.

89. Maurice Merleau-Ponty, *Phenomenology of Perception*, trans. Donald A. Landes (London and New York: Routledge, 2012), 156–178.

90. Lacan Jacques, *Séminaire XX: Encore,*ed. Jacques-Alain Miller (Paris: Éditions du Seuil,1975), 59. In this context, he actually says "the necessary" "doesn't stop . . . being written." What he has in mind is that tendency of philosophy to frame our desires and pursuits tends toward the Good, Beauty, and Truth, but in our actual desiring, the objects that we desire never stop being written.

91. Fredric Jameson, *Postmodernism: Or, the Cultural Logic of Late Capitalism* (Durham, NC: Duke University Press, 1991), 14.

92. Jameson, *Postmodernism*, 15.

93. Freud, *Civilization and Its Discontents*, 12–13.

94. Jacques Lacan, "The Subversion of the Subject and the Dialectic of Desire," in *Écrits*, trans. Bruce Fink (New York & London: W.W. Norton & Company, 2006), 671–702..

95. Rei Terada, *Feeling in Theory* (Cambridge, MA: Harvard University Press, 2001), 3, 6, 90–127.

96. Terada, *Feeling in Theory*, 10–11.

97. See Terada, *Feeling in Theory*, 43, 49, 50, 78, 85, 97, 101, 113, 162, 174. She does not make anxiety central to her analysis of "feeling," but it nevertheless occurs again and again in her account.

98. Lacan, *Seminar X: Anxiety*, 96–97, 136, 204.

99. The term is only mentioned once in Jacques Lacan, *Seminar VII: The Ethics of Psychoanalysis,* ed. Jacques-Alain Miller and trans. Dennis Porter (New York and London: W.W. Norton & Company, 1992), 139. There he says,

what we have described as the central place, as the intimate exteriority or "extimacy," that is the Thing, will help us to shed light on the question or mystery that remains for those who are interested in prehistoric art, namely, its site as such.

Such an apparently obscure reference, which did not become a central term in Lacan's own discourse, has become a useful tool for many Lacanians, Rothenberg among them.

100. Molly Anne Rothenberg, *The Excessive Subject: A New Theory of Social Change* (Cambridge and Malden, MA: Polity Press, 2010), 35.

101. Rothenberg, *The Excessive Subject*, 31.

102. Lacan, *Seminar X: Anxiety*, 237.

103. Rothenberg, *The Excessive Subject*, 41–42.

104. Rothenberg, *The Excessive Subject*, 42–43.

105. Rothenberg, *The Excessive Subject*, 45.

Chapter 2

Anxiety and the Contradictions of Culture

In the film *Barbie,* Ruth Handler (Rhea Perlman), creator of the Barbie doll, claims that the reason we have things like "patriarchy" and "Barbie" is because "being human can be pretty uncomfortable."[1] On the surface, this is a strange and facile causal analysis that suggests that it is our discomfort with our very condition as humans that causes us to make up things like Barbie and patriarchy. This claim is not explicitly developed in the film, but we can see traces of it everywhere. The film's opening scene reimagines Barbie not as a child's toy that oppressed women by getting girls to think of themselves as objects meant to embody an impossible form of beauty, but as a liberating alternative to the maternal roles assigned to women under patriarchy. Barbie is an excessive object, overflowing with meaning. She is something to be played with in every sense of the term. Alternately, isn't it Ken's anxiety about where he fits into Barbie's desire that leads him to quickly and totally commit to patriarchy so completely and toxically? The causal claim here not only focuses on discomfort as the "cause" of invention but on the very inventiveness itself. The universe did not come with either Barbie or patriarchy built in. They both arose and became popular for the way they responded to this discomfort. "Discomfort" as cause may still seem facile, but is this not more or less Freud's view of the origins of civilization? Did he not argue that civilization (*Kultur*, "culture") arose precisely in response to our discomfort? All the achievements and regulations of culture are meant to combat the very things that cause us to suffer. Yet Freud's "astonishing contention" was that this very civilization was also the source of our greatest misery.[2]

Without question, one of the effects of culture/civilization that makes being human uncomfortable is anxiety. If culture arises to combat suffering, and one of the effects of culture is to produce anxious subjects, one of the effects of anxiety is the production of more culture aimed at reducing and avoiding it. There is thus a kind of logic to "Ruth Hander's" claim that can serve to introduce how the theorization of anxiety developed in the last chapter might serve us in developing the kind of theorization of culture that has been so central to cultural studies. I take cultural studies not as a specific method, theory, or mode of thought, but rather as a movement of scholars from a variety of disciplines who seek to analyze culture in terms of its values, modalities, and objects in order to find more just and emancipatory ways to organize our lives. With a certain lack of justification, I use the English word "culture" as a literal translation of Freud's German "*Kultur*." I reject "civilization" as a suitable translation or effective concept for its historical tendency to mark off some cultures from others (civilized vs. uncivilized) or to frame conflict in terms of a "battle for civilization." Instead, I see culture as concerned with the whole realm of human activity, intersubjectivity, and expression, and I approach it as a topic with the concern to establish ways of intervening in culture to open up more just and emancipatory ways of living together.

Cultural studies arose first in the United Kingdom and then in the United States in direct opposition to the mode of thought that aimed at distinguishing between "high" and "low" culture. In this way, cultural studies has become known for its valuing of pop culture, everyday practices, and common objects for what they reveal about culture itself. But these scholars were also influenced initially by a desire to be critical of the way class, race, gender, and other social divisions in the social space were reflected, sustained, and even contested in the cultural sphere. Though Marxist critique had done much to show the relationship between culture and the modes and relations of production, they began to find a strictly Marxist approach inadequate. Stuart Hall expressed this in terms of contradiction. He saw something lacking in Marxism in terms of its ability to account for the diversity of antagonisms and contradictions that characterized the late twentieth century. He was seeking a mode of analysis that worked without seeing the "mode of production" as "command[ing] every contradiction," as Hall put it. For Hall, cultural studies was a project designed to bring theory into line with the complexities of the empirical problems confronting his analysis of culture.[3] But his project was less a wholesale rejection of Marxist analysis as it was a refusal to accept causal explanations that relied on the mode of production as adequate for explaining actual lived cultural conditions. For Hall, "culture" refers to precisely the place where the contradictions that characterize human existence are experienced. For all the acknowledgment he gave to the power of Marxism to analyze certain kinds of exploitation, he sought a way to think "new political subjects and subjectivities," claiming that the "domain of culture and ideology is where those new positions are opened and where the new articulations have to be made."[4] But how are we to understand these new subjects and subjectivities? We could argue that from at least 1968 until today, this has been the question that has preoccupied many thinkers around the world.

The aim of this chapter is to elaborate on the way Lacanian analysis of anxiety is one way to respond to Hall's project, one that articulates new ways of thinking subjectivities in relation to the domain of culture and ideology. In the first place, we will work out the implications of Rothenberg's development of the Möbius subject in relationship to Freud's thinking on culture to show how anxiety as a signal points to a specific way of thinking about culture.

THE EXTIMATE CAUSE OF CULTURE

Though I used Rothenberg's analysis of the Möbius subject in the last chapter to elucidate the kind of subjectivity that is implied by our affective experience of anxiety, Rothenberg is not particularly focused on anxiety. Her interest, like Hall's, is in how social change is possible. Rothenberg points out that there have been two major approaches to theorizing social change. The first, of which Marxism is the prime example, sees the cause of social change located entirely *outside the social field itself*. The second can be linked to Foucault, whose critique of Marxism focused on *the impossibility for an exception to the field of relations to be the cause of those relations*. While cultural studies may have its roots in Marxism, as Rothenberg points out, "Foucault's analysis of the implications of power and knowledge" serves as "the standard for cultural studies" today.[5] But, she argues, the weakness of this approach is that it ends up reducing "society to its immanent power relations, which are defined in terms of positive categories and properties."[6] This approach not only fails to distinguish causes from effects but also ultimately provides no path for changing these social relations.

For this reason, Rothenberg argues that the challenge for those interested in theorizing human culture in relation to social change is to "theorize a cause that is both exceptional to the social field, à la Marxist meta-cause, and internal to the field, à la the Foucauldian immanent cause." She argues that the "external/internal" (extimate or Möbius) cause outlined by psychoanalysis is the only way to both keep cause and effect distinct (unlike the Foucauldian model) while at the same time keeping cause and effect distinct but within the "social field of effects" (unlike the Marxist model).[7] Rothenberg's "extimate causality" refers to the "operation that generates subjects in their social dimension—that is, the operation that gives us social identities, properties, and relationships."[8] Because the extimate subject is inside/outside and because it creates this excess, the cause of social relations can be located within those relations themselves, but the cause (the excess) can be distinguished from the effects it creates. As Rothenberg puts it,

> the operation that bestows identities, properties, and relationships also leaves a residue, so that every subject bears some excess. At every point in the social field, then, an irreducible excess attends social relations . . . this excess is what makes the social field itself possible and makes its structure potentially analyzable.[9]

The extimate cause, found in the Möbius subject, is the only way to approach the social field that can account for a cause within the field of social relations itself that is distinct from the other relations in that field. This is what allows us to analyze culture and potentially change it. It is not for nothing that this same structure of causality is what Lacan deployed in explaining anxiety as the affect that does not deceive us.

This is because the experience of this extimacy, which persists largely within a field of reality supported entirely by fantasy, can be signaled in its extimacy through the experience of anxiety. While thought can bring us to assent to the truth of this extimacy, anxiety gives us the proof in experience. As Rothenberg put it, since the extimate cause always leaves "a remainder of indeterminacy, so that every subject bears some unspecifiable excess within the social field," the subject will necessarily be thrown into a relationship with the Other (and others) in order to resolve the meaning of the subject's excess. We rely on others because, as Rothenberg puts it, "the social field is the only place in which we can even try to find out what we mean to others."[10] The anxiety-fantasy dialectic is the extimate subject's relationship to the cultural world.

FREUD'S *KULTUR* AND LACAN'S *DISCOURSE*

For psychoanalysis, fantasy supports "reality" because our reality is always informed by desire. Just as Heidegger linked anxiety to the contingency of the world given the nothingness that is Being, in psychoanalysis, the fantasy structure of reality implies the constant potential for anxiety in our cultural life. Though anxiety is always potential, when we are immersed in fantasy as the support of our desire, anxiety slips into the background but persists as what drives our interest in and commitment to fantasy. To look at this from a different perspective, for Freud, repression occurs in order to avoid anxiety. Something must be repressed if we are not feeling anxiety. Things are not quite as simple as they seem in *Barbie*'s theory of causality. Seeing human discomfort as the cause of culture misses both the way culture itself causes us discomfort and the way something must be repressed for Barbie and patriarchy—to use the film's examples—to emerge.

For Freud, culture (*Kultur*[11]) was "the whole sum of the achievements and the regulations which distinguish our lives from those of our animal ancestors and which serve two purposes—namely to protect [people] against nature and to adjust their mutual relations."[12] Freud's definition is broad enough to include everything we would think of as "culture," achievements that range from buildings and vaccines to poems and sitcoms, and regulations that include not only the written laws that govern societies, but also the social conventions, ethical ideals, and unwritten rules at the heart of our social being.[13] For Freud, culture seems to be, for the most part, a set of solutions to our pressing problems, an attempt to combat the suffering we confront from our own bodies, the external world, and even our relations with others.[14] Culture (*Kultur*) ends up being something humans do in the world.

But at the last moment in this phase of his argument in *Civilization and Its Discontents* Freud says something causes him to "move in a different direction" in order to claim that culture is not only these achievements and regulations, but also a "peculiar process" that *we, as individuals, undergo.*[15] Culture does not merely change the landscape, produce tools, and domesticate plants and animals; it also transforms us. It also takes on a positive project. Not only does culture attempt to alleviate suffering, but it also attempts to satisfy our "familiar instinctual dispositions" (*bekannten menschlichen Triebanlagen*, "familiar human drives" or "well-known drive systems") *by changing them.*[16] It is these changes that characterize this process, transforming our satisfactions from what we can find in natural objects to what we can find only in cultural objects. Freud identifies three such changes. The first is what he calls "character-trait(s)" which are the result of a drive being "used up" (*aufgezehrt*, "consumed" or "eaten up") and replaced with something else (the character trait). The most "remarkable" example of such a process is "the anal erotism of young human beings" in which "the excretory function" is replaced by a "sense of order and cleanliness."[17] We have already discussed this phenomenon in the previous chapter. Here we should emphasize, as Freud does, how remarkable this is. The animal functioning related to waste and feces emerges in culture as an insistence on cleanliness and order. This emphasis on cleanliness and order not only appears at the level of the individual character trait, but it is also one of the characteristics of culture that Freud emphasizes.[18] Rather than an expression of a natural impulse to evacuate one's bowels, this activity becomes, as we pointed out in the last chapter, an intersubjective drama fraught with both anxiety and desire.

Second, Freud says that sublimation is another feature of the cultural process that points to the "similarity between the process of civilization and the libidinal development of the individual." As the example of anal erotism shows, this involves a displacement of the conditions that allow for our satisfaction, and this displacement, this finding of a new point of satisfaction, "coincides with that of sublimation." Freud says sublimation is "an especially conspicuous feature of cultural development; it is what makes it possible for higher psychical activities, scientific, artistic or ideological, to play such an important part in civilized life."[19] It means we can find things not only like Barbie, but like the *Barbie* movie, satisfying. Lacan famously summed up the nature of sublimation with his claim that the satisfaction he received from lecturing to an audience was the same satisfaction as "fucking."[20] What Lacan makes clear is that we do not engage in cultural activity in order to have sex. Rather, culture provides its own satisfactions. An even more astonishing example of sublimation is Lacan's account of a friend's extensive wartime collection of matchbooks. The collector's impulse to assemble these ordinary objects and to display them in his living room showed they had been elevated to the level of a sublime object.[21] There is an excess in culture that is inextricably linked to the excess of the subject. Not only do we create matches to make it easier to start fires, we can turn them into sublime objects to adorn our homes.

Finally, Freud says that repression is the third feature of the process that is civilization. Repression involves the "renunciation of instinct (*Triebverzicht*), that presupposes the non-satisfaction by suppression (*Unterdrückung*), repression (*Verdrängung*) or some other means of powerful instincts (*Trieben*)" and is a prerequisite for civilization. Here something emerges that seems to make the whole cultural process *self-undermining*. With the developing of character traits, the drives are *consumed*, while with sublimation they are *satisfied* but with a different object, and with renunciation, they are *repressed*. It is easy enough to see these as three *different* processes involved in the development of the subject of culture, but should we not also think of them as interrelated? They all point to something that occurs at the level of the individual that not only parallels the development of culture but seems to be its prerequisite. To use Freud's example, we can point out that the anal character seems to share in all three. Even when the feces is retained, the impulse to eject it is replaced by a drive toward parsimony, which finds a satisfaction therein, but that nevertheless makes the subject suitable for the larger cultural world where the disposal of waste products in approved ways is the *sine qua non* of entering that world (or at least of attending kindergarten).

Lacan highlights this same dynamic with his claim that the anorexic eats *nothing*.[22] There are days when probably all of us have had to go hours *without eating anything*; but only the anorexic *eats nothing*. Her satisfaction is found in *the nothing*. The anorexic is not merely repressing, though she is doing that, too. When she is standing in front of the mirror, seeing herself through the eyes of the Other, she sees something that is not measuring up to the Other's standards, and so she shifts the object of her satisfaction from food to nothing. She is sublimating—she finds satisfaction in her refusal of food—and in the process, a "drive" is "used up" in the sense Freud means it, namely, that a satisfaction is found. Culture, which aims at satisfactions, thus strangely requires both non-satisfactions and displaced satisfactions in the form of sublimation. Another way to put this is that culture requires satisfaction that is always sublimated, which is to say, found in a cultural object and not in the natural object, and even when the satisfaction is found in a natural object, it is mediated by culture. Culture is both the site of desire (beyond organic need) and the site that requires the non-satisfaction of powerful drives in order to produce and acquire these sublimated objects. It is also both the place where the desiring subject emerges and the place where the subject finds satisfaction. It is not that culture offers no satisfactions (which is the reading of Freud we would get from reading *Trieb* as *Instinkt*) *but of those satisfactions that are found precisely through the repression of those drives.* This is why Lacan said that even though he was not "fucking," he was still getting off, even when he was just fucking around in a lecture hall. One can imagine a religiously devoted person who gets off on not getting off. This remarkable process is what culture is, and it is a process functioning at the level of anxiety and fantasy (which, remember, Lacan claims, have the same structure: S/◇a).

Since culture involves exactly this kind of displacement—a shifting of our drives from natural objects to cultural ones—the desirability of these cultural objects, as well as culture itself, requires fantasy. The hungry, divided subject is rarely satisfied with food that can be foraged from an uncultivated environment and water found in the nearest pool or spring (or even tap) but seeks cheeseburgers and pizza, escargots and filet mignon, well-crafted IPAs and oaky cabernets. Such notions, so clearly beyond the level of organic need, suggest a kind of hedonistic excess that can, paradoxically, be understood in terms of repression. This is true, in the first place, because these more excessive objects require more excessive sacrifice. The cultivation of vineyards, the raising of livestock, the fermentation of beverages, and so on requires sacrifices by the laborers, the land, and animals. But the consumer must also sacrifice. Rather than simple activities to acquire the raw foods easily accessed in the environment, the consumer must work and save to afford these more excessive satisfactions. Rather than seeking satisfactions along the shortest path, the cultured subject takes long, winding detours toward satisfactions, and in general, the longer the detour (at least for someone, whether laborer or consumer) and the more sacrifice involved (even if it is the sacrifice of others), the more satisfaction is promised in our fantasies of the good life. This linking of repression to fantasy, which at first seems like a strange idea, can quickly be seen to be central to cultural life.

We can now begin to think through the relationship between the subject, culture, repression, fantasy, and anxiety. Heidegger's notion of the relationship between anxiety and the worlding of worlds does point to an important insight about the nature of the world as contingent and constructed in some sense. That is, anxiety shows us that the "world" is not natural and inevitable. It shows us that the "world" is culture and not nature. While this insight can be linked to anxiety, does it really explain it? After all, why should the fact that culture is culture cause anxiety by itself? When playing a video game or a role-playing board game, one can be fully aware that the rules of the game and all its features are constructed and contingent without feeling anxious at all. It is all a game, and so there is no reason to feel anxious. Furthermore, it is hard to see what would be authentic about playing the game in a knowing way. In Heidegger's "call to conscience," we come to realize that our choices are not compelled, and we take responsibility for them, but couldn't that all happen without anxiety? Similarly, Sartre's notion of "bad faith," while taking us further in the direction of authenticity by pointing to the freedom he locates in the subject, does not really explain anxiety, either. Yes, I have the freedom to throw myself off a cliff, but why should that cause me anxiety unless there is a part of me that might actually do it? Sartre has plenty of negativity introduced into the world by the subject, but no death drive. If Heidegger's Dasein is just "there," Sartre's subject is there too much. Indeed, Sartre's subject is troubled by the negativity that slips into being, but not by the possibility that the subject itself might not be in control of its own thoughts, meanings, and desires. Neither Dasein nor Sartre's subject have an unconscious.[23] By drawing out a theory of the subject that is not divided, they are not left with a dialectical relationship between the subject and culture, which is the only way to make sense out of our experience of anxiety, which signals the extimate nature of the subject. But this division in the subject is mirrored by a similar division in culture, which makes it always a potential site of the uncanny.

THE UNCANNY

Along these lines, Lacan thought that the uncanny was "indispensable for broaching the question of anxiety."[24] Similarly, Mladen Dolar has argued that the uncanny is "the dimension where all the concepts of psychoanalysis come together, where its diverse lines of argument form a knot."[25] Like other manifestations of anxiety, the uncanny confronts us as theorists with a problem that strikes at the very core of our subjective experience as intersubjective beings immersed in a symbolic world. As Freud points out in his essay on the uncanny, the German word *unheimlich* is ambiguous due to its being derived from another German word, *heimlich*. To say something is *heimlich*, "homey," is, at the same time, to point to its being concealed, or hidden away (within the walls of the home). So, while *unheimlich* ("uncanny") is formally the antonym of *heimlich* (the German "un" serves as a form of negation), it is not, strictly, an antonym. Another way to think about this, Freud argues, is that while some might think that the feeling of the uncanny is generated by something that is novel, there are many times when the experience of something new, or strange, does not cause us any sort of agitation at all, let alone the uncanny.[26] Something is uncanny precisely because there is something *familiar* about it.

Freud boils things down to two points related to the uncanny. First, he says that

> every affect arising from an emotional impulse (*daß jeder Affekt einer Gefühlsregung*)—of whatever kind—is converted into fear (*Angst*, anxiety) by being repressed, it follows that among those things that are felt to be frightening (*Ängstlichen*, anxious) there must be one group in which it can be shown that the frightening (*Ängstlichen*, anxious) element is something that *has been repressed and now returns*. This species of the frightening (*Ängstlichen*, anxious) would then constitute the uncanny, and it would be immaterial whether it was itself originally frightening (*Ängstlichen*, anxious) or arose from another affect.[27]

In other words, he claimed in *Inhibitions, Symptoms, and Anxiety* that repression is an attempt to avoid anxiety, but here he notes that the repression of some emotions and effects returns in the form of something anxiety-producing (i.e., the uncanny). Second, if this understanding of anxiety and repression is correct, Freud claims it would explain the German usage which allows the "homey" (*das Heimlich*) to become the uncanny (*das Unhemliche*) because "the uncanny element is actually nothing new or strange, but something that was long familiar to the psyche and was estranged from it only through being repressed."[28] Together, these two claims suggest that the experience of the uncanny is the result of *the return of the repressed*. Something repressed, by the individual, the culture, or both, has returned, opening up the anxious experience of the uncanny.

Freud notes that many of the experiences that people often associate with the uncanny—"animism, magic, sorcery, the omnipotence of thoughts, unintended repetition and the castration complex"—can all be associated with the same return of the repressed.[29] According to Freud, the paradigmatic experience of this kind is "represented by anything to do with death, dead bodies, revenants, spirits and ghosts." He notes that in some languages (including English) the German phrase *ein unheimliches Haus* (an uncanny house) is translated as "a haunted house."[30] "Haunting" evokes this return, but what exactly is returning and how is it repressed? Freud argues that for modern people who no longer believe that the dead go on living—even though, he notes, the idea is still peddled by religions, mediums, psychics, and so on—the "once highly ambiguous and ambivalent [feeling humans had toward the dead] has been toned down" and transformed into an "unambiguous feeling of piety." Older, more ambivalent attitudes, both mourned the loss of the dead and feared their return. But in the modern era, this has supposedly been transformed into an unambiguous, respectful sense of loss with, perhaps, *the hidden hope that they stay that way*.[31] What returns in the premodern world is the dead themselves, but what returns in the modern world is our repressed ambiguity about the very dead we consciously treat with only pious mourning and fond remembrance.

There are other examples, of course, but Freud's general point is that

> an uncanny effect arises when the boundary between fantasy and reality is blurred, when we are faced with the reality of something that we have until now considered imaginary, when a symbol takes on the full function and significance of what it symbolizes.[32]

It is a bit strange to define things in this way—*the uncanny as the blurring of fantasy and reality*—until we recall that Freud's point is that the "fantasy" is the site of a repression and, at the same time, so is reality, but reality as the other side of repression, the site where what is repressed is repressed.

But Freud is careful to point out that even though the uncanny is "something familiar ['homey'] that has been repressed and then reappears," not everything that reminds us of repressed desires is uncanny.[33] Furthermore, as he also points out, not everything that seems uncanny in one context is uncanny in another. In stories that assume a world of spirits and magic (like the world of *Harry Potter*), things can be fearful, but not uncanny. The uncanny requires repression in order for the "return," and without this return of the repressed, it would not be uncanny. Magic is not repressed in *Harry Potter*, so it cannot "return." Freud thinks this kind of thing is typical in fiction, but much rarer in our everyday experience, mostly being confined to "uncanny effects associated with the omnipotence of thoughts, instantaneous wish-fulfilment, secret harmful forces and the return of the dead." These are all uncanny because, Freud says, we no longer believe them, and "we do not feel entirely secure in these new convictions; the old ones live on in us, on the look-out for confirmation."[34]

Mladen Dolar has pointed out that French does not have a satisfactory way of translating Unheimlich (*l'inquietante étrangeté*), so Lacan invented one: *extimité*. For Dolar, extimacy is the uncanny. He explains that traditionally cultures focused on the attempt to draw a clear line of demarcation between inside/outside, mind/body, essence/appearance, subject/object, spirit/matter, and so forth, but Lacan's reading of psychoanalysis blurs this line with the concept of *extimité*, something neither interior nor exterior but "located where the most intimate interiority coincides with the exterior and becomes threatening, provoking horror and anxiety." It is uncanny in that it "is simultaneously the intimate kernel and the foreign body." For Dolar, all of the uncanny experiences cited by Freud can be read, via Lacan, as "the irruption of the real into 'homey,' commonly accepted reality." We can also characterize this uncanny experience as the "emergence of something that shatters well-known divisions and which cannot be situated within them." The uncanny is something that "puts into question" the "status both of the subject and of 'objective reality.'"[35]

The uncanny, for the way it calls into question the status of our objective reality, serves as a symptom of the repressed nature of culture itself. As extimate (Möbius) subjects, *we are all living in a haunted house.*

YELLOWJACKETS AS EXTIMATE SURVIVAL STORY

Following Dolar, we want to think of the uncanny in terms of Lacan's "extimacy," sensitive to where we might find instances of an "intimate interiority" that coincides with "the exterior" and becomes "threatening, provoking horror and anxiety." The Showtime series *Yellowjackets* exemplifies the uncanny in the exact ways we have been describing it and thus points to the uncanny, anxious nature of culture itself.[36] On the surface, the show seems to be a survival narrative about a group of teenage girls who, in the 1990's were marooned in the wilderness for nineteen months. The series switches back and forth between the 1990s survival narrative and the current-day stories of the survivors back in civilization. It becomes clear that the survivors are haunted in their modern adult lives by the events that occurred during their survival struggle. But nothing about this is necessarily uncanny. We could well imagine that the trauma of the survival experience would continue to be experienced in their current lives as PTSD.

But the uncanny enters the series in many of the ways Freud described: the repetition of symbols, the blurring of the lines between the living and the dead, fantasies of the omnipotence of our thoughts and wishes, the appearance of doubles, and the general sense of an otherly presence that registers in ambivalent ways. The first two episodes of the first season proceeded as a standard survival tale without the uncanny really intruding. With the third episode ("The Dollhouse"), we become aware that this might not be a straightforward survival narrative; it just might be a horror story. Taissa (Tawny Cypress) has a flashback to her childhood visit to her grandmother's deathbed. Initially the grandmother calms her fears by telling her that there is nothing to be afraid of, even in death, because God will provide a better afterlife. But then her grandmother starts speaking to someone who isn't there, telling him to stay away, and *not take her eyes*. At first, Taissa cannot see him, but then she looks in a mirror and sees a man with no eyes staring back at her. Later, toward the end of the episode, there is a scene that cuts between the young child Taissa, the marooned teenager Taissa, and the adult Taissa all walking slowly toward something. The teenage, marooned Taissa encounters a clothed skeleton in a rocking chair in the loft of the cabin in which the girls have sought shelter. The adult Taissa goes down into her basement and steps painfully on the eye of a toy, only to discover a small toy baby has been smashed and its eyes removed. The young child Taissa approaches her grandmother's open casket and lifts her eyelid to discover that her eyes have indeed been stolen. Taissa becomes an uncanny figure in the series as she increasingly seems to be controlled by a double of herself. When she asks her troubled young son who he is afraid of, he says "the other one," and we only later discover the "other one" is Taissa's double, that is, Taissa herself, but with a very different, malignant persona. In an extraordinary example of the uncanny, the show stages some scenes of Taissa staring into the mirror as her own reflection in the mirror suddenly changes facial expressions without Taissa changing hers. For Lacan, for whom the uncanny was a form of anxiety, this is the kind of thing he had in mind when he described the uncanny as "linked to anything that might appear at the place of the (-φ)." The (-φ) is Lacan's symbol for "castration." It points to the phallus as appearing as always missing. Lacan is saying that when something appears where that (missing object) is supposed to be, it is uncanny. Like the lack of lack we discussed in the first chapter, Taissa's double expresses something other than the normal experience of the mirror image. Normally, we expect the mirror to passively reflect back an image of a monadic subject who is master of its own house. But what Taissa sees is what we all repress, namely, that something else is living in "our house." The destruction of the mirror image's "homely" feeling by showing a reflection of an alien image not under control of the one standing in front of it is uncanny because it exposes the alien nature of the mirror image itself. It speaks to what the mirror image represses, namely the unconscious and the constitutional lack of symbolic castration that founds the subject. The image in the mirror is never "us"; it is an inverted, two-dimensional reflection of points of light reflecting off of the body placed in front of it. Even more deceptively, it conceals our own self-division—the idea that the discourse of the Other is at home in our house—that we are subjects of the unconscious.[37] *The uncanny we see in Taissa's mirror image is the return of what we all repress every time we look in the mirror.*

A different sort of instance of the uncanny in the show is the repetition of a mysterious symbol that the girls see carved into various trees in the forest when they are marooned. In the show, the adults again start to see the same symbol appearing in various contexts. In both cases, they do not know the source of the symbol or its meaning. The symbol is indecipherable yet seems to contain *an excess of meaning* both because it is clearly not a natural phenomenon and because of its repetition. Symbols mean something even when we don't know what they mean. They are a signifier of the other (as the source of the markings) and of the Other (for whom the enigmatic symbol has meaning). If the girls had been on a field trip to a museum and encountered hieroglyphics, the experience would not have been uncanny. It's uncanny when they encounter the symbol in the wilderness because, like something appearing where the (-φ) (i.e., only absence, loss) is supposed to be, the symbol evokes a presence in a wilderness devoid of human civilization. The girls increasingly come to believe that the wilderness, or some spirit living in it, is a presence that is keeping them alive but also demanding human sacrifices from them, leading to a troubling ambivalence. The symbol, with its excessive meaning, evokes the uncanny presence in the wilderness. As the narrative develops, the survivors begin to feel they have brought the spirit from the wilderness back with them, so it is not odd for them to see the symbol back in civilization. But it is uncanny for the audience. The doubling, the repetition, and the spiritual presence of the wilderness itself are all uncanny. The spiritual presence *first makes them a home in the strange wilderness, then makes their home in civilization strange by bringing back the repressed wilderness experience* (which included occultism, ritual hunts of other members of their party, and cannibalism). While the audience reacts with horror to this intrusion, the girls, now adults, seem far more ambivalent. The spirit of the wilderness, while initially uncanny for them, has become a subject with desires they can address. The spirit can inspire fear, but by conceiving it as a desiring subject, they fend off anxiety. This explains the relative ease with which the adult versions of the girls, now back in civilization, give in to the impulse to sacrifice yet another one of their own to appease this force. Through it all, the audience must endure an uncertainty about whether or not the spirit from the wilderness is a figment of the girls' imagination or something real. In either case, it is a Real that shatters objective reality.

What makes it so uncanny is that the show is not set at Hogwarts, where magic, demons, and occult rituals are normal. *Yellowjackets* exist in our world. But the return of these repressed forces triggers the uncanny in us, the viewers. We repress the fact that we are all subjects of the unconscious, so it is uncanny to see the image in Taissa's mirror indicating something else is in control of her. The repetition of the symbol whose occulted meaning cannot be deciphered points to the very nature of signification itself. The wilderness as the antithesis to culture serves as the object of culture's ultimate repression. The culture the marooned girls create in the wilderness, filled with violence and cannibalism, is the foundation of the culture from which they came and to which they return—a fact that we, as the audience, have repressed. The spiritual presence about which *we* as viewers feel so much ambivalence is *culture itself*, but we repress the demanding, bloodthirsty features of culture in order to compose ourselves as cultural beings in its (fantastical) nurturing embrace.

The experience of the uncanny, whether in our everyday experiences, or in literature, film, and television, discloses the nature of culture itself. It is not our personal, individual experiences that serve as the basis of the uncanny, but the repressions of culture (in both an objective and subjective sense). Culture is founded on repression, and we repress what culture actually is and does. The uncanny is a form of anxiety that *appears* on the side of culture in the dialectic that is the subject. The uncanny is a necessary, though perhaps rare, effect of the process of inculturation that we have all undergone. Because it can only occur from within the place we feel at home, it shows that *our home depends upon a repression, and that what is repressed can always return.*

The repression of cultural ideas of powerful supernatural forces, while a modern development, is a repression of a repression. To make ourselves at home in the universe, the world had to be transformed from a pure materiality into a subjective space—the space of the Other—in order to constitute subjects as cultural beings. Freud often thought of religion in exactly these terms, as a projection of the image of a powerful father-figure onto the empty universe as an antidote to the feelings of infantile helplessness that characterize our lives in the face of the superior powers of nature and fate. At the same time, this supernatural figure, the legacy of the murdered primal father, enforces the cultural order. Freud's just-so story of the bands of brothers in the primal scene can appear as a highly speculative hypothesis about a prehistorical occurrence that is beyond the ability of archaeology and evolutionary biology to confirm, even if it were predisposed to do so. But if we see this speculation as part of a sort of reverse-engineering process in which Freud is showing us what would have had to happen to make us like this—like what we are as Möbius subjects—then we can see it as a meditation on the nature of culture itself. Thus, the first repression, the ancient, even primeval one, was to repress the negativity in the universe itself in order to animate it, to give it a soul, to project a subjectivity onto it. (This is what happens to the girls when they are marooned in the wilderness.) This repression need not be seen as necessarily logically or temporally prior to the establishment of culture (and thus, of the subject), but rather as an essential element of that process itself. In this repression, the universe, or some important part of it, becomes a desiring subject. This desiring subject can become a source of fear, but it can thus fend off anxiety. The second repression—the repression of the repression—involves the modern, Enlightenment attempt to re-naturalize the universe, to remove the subjectivity from it. But in this repression of the original repression, the Other could not be eliminated. The Other persists. This accounts for Lacan's claim that "the true formula of atheism is God is unconscious."[38]

The uncanny, which Freud thought in terms of the homey/unhomey, can also be thought in terms of the animate/inanimate. When something thought to be inanimate—a corpse, a doll, a severed limb, a spacecraft's operating system—suddenly seems to be a (desiring) subject, we experience the uncanny (the return of the first repressed). But when we sense a "supernatural" force at work in the world (in a narrative in which it doesn't belong), we also experience the uncanny (the return of the second repressed that is characteristic of the modern world).

In other words, anxiety, in general, but here in terms of the uncanny, is the result of the return of the repressed. What has been repressed emerges in a form that generates anxiety (as a signal of the Real).[39] Earlier, we noted that Freud, in *Inhibitions, Symptoms and Anxiety*, argued that we repress in order not to experience anxiety. How do these two claims fit together? Though repression occurs as an attempt to avoid anxiety, what is repressed can always return. At the cultural level, this takes the form of the uncanny. Even in Heidegger's account, something like this dynamic between the subject and culture emerges. As Dylan Trigg has summarized it,

> Heidegger's argument is that in anxiety, the pregiven meaning of things in their everyday context slips away, including that of our own selves. In this slippage of things, the subject 'hovers' above and beyond their personal existence, revealing the 'pure Da-sein' that dwells beneath this personalized being.[40]

But whereas for Heidegger anxiety comes from the stripping away of the cultural modes of being in which Dasein exists, in the experience of the uncanny we see that it is not a slipping away, or even as Trigg describes it, a "hovering" above, but a return of what has been repressed in the constituting of both the subject and culture. However, there is no "pure Da-sein" to hover above (or below) the subject; *there is only the extimate subject*, who, in Dolar's terms, is "simultaneously the intimate kernel and the foreign body."[41]

The fact that we experience the uncanny is, as Dolar has suggested, because of the extimate character of the subject. This means that culture is not "out there" waiting for the subject to discover it, but neither is it "up there" imposing itself on the subject. Culture is the way the subject finds a home in the world, but this home is there only because of what has been repressed in the subject. This opens up possibilities for supplementing emancipatory theoretical projects with an extimate causality that is signaled by an anxiety that points to a return of the repressed. It suggests that our "reality" is in a real sense always the result of some sort of repression, and thus an acknowledgment of the return of these repressed elements is crucial to facilitating both critique and change since not only do we all live in a haunted house, we are, in some sense, the ones who haunt it.

THE ANXIETY OF BEING LEFTOVER

We can simplify both Freud's and Lacan's accounts of anxiety by boiling them down to two interrelated dynamics. One is the anxiety caused by the lack of lack. In our experience of culture, we can associate this with the uncanny. In the uncanny, something appears where there is supposed to be a lack. The other dynamic deals with the enigma of the Other's desire: I don't know what I am for the other. In this section, we look at this second dynamic in terms of what we can describe as a "hole" in reality. Lack itself, remember, does not cause anxiety. Here we can begin to understand how these two dynamics are really the same. When the "hole" in reality opens up, the important thing to do if one wants to avoid anxiety is NOT to fill it up. When it is filled up, we experience it as uncanny. But in this case, the anxiety comes in a form, reminiscent of Heidegger's account, that makes us aware that the hole only exists because of a Symbolic reality that is supported by fantasy. Lacan's position that there is no lack in the Real is crucial here. If a hole in the fantastic reality that sustains the subject appears, what is worse than the hole—which can be plugged—is the awareness that there is no "reality" at all—that the whole thing is just fantasy. This dynamic can be made more clear by analyzing the HBO series, *The Leftovers.*

The Leftovers, based on the 2011 novel by Tom Perrotta and broadcast in three seasons between 2014 and 2017, imagines a world in which 2 percent of the global population (140,000,000 people) simultaneously disappears without any explanation, an event they call "The Sudden Departure." The series ultimately revolves around the lives of two people who become romantically involved, Kevin Garvey (Justin Theroux) and Nora Durst (Carrie Coon), who each, in their own way, respond to the events of the Sudden Departure. In Kevin's case, the event has led to the dissolution of what appeared to be an ideal family situation. His psychologist wife, Laurie (Amy Brenneman), has left him to join a cult called "The Guilty Remnant." Kevin and Laurie's son, Tommy (Chris Zylka), has dropped out of college to follow a religious guru, "Holy Wayne" (Patterson Joseph), who claims he can hug the pain out of people. Their daughter, Jill (Margaret Qualley), has become sullen, alienated, and prone to risky and provocative behavior. Nora is the only main character in the series who has actually lost someone in the Sudden Departure; she lost her husband and two small children. In the aftermath, she found a job working for the "Department of Sudden Departures" which, among other things, runs a benefits program for family members. When she is not working, she sometimes hires prostitutes to shoot her while she is wearing a bullet-proof vest. Nora's brother, Matt (Christopher Eccleston), is a minister in their small town whose wife was seriously injured in the Sudden Departure when an unmanned vehicle suddenly struck their car. She has been in a coma ever since. Two other characters worth noting are Patty Levin (Ann Dowd), who was a patient of Laurie's before the Sudden Departure but who now leads the local chapter of the Guilty Remnant, and Meg Abbott (Liv Tyler), whose mother died of a heart attack on the day of the Sudden Departure, and thus her loss was never adequately acknowledged, lost in the chaos of the global catastrophe. Meg ends up joining the Guilty Remnant and in the second season becomes its most interesting member.

The first season of the series follows the reactions of the people in the small fictional town of Mapleton, New York, three years after the Sudden Departure. The second season moves Kevin, Nora, and Jill to the fictional town of Jardin, Texas, which is the only significant population center in the world with no departures. The residents of Jardin call themselves "the spared." The town is now dominated by religious/superstitious tourists who think of the site as sacred, and others who wonder if there might be some scientific reason why the place was immune. It has become a National Park. The third season basically moves to Australia on the eve of the seventh anniversary of the Sudden Departure, where Kevin's father, Kevin Garvey, Senior (Scott Glenn), a man with a recent history of being institutionalized for his mental illness, is attempting to stop an apocalyptic flood event by learning and performing traditional aboriginal rain songs, and where Nora is attempting to locate a group of people who are almost certainly con artists selling the opportunity to be transported by a machine to wherever it is the departed have gone. Though the locations change, each season continues to be an exploration of how people come to terms with *the disruption in reality* caused by a serious collapse of the shared cultural meanings that granted a kind of consistency to the Other (in Lacanian terms). As Žižek has pointed out, "what precedes fantasy is not reality but a *hole* in reality, its *point of impossibility* filled in with fantasy."[42] What the Sudden Departure does is reopen a hole that has normally been filled for us by "reality." The experience of this hole is what Lacan called a "signal of the real," or what we normally call "anxiety."

We might assume that a series premised on the disappearance of 140 million people would focus on mourning, but that is not the show's central concern. While some of the population did "lose" people in the Sudden Departure, most people did not. Two percent is a significant number, but not enough so that everyone would have lost someone close to them. Even worse for those who have "lost someone," they don't necessarily know that they are really gone. There are no corpses and there is no explanation for what happened to them. When Kevin expresses his sympathy to a woman in the community whose husband has "departed" by saying, "I'm sorry for your loss," she responds with, "Is that what it is?" (Season 1, Episode 1 "Pilot") We are not sure if the woman means she doesn't know what happened to him, or whether she means she doesn't know if her husband's disappearance should be considered a loss.

Nobody knows what happened or where the "departed" went. They don't even know if they should be called "victims," or if they are somehow the "chosen" ones. Therefore, the show is less about mourning and loss than it is about what they repeatedly call "the end of the world." In a world where nothing has materially changed and 98 percent of the population is still there, it is not immediately obvious how this could count for the "end of the world." But the world "ends" because it has brought an end to the "world" in the sense Heidegger understood it. More than anything else, the Sudden Departure creates a sense that there is a gap, an incoherence in the Symbolic order. This is crucial to seeing how the Sudden Departure provokes anxiety. Renata Salecl has argued that it is the inconsistency in the Other that creates the space for anxiety, and this is precisely what makes anxiety differ from those affects that arise out of loss, such as mourning or disappointment.[43] Losing people to death, break-ups, and so on creates a kind of loss but does not evoke anxiety. In cases of death and distance, traumatic as they may be, we have a story. The Symbolic order has a way to account for such events. Grief is not the same thing as anxiety. In grief, the Other can still appear consistent. In psychoanalytic terms, this consistency only comes from fantasy.

On the one hand, fantasy teaches us how to desire, not primarily in terms of identifying what I want, but more importantly in generating answers to questions regarding what others want from me. Žižek makes this point clear in his reading of Freud's story about his daughter, who delighted so much in eating strawberry cake. Freud had speculated that his daughter's desire was really based on the delight her parents took *in watching her enjoy eating strawberry cake*. As Žižek puts it,

> what the fantasy of eating a strawberry cake is really about is her attempt to form an identity (of the one who fully enjoys eating a cake given by the parents) that would satisfy her parents, would make her the object of their desire.[44]

In the Sudden Departure, a hole in reality is opened up that requires everyone to reorient themselves around the fantasy frames that have governed their lives. The Other has lost all consistency so that there is now no way to know what would please the Other.

In the pilot episode, which takes place three years after the Sudden Departure, we note a number of changes that have taken place to indicate this "hole" in reality. As already mentioned, the emergence of new state agencies and religious movements indicates a need to respond to this hole in reality with new fantasy frameworks. But we also see people expressing a kind of subjective destitution that has left them either melancholic or anxious (or vacillating between the two). Tommy dropped out of college because he could no longer "see the point." From watching Jill, we see that life in high school has also changed in some noticeable ways. During the morning announcements when students are asked to stand and recite the pledge of allegiance, nobody gets up, not even the teacher. After the pledge, students in this public high school are told they can, if they like, "pray for mercy and forgiveness and the return of those who left us." A few students do kneel on the floor and pray, but most sit sullenly in their desks. Students openly smoke marijuana on school grounds without any attempt by teachers or administrators to stop them. Parents seem to take no interest in where their kids are or what they are doing.

The town has also decided to celebrate the third anniversary of the Sudden Departure with something they call "Heroes Day." When the mayor is asked why they are calling it "Heroes Day" when the people who departed are not necessarily heroes (one cop clearly says they weren't heroes; his brother-in-law departed and "he was a dipshit"), she says they are calling it "Heroes Day" because nobody is going to come to a parade for "We-don't-know-what-the-fuck-happened day." As Heidegger would have suggested, we commit to the roles and ways of life—doing "what one does"—because that is how one lives in one's world as an alternative to confronting the nothingness of Being.[45] Or, for Lacan's extimate subject, who ex-sists, our reality, our sense of who we are and how we can matter to others, is based upon a set of understandings derived from our fantasies of the desires of the Other. To follow Lacan in this is to see "reality" not as something that we dream up, but as something we discover, albeit through fantasy. When we become aware of a "hole" in reality, we can't simply *produce* something on our own that would plug it. We have to *find* it. We have to *solve the problem.* In our fantasy we have to believe we have arrived at the secret. This is why attempts to solve such problems by creating things like "Heroes' Day" don't work, at least not in the way they are intended. Something like "Heroes' Day" can only work by expressly failing. In doing so, it keeps the object at a distance. We go through the motions but we know that "this isn't it." But the value of this "this isn't it" is that it sustains our belief in the "it." It doesn't plug the hole in reality, but by rejecting the emptiness of something like "Heroes' Day" it maintains the fantasy that the hole can be plugged, which sustains reality in general. Of course, there is no "hole" in the Real; the hole can appear only in "reality." The hole is the excess of the extimate subject who believes in the "it" because it believes in the Other, but so is the response to this hole in reality—the creation of new state agencies, commissions (like the Denziger Commission[46]), and religious movements—excessive, because the hole "exists" only because of the "reality" supported by the fantasy of the Other's desire. Because the subject is extimate, the subject finds its meaning from the Other, which expresses itself culturally in what Lacan calls the Symbolic, which is reality.

The holes in reality are the Real of which anxiety is a signal. While the initial appearance of a hole in the Symbolic order can produce anxiety, what would be even more anxiety-producing would be to realize that the Other which grants that reality its consistency does not exist, so there really is no hole to be plugged. This is why cultural responses to anxiety are successful only by failing so as to sustain the idea that there is something that could plug the hole. This keeps the subject in the realm of desire because it maintains the fantasy of the "it" that could restore consistency to the Other. In *The Leftovers*, the Guilty Remnant, who insist on "not forgetting" and show up on "Heroes' Day" just to make sure no one has a good time and forgets about the catastrophic Sudden Departure, live to make this point, namely, that there has to be an "it" to restore consistency to the Other and we have not yet found it. The Sudden Departure makes visible the excessive nature of the subject by showing how dependent we are on the Other to provide us with meaningful narratives that answer the questions, "what do you want from me? How can I matter?" It dramatizes the dialectic between anxiety and fantasy by showing the anxiety we feel first when we confront the hole in reality and then (again) when we realize that there is no hole and never was one. Fantasy returns us to the situation of having a "hole" in our reality, but one that can be plugged, if only we could successfully identify it. This sustains us in our minor projects of planning civic celebrations, conducting research, and committing to our "best lives" by seeing the hole in reality as a hole, and then believing that there is an "it" that could plug it.

In the case of the Sudden Departure, the only narrative on hand that was ready to plug the hole in reality was the evangelical "Rapture" narrative. According to this tradition, the "Rapture" is when Christ will return to earth seven years before the battle of Armageddon to "snatch" the true believers from the planet before the onset of the Tribulation—a seven-year period of intense suffering and violence as the Anti-Christ attempts to establish a new world order. Before the Tribulation begins, Christians will disappear from the planet and join Christ in the air where they will, presumably, be shuttled off to be with Christ for the duration of human history. The Sudden Departure had all the appearances of the Rapture, but as people begin to realize that there seems to be no rhyme or reason to the list of the departed, the narrative couldn't take hold. It was not like the best people were the ones who disappeared; it all seemed random. In the pilot, Kevin is sitting at a bar on the eve of the third anniversary as the television is playing CNN's anniversary coverage. Images of famous people who "departed" flash across the screen, to which the bartender reacts by saying, "The Pope I get, but Gary fucking Busey?" (Season 1, Episode 1 "Pilot") The Rapture narrative would have seemed to be just the thing to plug the hole opened up by the Sudden Departure, but it fails to account for what actually happened because it fails to restore a consistent Other. What causes anxiety is, in the first instance, the feeling that there is no answer to the hole (i.e., there is no way to understand what the Other wants in relation to the Sudden Departure; what did it mean?), but the second instance of anxiety, which is worse, is the feeling that there is no hole because there is no Other, which would mean there is no "reality" in that sense. This we cannot tolerate. It not only would mean anyone could disappear at any time for any reason but also that the subject, whose very existence as a subject is grounded on the desire of the Other, would lose its identity as such.

In asking why they are "leftover," the show's characters are approaching the trauma associated with Lacan's most famous "leftover," the *objet a*. They are really asking, what *objet a* am I for the Other? Were those who departed chosen? If so, what's wrong with me? This effect is pronounced in an ongoing gag that spans all three seasons involving the cast of the television comedy, *Perfect Strangers*. In Season 1 of *The Leftovers* all four of the main actors from *Perfect Strangers* "departed." In Season 2, we find out that one of them, Mark Linn-Baker, didn't depart but instead had been hiding out in Mexico, pretending to have departed. In Season 3, Mark Linn-Baker opts to put himself in what Nora describes as an "elegant suicide machine" in order to be "zapped" to wherever the other cast members are. He does this not because he misses his former cast members but because he cannot stand the thought that they were chosen—all three of them—and he was leftover. He doesn't know what *objet a* he is for the Other. In a way, Mark Linn-Baker is the paradigmatic "leftover" in the series. His anxiety ultimately leads him to what Lacan calls a "*passage à l'acte*."[47] It is a suicidal gesture. He lets himself fall from his own existence rather than live with the overwhelming anxiety of the "leftover," that is, to exist with no sense of one's place within the world of the Other's desire. But in doing this, Mark Linn-Baker affirms his ongoing confidence in the Other. He kills himself to maintain that consistency.

For Lacan, what makes all this so anguishing is that our reality is not simply something into which we have fallen or been thrown, but something to which we have been subjected. When he calls anxiety "the central affect, the one around which everything is organized," he does mean everything.[48] For Lacan, in both desire and anxiety the question to the Other is the same: "*Che vuoi*? What do you want from me?" and even "What *objet a* am I for the Other?" This is the same question lurking behind the bartender's "Why Gary-fucking-Busey?" that is, "What is the nature of the Other's desire that Gary Busey was chosen and I was not? What does the Other want from me? What *objet a* am I for the Other?" Of course, this questioning conceals the possibility that there is no big Other and the universe is not ultimately structured by a desire that I can satisfy, because it is not structured by desire at all.

The anxiety of this realization is too disorienting, leading people to acts as dramatic as that of the fictional Mark Linn-Baker's suicide.

In a telling scene from the second season, Kevin is being "haunted" by the now-deceased Patty Levin who appears to him in his (apparently) psychotic episodes. He desperately wants to be rid of her, so he asks her what she wants. She replies by saying,

> In Cairo, Egypt there is an ancient artifact, it's in a museum now, they found it in the tomb Amenhotep. Scholars call it "the wishing cup." You need to acquire this cup, it's more of a chalice actually. It's gonna be heavily guarded but you need to get it, any way you can, because once you do, you need to fill it with your cum, and then you need to drink it down, every, last, drop. (Season 2, Episode 7, "A Most Powerful Adversary.")

But then she laughs. It was a joke. She explains that she has no idea what to do. She is just as lost as he is. However, the scene reveals the nature of our situation. In our desperation to bring an end to our anxiety, we seek answers that manifest the excess associated with our extimate subjectivity. In studying analogous phenomena in culture, we should not be surprised that people fall for similarly ludicrous and extraordinary demands. In that same conversation between Kevin and his hallucination of Patty, he complains, "you're ruining my life" to which she replies, "*You're* ruining your own life, I'm just here to watch." This is the extimate subject, Dolar's simultaneous "intimate kernel" that is also the "foreign body." We fall for these ploys, pursue these difficult paths, and live in modes that seem to be "ruining our lives" not because of a "false consciousness" but because of our failure to confront what anxiety is telling us—that we are extimate subjects, whose excess escapes our conscious awareness but nevertheless keeps us up at night. This is why anxiety is the affect that does not lie. It does not depend on signifiers; it signals the Real that a chain of a million signifiers attempts to conceal.

In "The Subversion of the Subject and the Dialectic of Desire," Lacan argues that the neurotic "identifies the Other's lack with the Other's demand . . . so that the Other's demand takes on the function of the object in the neurotic's fantasy."[49] Lacan says this tendency to identify the Other's lack with the Other's demand "hides the anxiety induced in him by the Other's desire." The crucial question is: What am I for the Other? One of the ways fantasy defends against this anxiety is by providing an answer in the form of a demand, that is, *by identifying demand with desire*. In *Seminar X: Anxiety*, he says that "the fantasy the neurotic makes use of, which he organizes at the very moment he uses it, is precisely what serves him best in defending himself against anxiety, in keeping a lid on it." The neurotic does this, Lacan says, in a way that the "true object sought out by the neurotic is a demand that he wants to be asked of him. He wants to be begged."[50] Lacan associates this with what he calls the fantasy of "oblativity."[51] The speaking being, the castrated subject, avoids anxiety by situating himself in relation to the Other's demand, which he identifies with the Other's desire, and fantasy is the support of this "reality" structured as it is by the Other's desire.

This is basically the foundation for Žižek's "beyond-interpellation" account of ideology—an account that responds exactly to what Stuart Hall was seeking. For Žižek,

> Fantasy appears . . . as an answer to "*Che vuoi*?" to the unbearable enigma of the desire of the Other, of the lack in the Other; but it is at the same time fantasy itself which, so to speak, provides the co-ordinates of our desire—which constructs the frame enabling us to desire something . . . [fantasy] is the frame co-ordinating our desire, but at the same time a defense against "*Che vuoi*?" a screen concealing the gap, the abyss of the desire of the Other . . . The desire structured through fantasy is a defense against the desire of the Other, against this "pure," trans-phantasmic desire (i.e. the "death drive" in its pure form).[52]

What Žižek makes clear here is the alternative to reading the various manifestations of culture (films, state agencies, education, religion, etc.) as either "false consciousness" or "power relations" but as defenses against the Other's desire itself in the form of fantasy. What anxiety does is signal to us our dependence, in this way on the Other's desire that, in the experience of anxiety, is no longer working. We might be tempted to feel that a return to fantasy (what Heidegger would take to be a move toward inauthenticity and Sartre would take to be "bad faith") as unquestioned reality would be preferable to anxiety, but can we not rather see that when we are "destroying our own lives," as Patty tells Kevin in his hallucination, what is necessary is not to pursue another fantasy, but to come to terms with the fantastic nature of our reality itself? Only anxiety can signal that for us.

This is the real theme of *The Leftovers*. Every episode of the series pursues an understanding of the relationship between anxiety, fantasy, reality, and the Real, but one of the more stunning examples comes from the ongoing narrative involving the Christian minister, Matt Jamison. In the first season, Matt is occupied with two things: trying to prevent his church from being foreclosed on by the bank and distributing flyers around town depicting the sinful lives of the "departed." He is convinced that the Departure could not be the Rapture since he and his wife were not taken—or perhaps we would say, because he hopes that it was not the Rapture because he and his wife were not taken—he researches the lives of the Departed and publicizes his findings of their sins and crimes as proof that his worst fear has not been realized. The Rapture thus remains an option for him in plugging the hole in reality; that is, the Sudden Departure was not the Rapture. Not surprisingly, he gets beat up a lot and eventually loses the church. In the second season, he has moved temporarily to Jardin, Texas—the home of the "spared"—where, believing in the mystical powers of Jardin, he hopes that his wife will be restored from her coma and come back to life. Indeed, she does come out of her coma one night; they talk, make love (she becomes pregnant), and then in the morning she is back in her comatose state. Unable to make sense out of the strange workings of this "miracle," he attempts to remain in Jardin and becomes one of the most ardent spokespeople for the miraculous powers of the town—something the locals are actually more or less skeptical about—until everything comes crashing down on him. In the third season, he has become obsessed with the idea that Kevin is some sort of messianic figure who might be the key to all of the questions around his faith. Not coincidentally, though his wife did come out of her coma at the end of Season 2, Matt's stubborn religious commitment has prompted her to take their child and leave, and Matt has found out that a form of brain cancer he had suffered earlier has returned and is terminal. He pursues Kevin to Australia and on a ferry from New Zealand encounters a man named David Burton who many believe had come back from the dead. Burton has been traveling around ever since his "resurrection" claiming to be God incarnate. Of course, Matt is skeptical about Burton's pretensions to divinity, especially after he witnesses him pushing a man off the ferry into the open ocean. Matt kidnaps him and ties him up. What follows is a weird encounter that begins with Matt trying to force Burton to admit he is not God, but quickly turns to Matt talking to him as if he were talking to God. In a sort of redux of *Job*, he asks God/Burton about all the evil in the world for which God/Burton refuses to take responsibility or provide a reason. "There has to be a reason," Matt insists. God/Burton simply asks "Why?" and Matt responds that everything he, Matt, has done—helping people, letting his family abandon him, and so on—he has done "for you!" (i.e., God/Burton). To this, God/Burton replies, "Everything you've done you've done because you thought I was watching, because you thought I was judging, but I wasn't. I'm not. You've never done anything for me. You did it for yourself." To this, Matt responds, thinking of his terminal cancer, "Is that why you are killing me?" God/Burton simply nods. Matt tells him that when he was a child, he was sick (with the same cancer), and he prayed and "you" healed me. He asks if he can be healed again, and God/Burton tells him yes, and then commands Matt to untie him. Once untied, God/Burton slowly reaches for Matt as if he is going to touch his head only to snap his fingers and unceremoniously declare, "Ta-da, you're saved." Burton leaves and Matt is left alone, but we sense that something has changed in him. He has come to see the fantastic nature of the reality that has been governing his life. He sees his complicity in the events of his life. Events throughout the series have seemingly conspired to disavow Matt of this fantasy-reality, but he has stubbornly clung to it as a way to avoid anxiety. Only when through this encounter it becomes clear that "God" is part of the very extimacy that constitutes Matt as a subject can he finally let it go, finally understanding the nature of his "reality." His anxiety, which had been signaling the Real to him throughout the series, only to be met with more fantastic support, finally breaks through in this encounter with the Other (Burton/God), or rather with his awareness of the Other's nonexistence. As the ship prepares to dock in Melbourne the captain tells Matt that some fisherman did find a body, which verifies his claim that Burton had pushed a man overboard. When the captain asks if Matt has any pressing business in Melbourne, he says no, even though he had been maniacally trying to join Kevin in Australia before the seven-year anniversary of the Departure. We realize that Matt no longer believes. He has come face to face with the nonexistence of the Other of the Other (i.e., of that which would grant and confirm the consistency of the Symbolic order, i.e., "reality"). This encounter thus opened up the possibility for Matt to explore new paths of desire, but now with an awareness that there is no one watching him. No one judging him. It's as if Freud's daughter suddenly found out that her parents don't care if she ate strawberry cake or not; what does she eat now?

In his final scene in the series, Matt is with his sister, Norah, and he confesses to her that he is scared (not anxious). He's afraid of the chemotherapy and what it will do to his body, but also afraid it won't work. He is afraid of dying. He is afraid his son will forget his face and the sound of his voice. But then he says that most of all he is afraid that he will survive, because if he does, he will never be able to stand in front of a group of people and convince them that he has the answers when he has "no idea what the fuck [he] is talking about" (Season 3, Episode 6 "Certified").

This brings us to consider the so-called "end of analysis" and the idea of "traversing the fantasy." It is interesting to note that in one of Žižek's earliest expositions on the *sinthome*, he says that the "symptom in this radical dimension is unbound, it means literally 'the end of the world'—the only alternative to the symptom is nothing: pure autism, a psychic suicide, surrender to the death drive, even to the total destruction of the symbolic universe." He argues that this end of analysis comes when the analysand is able "to recognize in the Real of his symptom, the only support of his being." He says this is how we should understand Freud's *wo es war, soll ich werden*. In other words, Žižek says, "you, the subject, must identify yourself with the place where your symptom already was; in its 'pathological' particularity you must recognize the element which gives consistency to your being."[53] In Žižek's account of the traversing of the fantasy, "the desire with regard to which we must not 'give way' is not the desire supported by fantasy but the desire of the Other beyond fantasy."[54]

Žižek's tidy summary of this process points to a possible response to anxiety and also to the ways in which anxiety might be a very important signal for us. In this sense, I would like to offer a "defense of anxiety." Certainly, Heidegger was offering such a defense. For him, anxiety provides an opportunity for "authenticity." Of course, in Heidegger's account, it is entirely possible that nothing in the individual's life might actually change as a result of this authentic gesture. The subject could just be a more knowing participant in her absorption in the world, presumably always holding open the possibility of other possibilities.

Something similar can be said for Lacan's view. In the case of Matt Jameson, he of course realizes that he was not really talking to God, but following this encounter with Barton, he *comes to identify with his symptom*. Everything he has ever done, thinking he was doing it for God, he was doing for himself. He recognizes his own extimacy, which is to say, his own complicity in the events and meanings of his life. He thought he was doing it for God because God was watching and judging, but he wasn't. It was just Matt all along. Now, at the end, Matt has reached something like subjective destitution. But Žižek pushes this logic even further:

> What is at stake in this "destitution" is precisely the fact that *the subject no longer presupposes himself as subject*; by accomplishing this he annuls, so to speak, the effects of the act of formal conversion. In other words, he assumes not the existence but the *nonexistence* of the big Other; he accepts the Real in its utter, meaningless idiocy; he keeps open the gap between the Real and its symbolization. The price to be paid for this is that by the same act he also *annuls himself as subject* because—and this would be Hegel's last lesson—the subject is subject only in so far as he presupposes himself as absolute through the movement of double reflection.[55]

This is what the Sudden Departure makes possible, but most people in the world of *The Leftovers* do not choose this path. Instead, they continue to try to close the gap "between the Real and its symbolization." This can help avoid anxiety by maintaining the image the subject has of itself. It can close off the extimate real of subjectivity in favor of identity. But the cost for such a move is to foreclose the possibility of resistance and change.

From one point of view, a view that tries to understand the role of this anxiety-fantasy dialectic in terms of its implications for ideological critique, we must not assume that simply because we have identified the role of fantasy in supporting "reality" that all that is necessary is to decry this "reality" in those terms. Subjects are, by virtue of their own subjectivity, invested in this "reality." And yet, this "reality" is not coherent and complete. There is no Other of the Other. Though we may not have a Sudden Departure, the contradictions and inconsistencies that signal the hard kernel of the Real are always with us. In this light, the goal ought not to be challenging fantasy with "reality" (since they are the same) but seizing upon the real signal of anxiety to traverse the fantasy and find new modes of subjectivity that, to paraphrase Žižek, recognize in the Real of our symptoms the only emancipatory support of our being.

All of this demonstrates that the "reality" that shapes what Heidegger considered to be Dasein's normal mode of being is, as Lacan points out, structured symptomatically around a traumatic sense of loss. In the normal neurotic mode of life, the subject secures a defensive position against the abyssal desire of the Other in terms of a fantasy framework that takes refuge in the demands and desires of the Other. One thinks of Freud's characterization of religion as a kind of mass delusion, but one that could nevertheless spare "many people an individual neurosis."[56]

Though *The Leftovers* has sometimes been characterized by critics as engaging in a sort of "magical realism," it would be more apt to frame it as an attempt to engage the audience with the fantastic nature of "reality." Thus, the audience often doesn't know what is "real" and what is "delusional," and in fact, it raises the stakes on our purchase on "reality" by suggesting that our commitment to such delusions seems to be unavoidable. The main characters never arrive at a point at which they can claim to live without fantasy, but some of them do come to the point where they can keep open "the gap between the Real and its symbolization." This extimate point is the only one from which we can launch a critical appraisal of culture.

NOTES

1. *Barbie*, directed by Greta Gerwig (Warner Brothers, 2023).
2. Sigmund Freud, *Civilization and Its Discontents*, 38. References to the German text are from Sigmund Freud, *Das Unbehagen in der Kultur* (Berlin: Dearbooks, 2016. Originally published in 1930).
3. Stuart Hall, *Cultural Studies 1983: A Theoretical History*, ed. Jennifer Daryl Slack and Lawrence Grossberg (Durham, NC and London: Duke University Press, 2016), 185.
4. Hall, *Cultural Studies 1983*, 190.
5. Rothenberg, *The Excessive Subject*, 7.
6. Rothenberg, *The Excessive Subject*, 7.
7. Rothenberg, *The Excessive Subject*, 9.
8. Rothenberg, *The Excessive Subject*, 10.
9. Rothenberg, *The Excessive Subject*, 36.
10. Rothenberg, *The Excessive Subject*, 10.
11. In the Standard Edition, *Kultur* is translated, generally, as "civilization." Freud refused to draw a line between civilization (*Zivilisation*) and culture (*Kultur*). In fact,

he said, "I scorn to distinguish between culture and civilization," Sigmund Freud, *Future of an Illusion*, ed. and trans. James Strachey (New York and London: W.W. Norton and Company, 1962), 6. I use culture throughout both to avoid any exotic or fetishizing associations with the term, "civilization," and to emphasize the ongoing relevance of Freud's work for cultural studies.

12. Freud, *Civilization and Its Discontents*, 42.
13. Freud, *Civilization and Its Discontents*, 38–50.
14. Freud, *Civilization and Its Discontents*, 23–24.
15. Freud, *Civilization and Its Discontents*, 50.
16. Freud, *Civilization and Its Discontents*, 50. The original text reads: "*Diesen Prozess können wir durch die Veränderungen charakterisieren, die er mit den bekannten menschlichen Triebanlagen vornimmt, deren Befriedigung doch die ökonomische Aufgabe unseres Lebens ist.*" Freud, *Das Unbehagen in der Kultur*, 38.
17. Freud, *Civilization and Its Discontents*, 50–51.
18. Freud, *Civilization and Its Discontents*, 46.
19. Freud, *Civilization and Its Discontents*, 51, but also see 29–30. In a long footnote on this second reference, Freud makes a special case for professional work as an important site of satisfaction by way of "displacing a large amount of libidinal components, whether narcissistic, aggressive or even erotic, on to professional work."
20. Lacan, *Seminar XI: Four Fundamental Concepts*, 165–166.
21. Lacan, *Seminar VII: The Ethics of Psychoanalysis*, 113–114.
22. Lacan *Seminar XI: Four Fundamental Concepts*, 104.
23. Sartre, *Being and Nothingness*, 92–95, 589–592, 727–734.
24. Lacan, *Seminar X: Anxiety,* 41.
25. Mladan Dolar, "'I Shall Be with You on Your Wedding-Night': Lacan and the Uncanny," *October*, 58 (Autumn, 1991), 5–23.
26. Sigmund Freud, *The Uncanny*, trans. David McLintock (London and New York: Penguin, 2003), 123–134. The German text of this essay can be found at the Internet Archive: https://www.gutenberg.org/files/34222/34222-h/34222-h.htm . Originally published in *Imago. Zeitschrift für Anwendung der Psychoanalyze auf die Geisteswissenschaften V* (1919). S. 297–324.
27. Freud, *The Uncanny*, 147-148; "Das Unheimliche," 314-315.
28. Freud, *Uncanny,* 147–148.
29. Freud, *Uncanny,* 149.
30. Freud, *Uncanny,* 148.
31. Freud, *Uncanny,* 149.
32. Freud, *Uncanny,* 150.
33. Freud, *Uncanny,* 152.
34. Freud, *Uncanny,* 154.
35. Dolar, "Lacan and the Uncanny," 6.
36. At the time of writing, only two seasons of the series have been released.
37. For a fascinating and compelling account of this dynamic, see Jacques Lacan, "Remarks on Daniel Lagache's Presentation: 'Psychoanalysis and Personality Structure," in *Écrits*, ed. and trans. Bruce Fink (New York and London: W.W. Norton & Company, 2006), 559–572.
38. Lacan, *Seminar XI: Four Fundamental Concepts*, 59.

39. Lacan, *Seminar X: Anxiety*, 132, 185.
40. Trigg, *Topophobia*, xxxi.
41. Dolar, "Lacan and the Uncanny," 6.
42. Žižek, *Plague of Fantasies*, xiv.
43. Salecl, *On Anxiety*, 13–15.
44. Žižek, *Plague of Fantasies,* 10.
45. Martin Heidegger, "What is Metaphysics," in *Basic Writings*, ed. David Farrell Krell (London, Toronto, Sydney, New Delhi, Auckland: Harper Perennial, 2008), 102–105.
46. When Kevin is in the bar, we see a CNN report on the release of the "Denziger Commission Report." This is the dialogue from the CNN broadcast:

Denziger: To quote Wittgenstein, "whereof one cannot speak, thereof one must remain silent." Thank you.

Senator: Thank you, Doctor. So we're clear. . . We convened a council of clerics, representatives of most world religions, who, as you know, were somewhat conflicted about October 14th and were thus unable to reach any kind of consensus, which, in turn, led us to the scientific community for answers.

This document, the findings of your Commission, as to the instantaneous disappearance of 2 percent of the world's population, some 140 million souls, your conclusion as to what happened to them, why them, and where they've gone, is . . . and I'm paraphrasing here . . . "I don't know?"

Denziger: Sir, I am a scientist, and I was asked to look at data. In fact, I was asked to identify patterns that weren't immediately obvious and address related events like the Chef Anomaly and the Brandenburg Carousel that were, and still are, considered miracles. But they are simply statistical hiccups that we can't explain because, sir, in my opinion, miracles do not exist.

Senator: Miracles do not exist?

Denziger: Scientifically speaking, no, sir.

Senator: Doctor, pardon my tone, but who are you, sir, to tell the American people that millions of mothers, fathers, sons, and daughters disappeared, gone in an instant, and that's not a miracle? What in God's name do you call it?

Denziger: I don't know, but if you are implying it was a miracle, I am fairly certain, sir, that God sat this one out.

(Season 1, Episode 1, "Pilot")

47. Lacan, *Seminar X: Anxiety*, 77, 110–111, 113, 115–116, 186–187, 249, 261, 321, 333.
48. Lacan, *Seminar XVII*, 168.
49. Lacan, "The Subversion of the Subject and the Dialectic of Desire," , 823.
50. Lacan, *Seminar X: Anxiety*, 51.
51. Lacan, *Seminar X: Anxiety*, 52.
52. Slavoj Žižek, *Sublime Object of Ideology* (London and New York: Verso, 1989), 118.
53. Žižek, *Sublime Object of Ideology*, 75.
54. Žižek, *Sublime Object of Ideology*, 118.
55. Žižek, *Sublime Object of Ideology* 231.
56. Freud, *Civilization and Its Discontents,* 36.

Chapter 3

Anxiety in the Field of Vision

This chapter is the center of this book and can be seen as transitional, taking up what has preceded it (anxiety in the dialectic of Möbius subject and culture) and laying the foundation for what will follow (an analysis of anxiety in relation to sex and race). The visual field has a special relationship to anxiety, especially anxiety as understood in relationship to its dialectical relationship to fantasy and its signaling of the extimacy of the subject. In his last lecture in the *Anxiety* seminar, Lacan made it clear that of the five levels at which he had been trying to articulate the nature of the subject in terms of desire—oral, anal, phallus, gaze, and voice—it was only at the level of the gaze, the image, the visual that we find what is "characteristic of the subject's constitution in his relation to the Other, in so far as we can articulate it as being centered around the function of anxiety." Only at the scopic level can we see "this specific form fully articulated," and only here do we find an "exemplary form which is fully fleshed out, this specific form whereby human desire is the function of the desire of the Other."[1]

Furthermore, it is necessary to emphasize and attempt to isolate the visual field in our analysis of anxiety because it cuts against our intuition that seeing brings with it a kind of immediacy that should be immune from the effects of desire. "Seeing is believing," we like to say, without asking if beliefs based on vision are really as reliable as they seem to be. Furthermore, to be a subject in the twenty-first century is to be simultaneously acutely aware of the power of the gaze to inflict anxiety on us and simultaneously oblivious to the ways in which the field of vision is always mediated by the desire of the Other. We tend to assume that the way things "look" to us is related to properties intrinsic to those objects rather than to understand the role of intersubjective relations in the constitution of how we see.

We can sense this on a personal level in ways almost all of us understand that to be looked at can be a cause of anxiety, while at the same time finding nothing particularly anxiety-producing about looking at objects. But even our looking at objects can be a cause of anxiety once we understand this dynamic in relationship to our own extimacy. But provisionally, and for the most part, we might claim that an engagement with images, wherever and however they are encountered, offers the subject a sense of plenitude and wholeness, while being looked at provides a different experience that can be anxiety-producing. But the extimacy of the subject would suggest to us that things are not so simple. Because of its Möbius quality, the subject can never look at something without also being, in some sense, looked at. When we start to consider the implications of this we can begin to see why Lacan claimed that the visual field was where we could most clearly perceive what was most characteristic of the subject's being (in relationship to the Other) and where we could most clearly see the role anxiety plays in our lives.

Furthermore, the dynamic of the dialectic between anxiety and fantasy developed in the previous chapters applies to the visual field. Lacan goes so far as to claim that at the scopic level "the subject is most assured in relation to anxiety" ("*le sujet est le plus sécurisé quant à l'angoisse*").[2] The reason for this assurance, Lacan tells us, is because at the scopic level the *objet a* is "most fully masked." To frame it in terms of the extimacy we have made central to subjectivity, in the visual field the extimate nature of the subject is hardest to see because in "seeing" we find ourselves always in a field that seems to be divided in two between someone looking and someone being looked at. The value of centering anxiety in our consideration of the visual field is to see the way it disrupts this easy division into inside/outside that normally governs our thinking about seeing. In the typical way of thinking about looking, the visual field is divided between subjects and objects with the gaze always on the side of the subject. But the extimacy of the subject suggests this cannot be the case. The coincidence of the internal and external is what the subject is, and the gaze should be thought of in those terms. It is located where everything is with the Möbius subject, in the subject's relationship with the Other. To make this shift in thought is to move from a mode of analysis that is always looking for what effects are generated by the gaze of this person or that type of person and instead to see that what happens in the act of seeing as already mediated before the point of vision itself. Where then is the anxiety?

The anxiety I experience relative to my appearance to others seems obvious. When I am aware of being looked at, I am aware that this is potentially a scene of encounter with the Other. What do I look like to them, and what does that mean? Less obvious is the way in which fantasy shapes the way I look at the world. Looking is never a matter of what Lacan called the "geometry of vision"; it is never about what points of light can contact the lens of my eye. Rather, my looking is always mediated by desire, which is to say, by the desire of the Other. Beyond this simple opposition—appearance/anxiety versus looking/fantasy—is the realization that this is not a simple opposition, but a dialectic that reflects the subject's extimacy. The dialectic form of looking/appearing is also structured by the dialectic relationship between anxiety and fantasy. When I experience anxiety over my appearance to others, I am already in the field of fantasy. Similarly, when I view the objects in the world as mediated by fantasy, I do so in relation to the anxiety that haunts me as a subject. But at this level, more than the others, we tend to escape anxiety because of the capacity of the gaze to offer us a vision of a world without lack. Lack cannot be grasped in the visual field. But at the same time, it is here, at the level of the visual, that anxiety comes in the most obvious way.

LACAN'S GAZE

We have shown how Lacan locates anxiety in relationship to five zones, levels, or rims in the body: the oral, the anal, the phallus, the scopic, and the superego (the voice). The object associated with the scopic was the gaze. In *Seminar XI: The Four Fundamental Concepts of Psychoanalysis*, the gaze becomes a major focus of Lacan's, but this was not his first foray into the visual field. Lacan's first major contribution to the field of psychoanalysis was his elaboration of the mirror stage. He located this stage in children ages six to eighteen months. Lacan claims that during this period children are fascinated by their own image in the mirror. According to Lacan, this is because their bodies are still lacking the level of motor control that would allow them to act in competent and independent ways. The child's body is disorganized, lacking a sense of unity and cohesion. But in front of the mirror, the child finds an image of wholeness to bring a sort of unity to the mass of sensations, movements, and impulses that operate at the level of the organism. She sees her own image in the mirror, and this image forms the basis of an identity. The image does not even have to be a full-body image (for such a thing cannot be captured by a mirror, even a full-length mirror, because the body is a three-dimensional object, and the mirror image is only a two-dimensional reflection of some of the points of light on the surface of the body). Lacan will call this specular image the *ideal ego*. Often, the child will turn away from the image in the mirror to look back at adult caregivers who confirm, "yes, that's you!" This gives rise to a "jubilant assumption" based upon the mirror image (and the confirmation by the parents).[3] This identification forms the basis for the development of all identities that are commonly associated with the ego.

Lacan summarizes his position nicely when he says:

> This development is experienced as a temporal dialectic that decisively projects the individual's formation into history: the mirror stage is a drama whose internal pressure pushes precipitously from insufficiency to anticipation—and, for the subject caught up in the lure of spatial identification, turns out fantasies that proceed from a fragmented image of the body to what I will call an "orthopedic" form of its totality—and to the finally donned armor of an alienating identity that will mark his entire mental development with its rigid structure.[4]

Several observations can be made about Lacan's development of the idea of the mirror stage that are relevant for our project. First, we can note the centrality of the image in the establishment of the ego. For Freud and Lacan, the ego is not in control of things. *The ego does not mediate between the desires of the id and the demands of the superego*. Freud often refers to an "ego feeling" and even calls the ego a "façade."[5] This is part of why Lacan emphasizes the "subject" and not the ego in his development of Freud's teaching. Similarly, his reference to an "orthopedic" form of the body's totality mirrors the way Lacan will later describe ego psychology as an attempt to straighten out the subject (as opposed to an exploration of desire). The ego is not the subject, nor is it the focus of psychoanalysis. It is, in a way, a mistake—a mistaken identity—and not the center of the subject's authentic self, but rather the basis of identifications. Furthermore, the mirror image is an alien image. The mirror image is only a two-dimensional reflection. The infant identifies itself with something that is not itself, but a mere projection. It is also reversed. So, it is not even an accurate two-dimensional image. Finally, the image gives an impression that is false. It leads the infant to believe that it has achieved a level of competence it has yet to reach (and never will). Nevertheless, the infant, confirmed by the adult caregivers, takes this alien, false, misleading image to be "me." Probably most important for Lacan's later work, the image does not show castration.[6] What is missing cannot be seen, and this is the very nature of the Imaginary (i.e., to do with images, not "make-believe") relationship, to cover up our lack.

Of course, the penis can be seen, and this is part of the dynamic. Certainly, one of the things an infant may come to realize, in this imaginary relationship, is that some people have penises and others do not. The tendency to invest the penis with phallic power is one of the more pathetic features of patriarchy, but one that has been rather resilient. The young child who has a penis may not make much of it until, in a Symbolic relationship, he begins to wonder why Mommy sleeps in Daddy's room. Perhaps Daddy's penis provides him with a theory, but a theory that can only be castrating. But the infant's rival need not be "Daddy" but can be anything the child sees as diverting mom's attention and capturing her desire: for example, work, God, saving the planet, and so on. Similarly, "mom" need not be "mom" but can be the caregiver to whom the child most attaches and on whom the child most depends. All of this happens at the level of the Symbolic. At the level of the image, at the level of what the subject sees, there is not lack, but there can be a stain (to be discussed below).

This sets a pattern for future development in the sphere of the ego. The ego will continue to see itself in similarly alien, false, and misleading images that become objects of aspiration and paths to the disavowal of lack. These images, even in the mirror stage, need not be only those from the mirror. The child can begin to see, in others (siblings, playmates, etc.), an image that will reinforce this notion of wholeness. The phenomenon of such images, which in one sense are nothing, can take on significant emotional importance for the child.

But this is not the gaze, for Lacan. In *Seminar XI: The Four Fundamental Concepts of Psychoanalysis*, Lacan, responding to the recent posthumous publication of *The Visible and the Invisible* by his friend Maurice Merleau-Ponty, praised the way Merleau-Ponty had pushed the limits of his phenomenology in relation to the eye, but critiqued Merleau-Ponty's approach for going "too far." He characterizes Merleau-Ponty's approach to the visual field as a "regulation of form, which is governed, not only by the subject's eye, but by his expectations, his movement, his grip, his muscular and visceral emotion—in short, his constitutive presence, directed in what is called his total intentionality." Lacan says that the problem with this approach is that Merleau-Ponty does not realize that the "eye is only a metaphor" of something that Lacan would prefer to call "*la pousse du voyant*" which is something "prior to [the] eye."[7] "*La pousse du voyant*" is strange. Sheridan translates the phrase as "the seer's 'shoot,'" which is also strange. The contrast here is between the "total intentionality" characterizing Merleau-Ponty's approach with the "*pousse*" ("growth," "shoot") of Lacan's approach. Lacan would certainly have understood that "intention" for Merleau-Ponty would not have been a conscious intention, but rather an orientation toward the world that is pre-reflective. With that, we might understand this as a reference to the evolution of the eye itself. Lacan says as much in his seminar on *Anxiety* where he says that the eye does not refer simply to mammals, vertebrates, or "even chordates," but "appears on the animal ladder right down at the level of organisms that have nothing in common with us."[8] Before the evolution of the eye there were cells, "growths" if you will, that were sensitive to light, able to alert the organism to a shadow that might represent a predator.[9] These eyes functioned as a "*voyant*"—a "warning light"—before the function "of seeing" (also "*voyant*"). Thus, Lacan insists on the "pre-existence of a gaze—I see only from one point, but in my existence, I am looked at from all sides."[10] In evolutionary terms, before the eye was good enough to see, it was good at detecting when an organism might be seen. The gaze does not work in one direction. It speaks to the way the subject is seen when it looks, that is to its extimacy.

This is crucial to understanding Lacan's notion of the gaze. It is not about what I see but about the prior situation of my being seen in relation to what I see. The gaze is not a site of mastery but rather a way of locating the subject within the visual field. Rather than being constituted by passing through the poles of the visible and invisible, as Merleau-Ponty would have it, Lacan says that the "gaze is presented to us as a strange contingency, symbolic of what we find on the horizon, as the thrust [*butée*, more accurately, the "limit" or "end point"] of our experience, namely, the lack that constitutes castration anxiety."[11] It is, at first, strange to see the eye associated with castration anxiety, but in our previous discussion of the uncanny, we saw how Freud had already sketched the eye's role in relation to castration. Our fear of losing an eye is perhaps rivaled only by the fear of losing the (male) sexual organ. Perhaps this is because we tend to associate a kind of mastery with both organs. But it is more than that.

In his seminar on *Anxiety*, Lacan suggests the eye "is the object without which there would be no anxiety."[12] At the same time, in the same context, he points to Oedipus, who tore out his eyes but could still see. According to tradition, he could see into the future. Lacan describes Oedipus as the man who gouged out his eyes for "seeing too much" only to become a "seer," a paradigm of the moment of anxiety in which one encounters "the impossible sight . . . of your own eyes lying on the ground," which is "the surest key to what you can always find in the phenomenon of anxiety."[13] The two apparently opposing claims, one that asserts that the eye is crucial to anxiety, the other that pictures the moment of anxiety with the eyes dislodged from their sockets, are in fact dealing with the same problem: the emergence of castration in relation to the visual field, which is another sign of the subject's extimacy. (This passage is also quite suggestive in relationship to disability studies. For Lacan, the gaze is not about eyes. It is about seeing, but seeing that is not linked to an organic ability per se.)

In the same seminar, he sees that we are gazed at by the "white glaze of the blind man's eye," the "marine creature" hauled from the sea in *La Dolce Vita*, and also from tattoos. The non-seeing points of vision gaze at us precisely because the object of the gaze is non-specular: it is the *objet a*. We want to see, when we look with our eyes, what we can never see, because the object we seek—*the objet a*—is a non-object that cannot be accessed in the visual field. When looking with our eyes, we try to find mastery over the world, but when something like the uncanny objects Lacan describes here looks back at us—that is, something appearing where the (-φ) is supposed to be—that mastery is disrupted, and castration is made evident. Lacan's most celebrated example of this dynamic is in Holbein's *The Ambassadors*. The painting contains a stain, a blot in the lower region of the image that can only be made out from an extreme angle. The stain is what gazes back at us. It is a nothing in the image of the fullness exhibited by the two figures in the painting, surrounded by their exotic collection of gifts and souvenirs from their travels as dignitaries. In the midst of this image of abundance, Holbein installs an anamorphic image that reveals itself to be a skull. In doing so, it literalizes the nothing in a *memento mori*, reminding us that all our accumulations will come to nothing in the end, which is death. That is its meaning once the meaning emerges by shifting angles. However, as the stain, it haunts us by gazing back at us from where no fullness can emerge. It appears as a meaningless blot to stain the image of mastery and fullness. Indeed, it is what we cannot see, the stain on the image, that both disrupts and attracts our eye. This is Oedipus' eyes on the ground. They were, during all their time in Oedipus' skull, looking at things without seeing the lack that motivated the desire that shaped all of his experiences of knowing. Now that they are on the floor, Oedipus can finally see. This is the point of anxiety, seeing what our encounter with images could never bring us. This is because, as Lacan says, "castration . . . is always elided at the level of desire when it is projected into the image."[14] But once the eyes are on the floor, the image can no longer elide the reality of our castration.

And yet, without the eye, Lacan tells us, there would be no anxiety.

Lacan recounts an event from his youth in which he had gone to a small fishing port in Brittany where generations had made a living braving the dangers of the sea and confronting the elements. He wanted to "see something different, throw [himself] into something practical, something physical." One can imagine the handsome young student, prone to jokes, well-versed in the classics, wanting to be someone else, which is to say, wanting to appear like something other than what he was. We can imagine him congratulating himself on doing something other Parisian intellectuals would have shunned, seeing himself as "one of the guys" on their small boat. While he is out with the fishermen one day, one of them, Petit-Jean, spied an empty sardine can floating on the surface of the sea, sparkling in the sun. He turned to Lacan and said, "You see that can? Do you see it? Well, it doesn't see you!" Petit-Jean found the comment very amusing; Lacan did not, but he later asks himself why it was so funny to Petit-Jean, and to him less so?[15]

Lacan explains that the can was, in fact, "seeing him." Not that it had eyes, but from the point of view of the geometry of light, *the can could see him*. Lacan was within its view. But Petit-Jean said *it did not see him*. The point that Petit-Jean is making is that Lacan did not belong in that picture. Lacan does not find this amusing because the whole point of his slumming it with the fishermen was to prove that he did, in fact, fit in. In one sense, this is not surprising, given that our identifications tend to operate at the level of the Imaginary. But Lacan's point here is even more perceptive. He says the reason it was funny to Petit-Jean and to him "less so," was because "I—at that moment—as I appeared to those fellows who were earning their livings with great difficulty, in the struggle with what for them was a pitiless nature—looked like nothing on earth. In short, I was rather out of place in the picture."[16] This event illustrates and supports his view that vision is an extimate process, one of being seen and seeing. In a sense, the being seen is first. It is the being seen, or rather, how I understand my being seen, that shapes how I see. But in another sense, it is extimate the whole time. The sardine can is an external object that coincides with the internal kernel of Lacan-as-subject. Lacan puts it pithily: "The picture, certainly, is in my eye. But I am in the picture."[17] The *normal* understanding of this process would be to claim that while a picture does form in the eye, I can never be in that picture. This is how most people, including scholars in various branches of visual studies, understand the dynamic of looking. Indeed, Sheridan's incorrect translation ("but I am not in the picture") seems to be making that point. Lacan's point is the opposite. The picture that forms in my eye already includes me. Just as Lacan emphasized the evolutionary history of the eye to point to its earliest function as a warning light (*le voyant*), the gaze is something located in the "picture," *not in my eye*. Yes, something forms in my eye, but the picture always includes me. This is the extimacy of the subject. This is because the unconscious, the discourse of the Other, is always operative in the subject, so that even in what seems to be a pure sensory encounter, a matter of the geometry of light, a mediation occurs.

This mediation occurs in relation to what Lacan calls the "screen." A screen both blocks my field of vision—it hides something—and becomes a surface upon which an image can be screened.[18] What cannot be seen is the *objet a*. We cannot see an image of our loss or lack directly, so it appears only as a blot, or stain. Lacan says in his story about the sardine can, he himself was in the picture as "the screen . . . the stain, the spot."[19] He was the element that did not fit. Ironically, the fantasy of going to Brittany was one where, we can imagine, he sought to fill out his own image of himself. He wanted to see himself in a certain way. He was fine, absorbed in his fantasy image of himself in that picture until Petit-Jean pointed out that Lacan himself was the stain, the point of lack, the indicator of castration, that spoiled the picture of fulfillment Lacan had hoped to find. The sardine can, as an extimate object—as all objects are for the subject—could not only serve as a source of comedy for Petit-Jean, but as an object of anxiety for Lacan.

The same point is made in a slightly different way in Lacan's retelling of the ancient story of Zeuxis and Parrhasios. The two were having a contest to see which was the better painter. Zeuxis painted a picture of grapes that were so realistic that birds swarmed the painting trying to pick at the fruit. After such a convincing rendering of an edible object, he confidently turned to unveil Parrhasios' painting only to discover that the veil itself was the painting. A surface reading of the story awards the victory to Parrhasios, whose painting fooled a man, while Zeuxis' painting only fooled birds. But Lacan is not satisfied with this conclusion. It is not so much the skill of Parrhasios as it is his choice of object that awards him the prize. Lacan concludes that "if one wishes to deceive a man, what one presents to him is the painting of a veil, that is to say, something that incites him to ask what is behind it."[20] We are lured, in the visual field, by a veil. What we want to see is what we cannot see, the *objet a*, but an image captures our desire if we think what we see is merely veiling that lost object. An effective advertising image must present to us an image of the product as a veil. It must imply that the product is concealing for us the *objet a*. Like the *agalma* Alcibiades sees in Socrates, our attraction to objects (and people) is based on what we do not see; not what we see.[21] We are fascinated by such images because they capture us by promising to satisfy our desire. This is also why Lacan claims that the Other sees the voyeur for what he is, impotent.[22] The voyeur does not master the scene; his activity displays his own castration.

Jennifer Tyburazy reads the Lacanian gaze in relation to what she calls the "choreography" of display around one of Lacan's prized paintings, Gustave Courbet's *L'origine du monde*.[23] Lacan was the last private individual to own the painting, and he kept it at his country house, *La Prévôté* in Guitrancourt, which he and his wife, Sylvia Bataille, had purchased after the war.[24] The home was filled with an impressive collection of books and artworks, but Lacan kept the painting in his studio where he worked when in the country. He had concealed the painting with a woodcut representation of the Courbet done by Sylvia's brother, André Masson, in a surrealist style that only hinted at the image beneath. Using a concealed locking mechanism, Lacan would open the painting to reveal the Courbet underneath as he observed the reactions of his guests. Tyburazy notes that Amelia Jones has suggested that Lacan's experience of such exhibitions contributed to his theorization of the gaze, especially the idea that all pictures are "traps for the gaze." Tyburazy follows Jones, suggesting that perhaps Lacan's home in Guitrancourt was an "observational laboratory" in which he "used Masson's woodcut sketch as the sublime precursor to the overwhelming backdrop of the cunt."[25] She quotes the account of the memoirist James Lord, who saw the painting with Dora Maar (Picasso's muse and mistress, who was also supposed to have had an affair with Lord, who was known to be gay). In Tyburazy's reading of Lord's account, which emphasizes the theatricality of the display, Lacan's attention to Lord's reaction, and the "almost rude" way he dismissed them from his studio so he could read "a volume" he had brought to the studio with him, leads her to conclude that "the location of [castration] anxiety became allayed or at least temporarily displaced through the intermediary role of he who displayed."[26] What she means by this is that the reactions to the way the object is displayed, and not the object itself (i.e., the representation of female genitalia), was the point of Lacan's choreography. Lacan, Tyburazy suggests, was transferring his own anxiety onto his guests by assuming the role of observer.

By seeing Lacan as shifting his anxiety away from his own castration by displaying the image to the viewer, Tyburazy's focus on the "choreography of display" and the mediating role it plays in the viewing of sexually explicit images adds a different layer to how we consider the gaze. It forces us to think about what is achieved through the act of looking at looking, which, for Tyburazy is conceived here in a very specific way. Whether this deduction applies to Lacan or not is difficult for us to judge, but it may help us understand how displays of sexually charged images are choreographed in order to avoid the very anxiety they might provoke by staging the display in ways that create anxiety rather than feed fantasy.[27] This paradigm would tend to put "high art" on the side of anxiety and pornography on the side of fantasy.

But her reading of the scenario depends, in the first case, on her assumption that the confrontation with female genitalia arouses castration anxiety in the male viewer. I think this point could be debated. Furthermore, the reading of anxiety we have been pursuing in this book would not so easily divide fantasy and anxiety from each other. The fantasy is there to dispel the feelings of anxiety, but castration anxiety exists for structural, that is semiotic, reasons and not because of any particular image. (See chapter 4.) There is nothing natural about the revulsion someone might feel at the sight of female genitalia. It is always a matter of how the signifier has brought such an image into the unconscious life of the subject. But the more serious problem with her reading of Lacan's reaction is that she characterizes Lacan's understanding of the gaze as depending on the "stability of a spectator identity" and on the "supposition of an absolute 'eye,' understood to be white, heterosexual, and masculine." She bases this on Lord's saying that he feigned admiration for the image in a way that disrupted Lacan's expectations about Lord (who was known to be homosexual). After the display, Lacan sat down at his desk with a book he had brought into the study and dismissed the two guests in a way that seemed "almost rude." Tyburazy takes this rudeness as a possible expression of Lacan's disappointment that Lord's reaction did not match his expectations. (I wish I could be this forthright with guests when I have work to do, so I am not sure it makes the point she thinks it does. Perhaps it just demonstrates Lacan's willingness to be rude in order to do what he wants to do, in this case, read a book after showing two of his guests a prized work of art he thinks they will appreciate.) By this she must mean that Lacan expected to find revulsion in Lord's gaze, but was disappointed. But would not this show that Lacan did not, in fact, believe in the "stability of spectator identity?"

Tyburazy claims that her analysis of Lacan's display of *L'origine du monde* suggests a "slippery embodiment of spectatorship that is neither the detached voyeuristic male gaze" nor the female spectator who "sadistically" identifies with the male gaze or "masochistically" identifies with the objectified female nude. Her analysis suggests that "this reconfigured standpoint requires the curatorship of a different kind of viewing experience through queer praxis."[28] This perspective seems to follow John Berger's understanding of the role of the (white female) nude in Western art but with an attempt to make room for queer pleasure in seeing. Tyburazy's analysis, with its emphasis on the choreography of display, has the advantage of moving the looking relationship into a realm where the object is not the source of the observer's reaction, but rather the way that it is displayed.

But here, Lacan's display practice points to the special nature of the object in this case, *L'orgine du monde*. In Courbet's painting, the "sublime object" is exposed and centered, removed from its context in the female body. Normally, in the "high art" female nude, the vagina, the labia, even pubic hair are often concealed, just as the painting is obscured, in Lacan's studio, behind an abstraction (Masson's woodcut). The object sustains its sublimity by being concealed. What causes anxiety is not the suggestion of the absence of the penis, but the proximity of *the objet a*. The *objet a*, as a non-object, can only function properly when it is concealed and kept at a distance. Small children and other animals do not feel any anxiety (let alone revulsion) in the face of genitalia; it is the cultural intervention in the field of sex that both creates desire around the hidden and forbidden and thus presents the possibility for anxiety when the "lack is lacking" in the visual field. Lacan's display choreography, even if the veiling of the painting with another painting was Sylvia's idea, reinstates the possibility of making the vagina a sublime object.

There is no reason to think pornography functions in a different way. Anyone who has ever been to a nude beach, a nudist colony, or simply a European sauna can testify to the banal nature of those encounters with genitalia. This is because the concealment of the object, whether by Lacan's abstract woodcut in the display of "high art," or, in the case of pornography, placing it behind a counter or wrapping it in brown paper, the use of private browsing practices, and so forth, all elevate the object by removing it from view. But this is how the *objet a* functions in the field of vision. To trap a subject with a picture one must paint a veil. Tybyurazy's description of the choreography of display shows why visits to museums (and pornographic websites) are not like a visit to a nude beach.

Thus, Lacan sees the relationship between the eye and the gaze as a dialectic one, reflecting the extimacy of the subject. He is very clear that the eye-gaze relationship is "not a coincidence, but fundamentally a deception (*leurre*). When, in love, I ask for a look, what is fundamentally unsatisfying and always missed is that you never look at me where I see you."[29] Not only does the gaze not emanate from the eye, but the eye is also not the place from which I see. This conception of the gaze robs from us the sense of immediacy and mastery we want to associate with the gaze.

I grew up in the 1970s in a very conservative Christian home. I began to formulate imaginary relationships with images of competence and desirability based upon the fashions of the day, which, for men, included bell-bottom jeans, colorful tight-fitting silk shirts with wide collars, and long hair and sideburns. I was not allowed to wear such clothes. Instead, I was forced to keep my hair (and eventually sideburns) short and wear conservative clothes more in keeping with the styles of 1950s clothing (think *Leave it to Beaver*). Through my middle school and high school days, I lived in a state of constant embarrassment, feeling that I always looked out of place in a way that evoked (mostly silent) ridicule from those around me.

As soon as I left my parents' home to go to college, I let my hair and sideburns grow long, and within a year, I grew a beard. I shopped in thrift stores, which were the only places I could find the fashions that seemed desirable (i.e., would make me desirable). It did not occur to me to wonder why I could not find the "cool" styles in stores anymore. I spent three years wearing bell-bottom jeans and tight-fitting polyester shirts with wide collars (silk shirts not being widely available, and me not really knowing the difference between silk and polyester). I finally felt "cool." I no longer felt embarrassed to be in public. The problem was, of course, that it was now the 1980s. My peers were wearing 501 jeans with Sperry Topsiders and pastel-colored Oxford button-down shirts, or Ralph Lauren Polos with the collars flipped up, crew-neck sweaters tied around their necks. But I did not see that. My fantasy, based on the images that dominated when I was coming of age, shaped my vision. Despite what was happening at the level of my eye, the gaze was shaping what I saw.

One day, a good friend of mine asked if I would come by her apartment so we could talk about something. I was surprised to find out that what she wanted to tell me was that she thought the way I dressed was "holding me back" and wondered if I had considered perhaps changing my style a bit. I asked her what she meant, genuinely shocked by what she was saying. She described for me what guys my age were wearing at the time. Her comments came from a place of kindness (when I tell this story, people are often offended for me in ways I was not), and I am grateful for her willingness to do something that I imagine was hard for her out of genuine interest in my welfare.

When I left her apartment, a shift had taken place. I suddenly saw the world in a different way and realized that I was the stain. Choosing to follow one's own style, regardless of current trends, is not something to be shunned. But that is not what I had been doing. I was not a nonconformist. Rather, I had been conforming to an image that was no longer current. The stain that I was when I walked out of my friend's apartment was a stain on my own image of competence and plenitude. I suddenly realized that the Other was not seeing me as desirable. My polyester shirts, bell-bottom jeans, long hair, and beard were all external objects coinciding with an intimate kernel, but the Other no longer confirmed them.

The gaze is not mastery of the visual field, but the dialectical relationship between the place from which we see and the place from which we are seen by the Other. This is why others can never look at me from the point from which I see them. We are both, as subjects, always already caught up in this dialectic. This is what Lacan meant by the gaze.

OTHER GAZES

The term "gaze" has taken on a technical meaning in media studies and cultural studies. In these fields, the gaze is about looking, being looked at, and the relationship between the two. The use of the term "gaze" itself seems to have its origin in translating French theory, especially Lacan, into English. The French noun, *le regard*, related to the French verb, *regarder*, both refer to looking, but the verb form more clearly so. To say "*elle le regarde*" is simply to say "she looks at it/him," while "*le regard*" is literally the look. To speak of "the look" or "*le regard*" is already to be theorizing, to abstract the very process of seeing by thinking of it apart from the acts of seeing and being seen. When this line of thought is translated into English from French thought in theoretical discussions, its level of abstraction is inflected by using the English "gaze" for the French "*regard*" which has greatly influenced English speakers working in media studies, cultural studies, and critical theory (broadly conceived).[30]

Though it might be better to just speak of "looking," the notion of the gaze has become a critical tool in the analysis of both visual culture and social control. The importance of the gaze for media studies and cultural studies is hard to miss. A range of related concepts have emerged which might be clustered around four related positions: the gaze as a principal site for the emergence of subjectivity and intersubjective experience (Jean-Paul Sartre), as a technique of social control (Michel Foucault), as a site of pleasure (Laura Mulvey), and as a point of resistance (bell hooks). In the development of these ideas, the gaze has been connected with patriarchy, imperialism, racism, and anthropocentrism. While all these conceptions of the gaze share features with Lacan's gaze, they differ in their not being dialectical. Even though they all recognize that looking inevitably involves a subject-object relationship, rather than adopting Lacan's view that the looker is always in the picture, mediated by the desire of the Other, these "other gazes," seeing a polarity rather than a dialectic, privilege the side of the one looking as the place from which meaning emerges. In Lacan's gaze, things are more complicated. Meaning is to be found in the picture, but the gaze is located not with the one looking nor with the one looked-at, but with the way that meaning *fails to emerge* in the field of vision, thus locating the subject in the dialectic of desire that both constitutes subjectivity (as extimate) and undermines the subject's pretentions to master at the same time.

Lacan seems to have developed his conception of the gaze not only in response to Merleau-Ponty but also in response to Sartre. For Sartre, the "Other's look" (not to be confused with Lacan's big Other) plays an important role in the way the one looked at comes to develop a consciousness of a self by first seeing itself as an object for the other. His most famous example concerns the person bent over, staring through a keyhole into a hotel room, only to hear footsteps behind him. Before the experience of the footsteps, that is the experience of being seen by the other, Sartre says, "I *am my acts* and hence they carry in themselves their whole justification" so that behind the door a "spectacle is presented as 'to be seen' . . . No transcending view comes to confer upon my acts the character of a given on which a judgment can be brought to bear."[31] The idea is that I am absorbed in looking through the keyhole until I sense I am the object for the look of the other. When the presence of the other is registered by the sound of footsteps, it converts the subject into an object, giving the actions (looking through the keyhole) a value that is beyond their own justifications ("I want to see something inside that room" versus "how does what I am doing appear to the other?"). This encounter with the other's gaze brings with it, according to Sartre, spatiality, temporality, simultaneity, and a sense of the other as a subject.[32] The look of the other mobilizes a locating set of values that situate the self in a world. He claims that "the *Other's look* as the necessary condition of my objectivity is the destruction of all objectivity for me." The "Other's look," which is a "look-looking" and not, like me, a "look-looked-at" enacts "not only a transformation of myself but a total metamorphosis of the *world*."[33]

Lacan is clear that this is wrong. First, he rejects the idea of a polarization in the gaze: "It is not true that, when I am under the gaze, when I solicit a gaze, when I obtain it, I do not see it as a gaze." Instead, "the gaze sees itself," even when, as Sartre takes it, the gaze of the other "surprises me and reduces me to shame." Lacan points out that even in Sartre's own account "the gaze that I encounter . . . is, not a seen gaze, but a gaze imagined by me in the field of the Other." One does not need to see the eye of the other to imagine the gaze of the Other, even if its only manifestation is in the form of the rustling of leaves in the forest. The key for Lacan is that Sartre's gaze involves an "annihilating subject, correlative of the world of objectivity" but fails to account for the way that desire functions the entire time in sustaining the subject as a subject.[34] While Sartre is correct, in a way, to see the gaze disorganizing the field of perception, this can only happen if the subject is not a reflective consciousness, as Sartre takes it, but a subject of desire, as developed by Lacan.[35] In other words, the critical difference here is that Sartre asserts that the occasional and accidental gaze of the other transforms me into an object, while Lacan sees my situation as always being a subject whose looking is governed by my desire, which is a desire of the Other. I am always in the picture. But this does not mean that I am always simply an object; I am, rather, a coincidence of externality (object for the Other/others) and intimacy (one who is looking at the world).

This is the second problem Lacan finds with Sartre's conception of the gaze. When Lacan revisits Sartre's evocative scenario, he does not assume, as Sartre does, that the subject has disappeared in the intentionality of his looking through the keyhole only to reemerge by way of becoming an object for the other as a sort of steppingstone to a self-awareness. By contrast, Lacan says the other surprises the voyeur, the subject, "as entirely hidden gaze." Here Lacan is connecting the gaze to the "scopic drive" which contains an "ambiguity." He says the gaze is the "object lost and suddenly re-found in the conflagration of shame, by the introduction of the other." The subject, peering through the keyhole, is trying to see the "object as absence." What the voyeur is looking for, and finds, is a "shadow behind the curtain," where he can "fantasize any magic of presence, the most graceful of girls, for example, even if on the other side there is only a hairy athlete." This means, Lacan explains, that the voyeur is not looking for the phallus, but for its absence, which is what determines the objects of his gaze. "What one looks at is what cannot be seen," Lacan tell us.[36] This is not to discount the way victims of such invasive acts have been violated and traumatized as a result of the acts of a voyeur, but to emphasize what it is the voyeur wants to see, which is, in fact, nothing, or rather, a "less than nothing," an absence of the phallus. Why? The phallus, which we experience only as castration, cannot appear in the visual field because it does not exist, and if it did, we do not have it. So, the voyeur is always looking for the absence of the phallus in order to disavow his castration. In place of his missing phallus, he positions the image of a passive, unknowing object (another person) who veils the *objet a*. For Sartre, the gaze only emerges with something like the footsteps down the hall that trigger a sense of shame that creates self-consciousness. For Lacan, the gaze was there all along. What is not there is the phallus and if anything is brought to the fore in the steps down the hall, it is the awareness of the voyeur's own castration.

This brings to mind Laura Mulvey's famous essay on visual pleasure in the cinematic experience. Mulvey's explicit intention was to use psychoanalytic theory as a "political weapon" in order to "demonstrate the way the unconscious of patriarchal society has structured film form."[37] But she wields this weapon in an odd way since she finds in psychoanalysis an "exact rendering of the frustration experienced under the phallocentric order."[38] Unlike Lacan, who sees universal castration and absence as the core constitutive features of the gaze, for Mulvey, the gaze is phallocentric and "depends on the image of the castrated woman" whose lack "produces the phallus as symbolic presence" and "her desire to make good the lack that the phallus signifies."[39] Like Sartre, she displays a tendency to polarize the gaze between the viewer and the object, but like Lacan, she introduces some ambiguity into the experience. For her, the image of the woman is crucial to meaning production, even though the meaning this image produces serves to help the male viewer disavow castration. On the one hand, she argues that "in a world ordered by sexual imbalance, pleasure in looking has been split between active/male and passive/female" with the "determining male gaze project(ing) its fantasy on the female figure" which takes on the quality of "to-be-looked-at-ness."[40] In cinema, this effect is extended by the split between spectacle and narrative in which the male character typically advances the story while the female character is there as a spectacle. The male character thus "articulates the look and creates the action."[41] But on the other hand, the meaning is ultimately dependent on the female character, even though she functions in a passive way. The gaze, undergoing a sort of sexual division in Mulvey's reading, cannot be truly binary given the dependence of the gaze on its object. There is something implicitly extimate about this formulation, but then she brings it back to something like Sartre's polarity. But we should not overlook the way Mulvey sees this dynamic as not functioning in the service of some kind of necessity, but as a result of living "in a world ordered by sexual imbalance." The inadequacy of Mulvey's view lies, rather, in the constant insistence on a polarity that tends to disavow the extimate nature of the subject.

The issue here is not that such views of the gaze are not intersubjective, but that their view of subjectivity is not extimate. This makes the experience of anxiety one that is located only on the side of the person subjected to the gaze, which would be fine, if this model understood that when two people are looking at each other, they are *both* always already being looked at by Lacan's big Other, and it is the look of this Other that both implicates each subject in their own looking and creates the feeling of anxiety in the subject. This is why looking is so paradigmatic for the Lacanian mode of understanding both anxiety and subjectivity; in looking, when properly understood, we see the extimacy of the subject that locks them into the anxiety-fantasy dialectic.

Bell hooks' "oppositional gaze" makes intersubjectivity central to the act of looking; it deviates in key ways from the duality that characterizes Sartre's approach. Like Mulvey, hooks is interested in the role of gaze in cinema, and like Mulvey, she has concerns regarding the way cinema reinforces patriarchy. But she is also concerned with the role race plays in the visual field of Hollywood cinema. She says, "identifying with neither the phallocentric gaze nor the construction of white womanhood as lack, critical black female spectators construct a theory of looking relations where cinematic visual delight is the pleasure of interrogation."[42] She seeks to develop an "oppositional gaze" that "resists the negation" of the dominant (Hollywood) gaze. This negation that must be resisted takes several forms. She notes that under slavery, as well as under Jim Crow and other racist cultural regimes, the look of the slave (and later the black citizen) was regulated. They were expected not to look. Though she does not name it this way, this resistance to the look of the racialized black subject was a site of anxiety for the white racist subject. We can thus see restrictions on the black person's looking as a denial of subjectivity, as Sartre's theorization might suggest, but we can also see it as an expression of the power dynamic in a slave society and racist culture. As hooks' analysis suggests, these regulations were negating opposition. It was the black person's negating gaze that was negated. This is the logic of her oppositional gaze.

While her "oppositional gaze" seems to be based on something like Sartre's polarity since she seeks to put meaning on the side of the one looking, a closer analysis of the logic of this look suggests something more dialectical. First, she notes that black women do not normally "see differently" than other people because "their perceptions of reality are so profoundly colonized, shaped by dominant ways of knowing."[43] This nod to the way one's look can be "colonized" points to a way of theorizing looking that goes beyond the subject-object paradigm. The problem presented by black female spectatorship suggests that resistance is not as simple as seeing oneself as a subject by objectifying the other. Instead, what she calls "critical black female spectatorship" can only emerge when black women, as individuals, develop resistance to those "dominant ways of looking and knowing" that characterize American culture. But how would something like this develop?

Her distinction between the normal way black women look at things and this new site of critical black female spectatorship demonstrates that it is not as easy as willing oneself to see critically. Nor can it be simply a matter of changing the racial identification of the actors and characters in a film. Her critique of Spike Lee's *She's Gotta Have It* suggests that Lee simply adopted the habits of Hollywood representation, substituting a black woman for a white woman.[44] For hooks, it is not a matter of changing the racist markers of the characters on screen, but of constructing different narratives around those characters, regardless of their racial identities. In this regard, she focuses on the power of non-Hollywood films to connect with viewers on a different level with different narratives and characters. Her own experience with foreign films offered a different kind of spectatorship. She started taking her sister to such films, who though initially upset about the more challenging experience, came to realize that "there was more to looking" than what was available in Hollywood films. Even though these foreign films typically had white actors playing white characters, these films were different because, as hooks' sister put it, "the lives they depicted seemed less rooted in fantasies of escape."[45] Here, Hollywood films are characterized as escapist fantasies that help the viewer avoid the troubling confrontation with lack and castration. By contrast, non-Hollywood films develop narratives that center themselves on the vicissitudes of lack and castration. They show absence as absence, rather than implying a kind of abundance, and thus undermine hierarchies of all kinds, including racist and patriarchal ones, for their refusal to disavow castration.[46] We can begin to see that for hooks, opposition comes not from the eye of the female, racialized viewer, but from the relationship of the viewer in general to the images on screen in terms of their relationship to lack. An oppositional gaze is, then, one that identifies with this lack and opposes the fantasy of wholeness characteristic of Hollywood films. Hooks argues that such oppositional films, like Julie Dash's *Illusions*, can have this effect by showing that white people "are unable to 'see' that race informs their looking relations."[47] By showing the gaze as gaze, *Illusions* undermines the way of looking that empowers white privilege by disrupting its confidence in the power of vision to bring us the world as it is rather than as a representation shaped by our desires.

But hooks reading of *The Passion of Remembrance* is more problematic. Here she focuses on a scene in which Louise and Maggie first look at one another in mirrors, "completely focused on their encounter with black femaleness," and then are shown dancing in a display of their own bodies that is "not for a voyeuristic colonizing gaze but for that look of recognition that affirms their subjectivity."[48] What hooks sees here is a modeling of a type of oppositional gaze that takes place between Louise and Maggie that might demonstrate a resistance to dominant ways of looking at black female bodies. Without diminishing the value of that kind of exercise, such a position is not cinematically possible. By positivizing something that persists only in absence, one is engaging, again, in an attempt to locate meaning on the side of the viewer. Yes, hooks wants to locate the gaze at the point from which Louise and Maggie are looking at each other, but the gaze cannot be located there. Her analysis of *Illusions* already demonstrated that the white viewer of these scenes might very well not see the same thing she does. Despite what is going on in the picture that includes Louise and Maggie, when we view the picture we are already in it. Perhaps this is her point, that for a black woman viewing a film to establish what Mulvey would call a "narcissistic" relationship with the characters on the screen might be a more pleasurable experience than its alternatives, but we might ask if such a move is really oppositional? Her critique of *She's Gotta Have It* already demonstrated that simply substituting one racialized (female) object for another does not necessarily create an opposition to patriarchal and racist cultural influences that might be operating at the level of the gaze. Instead, an oppositional gaze would see the veil as a veil, that is, as a simple pretense to capture us in our desire. We need to see that a film can be nothing but a veil, which is to say a screen, that while showing us images of plenitude conceals our lack.

Perhaps this is why Amber Jamilla Musser prefers the experience of "opacity" to "opposition." For Musser, "opacity . . . offers a bulwark against the mandate of transparency foisted on minoritarian performers who are imagined to be without subjectivity or interiority." She is following Nicole Fleetwood here, who argues that the deployment of "excess flesh" in black female music video performance is a way of emphasizing the faulty notions of a "visual truth" of blackness, in which this excess is "an enactment of visibility that seizes upon the scopic desires to discipline the black female body through a normative gaze that anticipates its rehearsed performance of abjection." From this, Musser concludes that "excess flesh actually hides in plain sight—opacity is found in the inability to take it all in and produce coherence."[49] Could we not claim from this that opacity is "more true" precisely for its refusal of knowledge? If we do not take it this way, is not the "excess flesh" described here just as likely to negate subjectivity and interiority as it is to produce a sense of incoherence in the viewer?

My argument here is not to discount the importance of critiquing the role of patriarchy and racism in the visual field or the importance of developing a critical relationship to these modes of seeing. Rather, it is to critique these ways of conceiving the gaze *as not radical enough*. The limits of these kinds of approaches stem from the commitment to viewing the operation of the gaze in the terms outlined by Sartre that fail to account for the extimacy of the subject and thus neglect to understand the role of anxiety in these visual fantasies. This is natural enough. Our experience in the visual field is one of seeing and being seen, so to sense that we are always situated at one pole or another, vacillating between the two, so that seeing seems to be a contest for who will "control" the gaze. But this assumes that meaning is located at the point of the one looking, implying that vision provides a kind of mastery over the significance found in the visual field. But it does not.

This is why we need Lacan's intervention here. We must see that we are always already in the picture. The picture is shaped by desire. Rather than thinking of an oppositional gaze, we should think of ways to bring ourselves into opposition to the gaze. Put differently, we should come to see that our way of seeing is already implicated in the dialectic of desire. The white people in Dash's *Illusion* do not see that their looking is shaped by their own desire. The films that avoid the "escapist fantasies" that hooks' sister came to appreciate also provide a similar effect. *But when we see the gaze as coming from a subject, rather than as complicit in the emergence of the subject, we become complicit with it.* When Mulvey parses the gaze in terms of scopophilia and narcissism, she fails to see how these two are related. In Lacanian terms, the Imaginary relationship of the subject to the specular image that can never reproduce an image of castration provides an image of wholeness that aims to disavow the gaps in the Symbolic order. As Todd McGowan puts it, "Imaginary plenitude is a haven for the subject who would otherwise confront real impossibility." McGowan, like Mulvey, sees in the Imaginary an important site of identification between the viewer and the image of the star on the screen, but he more clearly links it to the ideological function of cinema in general where "an image of overwhelming plenitude" enables us "to forget our own lack" and thus produce an "ideological effect."[50] But McGowan is critical of the way screen theory "prioritizes the process of imaginary identification that takes place when a spectator watches a film" instead of the more psychoanalytic approach which "focuses on the way that a film relates to the spectator's desire."[51] As McGowan points out, the Lacanian Real is the gaps, inconsistencies, and contradictions within the Symbolic order. The Imaginary (image of wholeness, plenitude) gives us a sense that everything is there to be seen—that it is all seeable—while the Symbolic is the domain of desire, that is where lack emerges, where absence emerges as absence. Rather than focusing on the apparatus as the point wherein we can locate the gaze, McGowan locates it at the site of the screen which serves a "double function: it is a site for presenting the image and for marking what lacks within the image." For this reason, plenitude does not subsist in an "all-seeing subject" because, as McGowan puts it, "an all-seeing subject would have no desire to look, which is why nudist colonies are not hotbeds of desire but instead paradigms for desire's evacuation."[52] Any theorization of the gaze that depends on what the subject sees is to immerse oneself in fantasy in order to avoid anxiety.

But there is yet another theorization of an all-seeing subject that could be linked to anxiety (though not to fantasy), the panoptic gaze developed by Michel Foucault. There is no question that Foucault, in *Discipline and Punish,* foregrounds the role of looking in the exercise of power. As Foucault explains it, under the old regime, the body itself is a sort of screen upon which the power of the monarch can be displayed. The public torture and execution of criminals served the purpose of "justifying justice" often including a "theatrical" reenactment of the crime on the body of the perpetrator. But ultimately, for Foucault, what is displayed on this screen, which is the perpetrator's body, is the "unrestrained presence of the sovereign."[53]

But this sort of theatricality is replaced, according to Foucault, by surveillance. In the first place, by the modes of surveillance that emerged in response to waves of plague infestation. He cites a text from seventeenth-century Vincennes which declared that "the gaze [was] alert everywhere," with observation posts at every gate and sentinels on every street. Here, the gaze is part of a bureaucratic regulatory system meant to enforce strict quarantine measures.[54]

But the key passage in his argument focuses on his analysis of Jeremy Bentham's panopticon. This idealized vision of a modern carceral situation pointed, for Foucault, to a radical change in the figuring of power in the field of vision. He argues that the modern practices figured in the panopticon produced as their "major effect . . . a state of conscious and permanent visibility that assures the automatic functioning of power."[55] Placing an observation tower at the center of the prison from which guards could constantly view the prisoners while concealing the prisoners' view of the guards provided the mechanism for this "permanent visibility" that assured this "automatic functioning of power." Though the visibility was possibly, maybe likely, fictitious, "a real subjection is born mechanically from [this] fictitious relation."[56] This use of visibility through just such a mechanical technique (*dispositif*) provided the "automatic functioning of power." For Foucault, under this technique of visibility what we encounter is "not that the beautiful totality of the individual as amputated, repressed, altered by our social order" but rather that "the individual is carefully fabricated in it, according to a whole technique of forces and bodies" that characterize a "disciplinary society."[57] The more recent tendency to emphasize "legibility" in relation to race and gender identities finds an argument here where Foucault describes this disciplinary effect that "arrests or regulates movements," "clears up confusion," "dissipates compact groupings of individuals wandering about the country in unpredictable ways," and "establishes calculated distribution."[58] But for all the work Foucault's gaze does for the social order, it is not significantly different from Sartre's gaze. The same binary operates, and even the invisibility associated with Sartre's "footsteps down the hall" and "rustling leaves" in the forest that have a constitutive effect on the subject are operative in Foucault's panopticon. For Sartre, the awareness of the gaze has the effect of drawing a self-awareness out of the subject by seeing oneself as being-seen. For Foucault, the act of thinking one is seen has a disciplining effect that "fabricates" the subject in ways that make the subject socially useful.

Living in the first decades of the twenty-first century, Foucault's analysis of surveillance might seem tame and understated. At this point, we are all aware that we carry on our persons a surveillance device that records our every movement, tracks our web searches and consumer habits, maps our networks of relationships and associations, and aims at instantiating our desires and fantasies. We are aware that everything we say may well be recorded, if not listened to, for later data mining by intelligence agencies and marketing firms. In many cities, there are few blind spots where surveillance of one kind or another cannot capture images, and in suburbs, cameras are installed on front doors with the effect of recording much of the activity in these neighborhoods as well. All of this is to say, that we certainly do live in a regime of permanent and constant visibility. While it is possible to limit this visibility, it requires conscious and sometimes considerable effort to evade it.

There is no doubt that Foucault's articulation of this dynamic has given birth to thousands of analyses of visibility in the age of electronic surveillance and the capacity of the state to keep all of us under a near constant watchful eye. (It has also led to "sousveillance" where billions of citizens armed with cell phones can keep an eye on police, government officials, and corporations.[59]) There is also little doubt that this form of surveillance has real-world effects, from both state and corporate actors. Office employees are aware that their keystrokes and screen activity may be monitored. Drivers on the job know that their every move, speed, and stop are being tracked. This no doubt does have an effect on us, and it certainly can generate anxiety. So, there is no doubt that Foucault's conception of the panoptic gaze has been an incredibly fecund tool for thought and research in the last fifty years.

But two objections can be raised to his view. The first, raised by Joan Copjec, calls into question the "total visibility" and "automatic functioning" suggested by Foucault's model. Such a model of visibility, especially for her, as coopted by film theory, creates a scenario in which the subject of the gaze becomes "perfect" by virtue of this permanent visibility. She points out that the logic of Foucault's "fabricated" subject is to assume that the "very condition and substance of the subject's subjectivity is his or her subjectivation by the law of the society that produces that subject," so that one becomes visible, not only to others, but even to oneself by way of the categories of a "specific, historically defined society" such that these "categories of visibility are categories of knowledge."[60] She means that Foucault's subject is "perfect" in the sense of only subsisting within the social categories laid down by the society itself. In Foucault's account, the "other" that is the source of the gaze provides the very categories of legibility by which the subject understands herself. Copjec makes a similar point when critiquing the adoption of Foucault's panopticon in conceiving of the gaze as a mirror, rather than as a screen.[61] The mirror returns a reflection; the screen both blocks and displays at the same time.

Copjec develops this in more detail by comparing Foucault with film theory (of the 1990s). Foucault's concepts of the panopticon and power have their film-theory analog in the apparatus and the gaze. Both of them use a "model of self-surveillance" that parallels the psychoanalytic model of "moral conscience," but they both disavow this resemblance. In making this move, they both suggest that power, surveillance, the apparatus, and the gaze "produce the subject" without considering that if this were true, the power/surveillance and apparatus/gaze configurations would be redundant since the subject is produced by these very categories.[62] Bell hooks' oppositional gaze undermines this position as well. If, in cinema, the apparatus produces certain subjective effects, would not the subject of the gaze find themselves produced as a perfect viewer? Of course, no one would claim this, but that is Copjec's point. If the logic of the panopticon were truly operational in the ways outlined by Foucault, the subject produced thereby could never escape. His view also seems to assume that the subject is not only self-identical but also self-aware, able to clearly evaluate its own responses to the social demands enforced by this panoptic gaze.

By contrast, psychoanalysis conceives of the gaze in terms that do not trap the subject within it. As Copjec points out, the subject is "split from its desire" so that "desire is conceived as unrealized, it does not actualize what the law makes possible."[63] Following her lead here, when we think of the gaze, if we think of it, as Foucault does, in terms of power relations such that the gaze, by enacting a regime of visibility, fabricates a subject in alignment with expectations of the social order, then the subject would become the perfect tool for power. But this is not what happens, even when it is what the subject consciously desires. The categories coming from the tower of the panopticon, so to speak, must be transmitted by way of the signifier, and thus never arrive at the level of the subject intact. The gap between the signifier and the signified renders this impossible. If it were possible, there would be no queer or trans* people,[64] for example. We would all look like the set of the musical *Grease* and act like the characters in *Mad Men*. Certainly, Foucault is not wrong about the fact of surveillance as an especially ubiquitous feature of modern life, nor is he wrong about the role of historical situations in defining for us certain parameters of what can be intelligible and legible for us in the field of vision, but the subject emerges not from the internalization of a set of social demands because we think of ourselves under constant surveillance, but because in the field of vision our desire is awakened by what we cannot see. The panopticon is, at best, only a means to increase anxiety when the demands of "power" have been clearly articulated. But this articulation always leaves something unsaid. The enunciation is always excessive in relationship to the statement so that the response will necessarily be similarly excessive in the sense of ceaselessly failing.

It is interesting that Copjec reads Lacan's anecdote about the sardine can as a tragic retelling of Hegel's master-slave dialectic. She sees Lacan looking for recognition in the "mirror-like" sardine can in which the young Lacan hoped to find an image of himself conceived as a member of the "slaving-class." But, of course, he finds none. She takes the story as tragic because there is no sublation in this movement (according to her). She thus characterizes the encounter with the sardine can as "an attack of anxiety."[65] She is correct. Lacan seeks confirmation in the picture, but the mirror turns into a screen, if I can put it that way. The confirmation is denied and Lacan is left to wonder what he is for the Other and what the Other wants. This is the basic Lacanian position. As Copjec puts it, the gaze does not confirm us, nor validate us, but confronts us with an impossibility that is always registered in the visual.[66] It is this encounter with impossibility that Foucault's panoptic gaze denies. This is why Copjec can theorize anxiety in the field of vision in ways that Foucault cannot.

But we must point out, as Copjec does, that a superficial reading of Lacan might see his position as parallel to Foucault's since Lacan claims "the gaze is that which 'determines' the I in the visible."[67] But as Copjec points out, Lacan claims the subject is *photo-graphed*, inserting a hyphen that divides light (photo) from writing (graph). As she puts it, "semiotics, not optics, is the science that enlightens for us the structure of the visual domain."[68] For Copjec, "Foucauldian [theory] . . . tend[s] to trap the subject in representation . . . to conceive of language as constructing the prison walls of the subject's being," while for Lacan the subject "sees these walls as *trompe l'oeil* and is thus constructed by something beyond them." For Copjec, the subject is "the effect of the impossibility of seeing what is lacking in the representation." The gaze thus functions not only as the object-cause of desire but also as the object-cause of the subject of desire in the visual field.[69]

Thus, while Foucault's panopticon figures the gaze in ways that may be productive in terms of analyzing the role surveillance plays in modern societies, it fails to properly theorize the role of the gaze in the life of the subject. In all of my looking, I am already looked at, but what captures me, as a subject, is not the awareness of being surveilled, but the dialectical relationship in the field of vision by which we are *photo-graphed*.

FANTASY AND ANXIETY IN THE FIELD OF VISION

Anxiety appears in the field of vision in just this contradictory way. On the one hand, vision can offer us an experience of plenitude and wholeness, but only through a process of alienation (in the mirror image) or through the immersion in the Other's desire, and, for that very reason, it is also a site where anxiety might emerge. The objects we encounter in the visual field become veils, leaving us in a visual field that is not mastered by us but is always a place for the desire and anxiety that is linked to the nature of the subject. No doubt, this has been true for human beings for tens of thousands of years, but in the modern capitalist era, the dynamic has become intensified. When we see the image of a preferred semblable screened for us (in a film, on television, in an ad, or on social media), we identify with their power to achieve the competence and completeness we lack. We can identify with fictional characters in novels as well, but this never has the same imaginary effect. To be properly "drawn" as a fictional character requires the character to experience loss, trauma, and division. Even a confident narrator like Nabokov's Humbert Humbert constantly undermines his own story, and thus himself, revealing the division produced by the unconscious. But with the image, the lack of the phallus is not seen, allowing for an immediate identification with an image of competence and plenitude. To put it more crudely, an image of a character on the screen can provide us with a sense of wholeness and completeness, but a character will betray this unity and autonomy if realistically portrayed.

Is this what is at the heart of celebrity culture? Ironically, Indiana Jones, as a character, can be vulnerable, make mistakes, be bested by a female character, and so on in ways that Harrison Ford, as the cinematic icon, cannot. In the golden age of Hollywood, knowledge about the quotidian affairs of celebrities was closely guarded. We might think this was to protect their privacy in support of their work embodying characters, but was it not to confirm their role in this Imaginary drama? In fact, does not capitalism depend on such images of wealth and privilege to serve as a sort of "proof of concept" for capitalism itself? It is not simply that we see these celebrities in their fabulous clothes, driving expensive cars, eating at posh restaurants, lounging on yachts, and disembarking from private jets, but that by presenting the image alone we can avoid the confrontation with castration and lack that must inevitably be the human experience they all share with us. Today not only actors, musicians, and athletes occupy this Imaginary point, but business people and politicians. Even now, with paparazzi and celebrity news ubiquitous, do not these stories tend to confirm celebrities as basically non-lacking, un-castrated subjects? Even when they give us some little glimpse of some adorable human quality, or their own confrontations with tragedy, do not such disclosures strike us as, at best, endearing, or at worst, fabricated? This deception is not for their benefit as much as it is for ours. Though they may portray characters or write and perform songs that expose the lack at the core of their subjectivity (how often has Taylor Swift experienced heartbreak in her songs?), as a celebrity they provide us with the image of competence and control that sustains the disavowal at the heart of our own ego production.

But with the advent of social media, we have all been granted the opportunity, whether we take it or not, to construct our own images of wholeness and competence. Social media accounts become places where we display not our lack, our incompetence, or our insecurities, but our expertise, our competences, and the fullness of our lives. Here is where anxiety enters the visual field at the level of the image. In the first place, when the image upon which my ego was constructed, the specular image, as Lacan put it, that conceals what is missing and what does not work, confronts my own experience as a subject in the world. It can be gratifying to post an image of oneself—one's vacation, one's loving romantic partner, one's latest success—online and receive affirmation from others that confirms, "yes, that's you, and you're wonderful." This affirmation goes a long way in explaining why we do it. But in such activities, anxiety is there the whole time. It is felt in the act of posting as one awaits "likes" and comments, but in a deeper sense, it is there the whole time since the entire activity is designed to avoid anxiety. Yes, it might be true that in some cases our posts are meant to share our lives with friends and family who are genuinely interested and are just trying to "keep up" with our activities, but even when this is the conscious motivation, the need for this affirmation to forestall anxiety seems to almost always emerge. Our posting on social media is an avowal of our anxiety, both "I post, therefore, I am anxious" as well as "I'm anxious, therefore, I post."

But anxiety also emerges in relation to consumer culture, which seems aimed at keeping us in a constant state of difficulty and motion around the material demands of our lives. Annetta Grant and Jay M. Handleman have analyzed the role of what they call the "market-reflected gaze" in the home renovation phenomenon that occupies the minds of so many homeowners (though we can assume that renters are not immune to many of the same effects, but they were not part of this study). Grant and Handleman situate the gaze in relation to "ubiquitous social and mainstream media portrayals of home design" that present what is acceptable and unacceptable in terms of home décor.[70] Such homeowners find themselves torn between the desire to make their abode "their own" by styling it according to their taste while at the same time thinking of their home as an asset whose value of which must be protected by following expert advice on what will make their home appealing to a marketplace of consumers educated by the same round-the-clock programming and ubiquitous images generating this market-reflected gaze.

In this "market-reflected-gaze" we encounter the gaze of the Other. Since there is no big Other, everyone, including the experts, must seek to divine what the Other desires. Not only the value of one's home, but the ability of one to feel affirmed in one's home depends on creating a visual space that appeals to the cryptic and ever-changing desires of the Other. Décor that seemed pleasing to the Other twenty years ago now *looks* outdated, requiring constant renovations. Grant and Handelman report that homeowners who have just finished renovations are often already thinking about what to do next. Anxiety is at the core of this experience. They point out that this market-reflected gaze is also often a source of shame. Home-improvement shows typically show experts and potential future home buyers inspecting the targeted home with a "critical gaze" that induces this feeling of shame in participants and viewers alike. Grant and Handelman describe one show in which potential buyers examine a kitchen that features "dark brown cabinets, white appliances, a single oven, coil burners, and laminate countertops and floor." One of the buyers exclaims "it's so bad" and that they would be "embarrassed to have anyone over."[71] They describe one of the homeowners they studied who had selected some unique, handmade tiles for the backsplash in her kitchen but was filled with anxiety after watching an episode of *Million Dollar Listings* in which the English-style mansion of a Hollywood producer who had decorated it with many unique touches was bought for $26 million by owners who decided to just bulldoze it to the ground and replace it with a more "updated" home.[72] The homeowner in their study fretted over what her unique backsplash tiles would do to the value of her home and the perceptions others might have of it. Another homeowner had conducted a major renovation of the home they recently bought. She was excited by the new spaces that she had made "her own." The previous owners still lived in the neighborhood and had children who were friends with the new owners' children. They wanted to see the renovation, but the new owner "was not ready" to show it off. Her anxiety in the face of the original owners was too much. She feared their disapproval. Another homeowner "needed" to repaint her entire home because "the color was out-of-date." She now has a home with a lot of grays, which contrast with her childhood home in which her mother had painted every room a different color—something that used to "drive her crazy" and that she even now "teases" her mother about. The owners portrayed in Grant and Handelman's study are constantly imagining how others will view their homes, both guests and future buyers, in ways that disrupt their ability to make the space their own. Because of this, they often feel anxiety in their own homes when things don't have the "right look."[73]

When Grant and Handelman want to theorize their "market-reflected gaze," they turn to Foucault's panopticon that represents "an ever-present surveillance." On the one hand, they see the dynamic of the panopticon in the way "the consumer is confronted with the judgment of the market-reflected gaze that shuns the consumer's unique choices," and on the other hand, they point to a "market-embedded gaze" that comes from "smart-home technology" that "imposes real time, omnipresent 'guidance' on every aspect of the home, from room temperatures and lighting, to refrigerator content, and recommended music that creates an 'appropriate' home ambiance."[74] But in the first instance, the "market-reflected gaze" does not function like the panopticon. One is not permanently under surveillance in one's own home. Rather, it is the extimate Lacanian gaze that confronts the homeowner with the demands and shaming critique of the marketplace, even when no one else is home, and even if one never has guests. The smart-home technology is a form of surveillance that does, potentially, provide a way for both state and capital to surveil one in their own home, but the presence of such technology in the home, especially if it functions as they suggest to create an "appropriate" ambiance, is in the home not because of a panopticon installed by the state, but technologies of surveillance that were installed by the homeowner in pursuance of the desire of the Other as reflected in the gaze that Lacan describes. In all these examples, it is how things look that determines the subject's level of anxiety and satisfaction, but the "look" of a countertop is not grounded in the field of optics; it is all semiology. Just like my personal fashion story, the Other's desire is what determines how we see our home décor.

All of this takes place in the realm of capitalism, which thrives on the role of the gaze in the dialectic of desire. When our consumer choices become linked to the "look" of the things we consume, an object can no longer be judged in terms of its use value but must always become a sublime object as well. A car cannot be valuable because of its reliability; it must also become a sublime object in the field of vision. (For that matter, one must drive in a car, because it is hard to look cool on a bus or riding a bicycle.) Our kitchen is no longer a space for preparing meals and socializing with friends and family; it is a visual representation of our own competence as consumers. In such a context, it is impossible for us to look at items required to function in the world and simply say, "it'll due"; we must judge every item in terms of how it looks to others (i.e., the Other) in order to make us look good to ourselves, which is to say, to the Other. In consumer capitalism, we are in a constant state of anxiety about the "look" of the items that comprise our daily lives.

This extreme situation is obviously not a basic form of human sociability, but one that is produced by consumer capitalism. While it is not uncommon for people to bring items from home to their place of employment in order to personalize their workspace, the impulse in the home goes in the other direction because of the importance of protecting the home as an asset. Correspondingly, expertise in dressing appropriately, taking care of one's physique, eradicating gray hair and baldness, and so on are linked to our marketability in professional, social, and romantic settings. Yet, we still see a fair number of people tattooing themselves, a practice still sometimes frowned upon by the corporate world. Tattoos, too, are a message to the Other, but one that bears a stamp of personal taste. Similar to the photos, trinkets, mugs, and so on that decorate one's workspace, the tattoo represents an impulse to construct one's own message around personal commitments, values, experiences, and tastes even while the impulse toward body art may be a new form of conformity.

Still, life without the sublime would not be worth living. The capacity of simple objects to provide us with meaning and joy should not be undervalued, but these gestures should move in the direction of the lasting and durable in conformity with our personal values. The realm of the lasting and the durable is where old, worn objects, in the mode of Heidegger's Black Forest House and Van Gogh's *Peasant Shoes*, persist in their sublimity because of the way they link us to others. When anxiety haunts our relationship with objects, we must ask whether or not the path we have chosen toward the sublime is in the service of human living or the expansion of the consumer economy.

NOTES

1. Lacan, *Seminar X Anxiety*, 325.

2. Lacan goes so far as to claim that in the scopic level "the subject is most assured in relation to anxiety" ("*le sujet est le plus sécurisé quant à l'angoisse.*"). *Seminar X Anxiety*, 325 (French edition, 376).

3. Jacques Lacan, "The Mirror Stage as Formative of the *I* Function," in *Écrits*, 76. French original (Paris: Editions du Seuil, 1966), 94.

4. Lacan, "The Mirror Stage," 78. French edition, 97.

5. Freud, *Civilization and Its Discontents,* 12.

6. Lacan, *Seminar X Anxiety*, 254: "castration . . . is always elided at the level of desire when it is projected into the image."

7. Lacan, *Seminar XI: Four Fundamental Concepts*, 71–72. French text from Jacques Lacan, *Les quatre concepts fondamentaux de la psychanalyse*, ed. Jacques-Alain Miller (Paris : Editions du Seuil, 1973), 84.

8. Lacan, *Seminar X: Anxiety*, 240. See also p. 254 about the "pigmented patch" that "is already specifically visual."

9. For a brief, readable account of the evolutionary history of the eye and other sensory organs see Richard Dawkins, *The Blind Watchmaker: Why the Evidence of Evolution Reveals a Universe Without Design* (New York and London: W.W. Norton & Company, 1996), 77–109.

10. Lacan, *Seminar XI: Four Fundamental Concepts,* 71–72 and *Les quatre concepts,* 84.

11. Lacan, *Seminar XI: Four Fundamental Concepts*, 72–73; *Les quatre concepts,* 85. Explanation mine.

12. Lacan, *Seminar X Anxiety*, 106.

13. Lacan, *Seminar X Anxiety*, 162.

14. Lacan, *Seminar X Anxiety*, 254.

15. Lacan, *Seminar XI: Four Fundamental Concepts,* 95.

16. Lacan, *Seminar XI: Four Fundamental Concepts,* 96.

17. Lacan, *Seminar XI: Four Fundamental Concepts,* 96. Sheridan's translation, "But I am not in the picture" is wrong. The French original is "*Mais moi, je suis dans le tableau.*" See Todd McGowan's comment on this in *Psychoanalytic Film Theory*

and the Rules of the Game (New York, London, Delhi, Sydney: Bloomsbury Academic, 2015), 74.

18. See Joan Copjec, *Read My Desire: Lacan against the Historicists* (London and New York: Verso, 1994, 2015), 36.

19. Lacan, *Seminar XI: Four Fundamental Concepts,* 97.

20. Lacan, *Seminar XI: Four Fundamental Concepts,* 112.

21. Plato, *Symposium*, Greek text edited by John Burnet (Oxford: Oxford University Press, 1905), 222a.

22. Lacan, *Seminar X: Anxiety*, 254.

23. Jennifer Tyburazy, *Sex Museums: The Politics and Performance of Display* (Chicago, IL and London: University of Chicago Press, 2016), 44–56. The painting is on display a the Musée d'Orsay and on their website: https://www.musee-orsay.fr/fr/oeuvres/lorigine-du-monde-69330.

24. Elisabeth Roudinesco, *Jacques Lacan* (Cambridge, UK: Polity Press, 1999), 183–184.

25. Tyburazy, *Sex Museums*, 50–51.

26. Tyburazy, *Sex Museums*, 52.

27. I think Tyburazy's reading is too influenced by a vision of the gaze that aligns more with Sartre's theory than Lacan's.

28. Tyburazy, *Sex Museums*, 55.

29. Lacan, *Seminaire XI* and *Les quatre concepts,* 118. It appears in the English edition (trans. Sheridan) on pp. 102–103. The translation here is mine. The French text reads: *qu'il n'y a point coincidence, mais foncièrement leurre. Quand, dans l'amour, je demande un regard, ce qu'il y a de foncièrement insatisfaisant et de toujours manqué, c'est que*-Jamais tu ne me regardes là où je te vois.

30. But something might be gained by simply saying "the look." Jacqueline Rose generally took this approach in *Sexuality in the Field of Vision* (London and New York: Verso, 1986, 2005).

31. Sartre, *Being and Nothingness*, 347–348.

32. Sartre, *Being and Nothingness*, 356–357.

33. Sartre, *Being and Nothingness*, 360.

34. Lacan, *Seminar XI: Four Fundamental Concepts,* 84–85.

35. Lacan, *Seminar XI: Four Fundamental Concepts,* 88–89.

36. Lacan, *Seminar XI: Four Fundamental Concepts,* 182.

37. Laura Mulvey, "Visual Pleasure and Narrative Cinema," reproduced in Laura Mulvey, *Visual and Other Pleasures* (Bloomington and Indianapolis: Indiana University Press, 1989), 14.

38. Mulvey, "Visual Pleasure," 15.

39. Mulvey, "Visual Pleasure," 14.

40. Mulvey, "Visual Pleasure," 19.

41. Mulvey, "Visual Pleasure," 20.

42. bell hooks, "The Oppositional Gaze: Black Female Spectatorship," in *Movies and Mass Culture,* ed. John Belton (New Brunswick, NJ: Rutgers University Press, 1996), 258.

43. hooks, "Oppositional Gaze," 261.

44. hooks, "Oppositional Gaze," 258.
45. hooks, "Oppositional Gaze," 260.
46. Stephen Felder, "Screening Neoliberalism in *Nightcrawler* and *The Wolf of Wall Street*," in *Screening the Crisis: U.S. Cinema and Social Change in the Wake of the 2008 Crash*, ed. Juan A. Tarancón and Hilaria Loyo (New York, London, Dublin: Boomsbury Academic, 2022), 91–95.
47. hooks, "Oppositional Gaze," 262.
48. hooks, "Oppositional Gaze," 263.
49. Amber Jamilla Musser, *Sensual Excess: Queer Femininity and Brown Jouissance* (New York: New York University Press, 2018), 10. She is citing Nicole Fleetwood, *Troubling Vision: Performance, Visuality, and Blackness* (Chicago, IL: University of Chicago Press, 2011), 29, 112.
50. McGowan, *Psychoanalytic Film Theory*, 39–41.
51. McGowan, *Psychoanalytic Film Theory*, 70–75.
52. McGowan, *Psychoanalytic Film Theory*, 72.
53. Michel Foucault, *Discipline and Punish: The Birth of the Prison,* trans. Alan Sheridan (New York: Vintage Books, 1995, Second Vintage Edition, 1997), 44, 49.
54. Foucault, *Discipline and Punish*, 196.
55. Foucault, *Discipline and Punish*, 201.
56. Foucault, *Discipline and Punish*, 202.
57. Foucault, *Discipline and Punish*, 217, 209.
58. Foucault, *Discipline and Punish*, 219.
59. T.V. Reed, *Digitized Lives: Culture, Power and Social Change in the Internet Era* (New York and London: Routledge, Second edition, 2019), 171.
60. Copjec, *Read My Desire,* 17.
61. Copjec, *Read My Desire*, 15–16.
62. Copjec, *Read My Desire*, 26.
63. Copjec, *Read My Desire*, 25.
64. I use the asterisk with "trans" following Jack Halberstam who uses the asterisk to "hold open the many histories of variant bodies and the many ways in which those histories have been deployed" and because the asterisk "embraces the nonspecificity of the term "trans" and uses it to open the term up to a shifting set of conditions and possibilities rather than to attach it only to the life narratives of a specific group of people." In Jack Halberstam, <i>Trans*: a Quick and Quirky Account of Gender Variability </i>(Oakland, CA: University of California Press, 2018), 51-53.
65. Copjec, *Read My Desire*, 31.
66. Copjec, *Read My Desire*, 36.
67. Copjec, *Read My Desire,* 31. She is citing Lacan, *Seminar XI*, 106. The French is: *Ce qui me détermine foncièrement dans le visible, c'est le regard qui est au-dehors.* This could be translated as "what fundamentally determines me in the visible is the gaze that's out there." The extimate quality of the gaze is made clear here. *Seminaire XI*, 120. It is not clear to me that "me" should stand for "moi," the "I," or the "ego." In any case, Lacan's use of photo-graphed (*photo-graphié*) confirms Copjec's reading.
68. Copjec, *Read My Desire,* 34.
69. Copjec, *Read My Desire,* 34–35.

70. Annetta Grant and Jay M. Handelman, "Dysplacement and the Professionalization of the Home," *The Journal of Consumer Research*, 49 (2023), 882–903. This quote is from p. 882.

71. Grant and Handelman, "Dysplacement and the Professionalization of the Home," 891.

72. Grant and Handelman, "Dysplacement and the Professionalization of the Home," 892.

73. Grant and Handelman, "Dysplacement and the Professionalization of the Home," 891–895.

74. Grant and Handelman, "Dysplacement and the Professionalization of the Home," 899.

Chapter 4

Anxiety as the Truth of Sexuality

For Lacan, "anxiety is the truth of sexuality."[1] By making this point, he is anticipating his later, more famous idea that "there is no sexual relationship."[2] The basic issue is that what "mediates" the relationship between man and woman is castration itself. As he puts it, "the phallus is what, for each of us, when reached, just alienates us from the other."[3] Rather than make the sexual encounter possible, as it promises, the encounter with the phallus, because it is always missing, leads to an alienation from the other. In heteronormative terms, which are the terms Lacan typically uses, the man is always looking for the *objet a* in his partner, while the woman is looking for the phallus in hers. Neither of them has/is what the other is seeking.

Would this be different in a homosexual relationship? It would not. The reason is that the phallus is not a penis; it is a signifier of the possibility of establishing a sexual relationship. In our pursuit of the sexual relationship—an emblem of perfect jouissance that would swamp our lack and make us whole again—we look to the phallus to accomplish this goal, but it is always lacking. The phallus, which promises to mediate our relationship with the good, is always already missing. It always exists as a negative, as something that is missing but nevertheless, in its absence represents what would grant the fulfillment promised by the sexual relationship. As Freud pointed out, there is nothing in the psychology of human beings that could distinguish us in terms of male and female.[4] Nowhere in the discussion that follows, or in Lacan's account of anxiety as the truth of sexuality, are we talking about biological difference. Sexual difference is all about how we reckon with our own castration.

The most famous anxiety associated with sex is castration anxiety. Castration marks the place where we must confront the fact that we do not have what it takes to satisfy ourselves or others. A typo in an email, the inability to open a jar, becoming befuddled in the face of some technology problem, these mundane and ubiquitous encounters can all be experienced as moments of castration. Though everyone experiences such things, only masculine subjects become anxious in such situations because they experience them as castrating (as opposed to frustrating, annoying, etc.). This experience of anxiety in the face of not having what it takes to get it done is masculinity because of the way it associates such experiences with the loss experienced in castration. What is lost in castration is something *none of us* ever had: the phallus. The phallus is the thing that, if we did have it, would allow us to control and satisfy the world and thus find a perfect *jouissance* for ourselves, a satisfaction with no barriers, limits, or ends. But getting this perfect *jouissance* depends on having the phallus, which none of us have, because by being cultural beings, we have been (symbolically) castrated. Culture has separated us from the simplicity of the natural world, which is ruled by the quest for homeostasis. Other species remove the disturbing element that causes pain, hunger, fear, fatigue, and so on, from their existence, and things get back to normal. Hunger can be solved with food. The need to mate can be solved with mating (or failing to mate until mating season is over). Fatigue can be solved with rest. But humans do not operate this way. We are *desiring beings*, which means that we are always seeking the lost object we never had.

We are also intersubjective beings whose very survival depends on being desired by others. The "phallus" is the psychoanalytic word for the way we all theorize our relationship to the desire of the Other *in relation to others*. Very early in our lives, our primary caregiver, let us call her, "the mother," seemed to have desires that we could not meet. *What does she really desire?* Someone or something out there seems to have what it really takes to satisfy her. Possibly, dad, or her job, or maybe her religion, but something seems to draw her away from us. From this dynamic, we conclude that someone or something else has "it"—what really satisfies "the mother"—and we do not. Not all children respond to this in the same way. To simplify, one could respond to this realization that one does not have the phallus by accepting it and then concluding that whatever it is "the mother" has that gives her access to "it"—the phallus—perhaps I can pretend to be. I will mimic her in her desirability. Or one can respond to this situation by pretending to have "it"—the phallus—basically living as an impostor.

The phallus is only the concern of subjects. If we lacked the extimacy that characterizes us as subjects, we would not relate to our experience in relation to the phallus. If we were not animals shaped by the intersubjective process of acculturation that takes place in the field of the signifier, we would not be castrated. We are castrated because to be subjected to the signifier means that we can never really get things to work out. We are always aiming at something we are going to miss, and even when we hit our target, it turns out not to be the right target. The phallus is the object that would make things work out for us. But of course, we never had the phallus; its existence depends on our not having had it. It is precisely because no one has it that the idea of the phallus exists at all. It is not a matter of "if it didn't exist, we would have to make it up"; it is a matter of "it doesn't exist, which is precisely why we have to make it up." If we were like other mammals, our organs would function apart from desire in the service of the species; things would always work out, not because all mating in the natural world is "successful," but because the natural world itself does not distinguish between success and failure. Species emerge, change, evolve, go extinct, and so on without any need for desire. Whether this individual member of a species manages to procreate or not is part of the whole process of natural selection. The universe without subjects is a world of disturbance and homeostasis. But for subjects, we have desire, and so in place of disturbance and homeostasis, we have the phallus and the *objet a*. It is how we reckon with the demand to establish satisfaction through the sexual relationship, which, according to Lacan, cannot exist, because in the sexual relationship each partner is looking to the other for something they do not have.

For Lacan, *masculinity* hinges on a disavowal of castration that occupies itself with pretending that it has not happened. Masculinity requires an exception in order to motivate this disavowal. Masculinity takes the position that "there is one who has not been subjected to the phallic function."[5] Masculinity is about this "one." This is why masculine subjects obsess over the "real men" they see in sports, movies, business, and politics. To be masculine is to look at this hypothetical exception to castration as an imperative to disavowal. This is why, in the first case, masculine subjects elevate those masculine figures who seem not to be castrated (even though they are) and then often proceed to mimic the disavowal of those figures. Masculinity figures itself as having the phallus precisely through these gestures of competence that are meant to mimic the one who is not castrated. "Mansplaining," the frequent trope where men explain something to women who already know all about it, is such an example. Whatever the mansplaining man is explaining, what he is always saying is, "Look! I have the phallus." He does this precisely because he unconsciously knows he does not have it.

For Lacan, "woman is more true."[6] To be feminine is to accept that one does not have the phallus, and thus there is no need to constantly try to convince oneself and others that they really do have the phallus when they do not, but this is not the same as giving up on the possibility of a phallic relationship. If, for Lacan, to be masculine is to become an impostor with the unconscious belief that "there is one not subjected to the phallic function," to be feminine is to revive the potential phallus in terms of a "not all have been subjected to the phallic function." In his discussion of anxiety,

Lacan references the "myth" of Don Juan which he describes as a "woman's dream." It is not, he says, that Don Juan arouses desire in women: "though he slips into women's beds, no one knows how he got there." Rather, Don Juan functions as an "absolute object" who has "accepted his radical imposture." He does not provoke anxiety in women precisely because he does not make them feel that they are the "center of his desire."[7] But this fantasy of Don Juan, which Lacan says is a "woman's fantasy," is a fantasy about a man that "always has it" and "can't lose it."[8] If this were a man's fantasy, the masculine subject would identify with Don Juan (mistakenly) believing that this would make him the object of woman's desire. But Lacan is clear that she does not desire Don Juan; rather, she feels no anxiety with him. Why? Because to be a feminine subject is to take on the responsibility for what is lacking in relation to the (missing) phallus. In a way, it is to be the support of the (missing) phallus. It is to feel anxiety in the situation where one imagines that the "success" of the sexual relationship depends on the effectiveness of one's masquerade in producing desire in the other. This is what provokes anxiety for the feminine subject.

In *Seminar X: Anxiety*, Lacan puts it this way: "For the woman, it is what initially she doesn't have that constitutes the object of her desire at the start, whereas, for the man, it is what he is not, and that's where he falters."[9] This corresponds to his claim that "in man's realm there is always the presence of some imposture," while "in the woman's . . . it's the masquerade."[10] In later seminars, he will develop this in terms of a set of formulas that lay out the impossibility of the sexual relationship in terms of his famous formulas of sexuation, but in his treatment of anxiety, he is focused on finding where anxiety emerges in the sexual relationship and elaborating on why it is the truth of sexuality. In this regard, he notes that anxiety is understood in relationship to a male fantasy of female masochism. The odd structure of what I have been calling the anxiety-fantasy dialectic is developed here by Lacan around this very fantasy: "it is by proxy and in relation to the masochistic structure that is imagined in woman that man sustains his jouissance through something that is his own anxiety."[11] The man's anxiety concerning his own disavowed castration prompts him to fantasize a masochistic woman who, despite the lack of jouissance she will find with him, is satisfied by being denied that satisfaction. Anxiety covers over the man's castration. But Lacan says that for women, "anxiety is only anxiety faced with the desire of the Other and at the end, she doesn't really know what it covers over."[12] The state of this situation leads Lacan to conclude that "woman is much more real and much truer than man" because "she knows the worth of the yardstick of what she is dealing with in desire."[13] She understands that it is all a masquerade. While she might feel anxiety over whether or not she will be able to make the sexual relationship work, the anxiety doesn't touch the "intimate kernel" in her because she understands that it is all a masquerade, but the man's imposture strikes directly at the extimate object—the phallus—associated with his sense of himself in this relationship. This can go a long way in accounting for things like misogyny and incel fury, all being motivated by intense anxiety around their own castration. But it can also explain the masochistic lengths to which many women will go in order to emerge as the desirable object in this doomed project.

Nothing about this forecloses the possibility of experiencing pleasure with another person in the sexual act, but as extimate subjects, our concerns are not so simple. We desire not only to get pleasure but to give it, and what we seek is not simply pleasure but satisfaction, and the satisfaction we seek cannot be found, ultimately, in something as fleeting as an orgasm. This is because, in sexuality, we are seeking a confirmation of our identity as subjects. In the sexual act, desire is no longer a matter of theory but the time for action. Our need to be desired is on full display. This is also where we see most clearly our extimacy in terms of anxiety. Lacan says that "men's anxiety is linked to the possibility of *not being able*"[14] but for women things are more complicated. Woman, he says, has a "bond to the infinite possibilities or rather indeterminate possibilities of desire in the field that stretches out around her."[15] For men, desire "covers over anxiety," which can reappear when his desire for a woman "can be seen," which for him "amounts to letting *what there is not* be seen." But for a woman, it is "*what there is*" which can be the cause of anxiety since that is what is seen. What Lacan means is that when a man lets it be seen that he desires a woman, he is showing his lack, which means he is letting "*what there is not*," that is, the phallus-as-missing, be seen, which provokes anxiety in him.[16] To put this less elegantly, but perhaps more clearly, the anxiety for "men," that is, those who find themselves processing castration in terms of disavowal, what causes the most anxiety is the possibility that they might be seen not to have "it"—that is, the phallus. This is what masculine anxiety revolves around. For "women," that is, for those who find themselves processing castration in terms of masquerade, it is what is seen that is anxiety-provoking. Feminine anxiety is all about the investment in a masquerade erected to arouse desire: "How do I look?" "Am I physically attractive?" "Do I know how to be sexy?" and so on. In both cases, we see anxiety indicating the Real of the strange extimacy we find at the level of the phallus, which is to say, at the level of the sexual relationship, where the external object is ephemeral (the phallus) and the intimate kernel is phantasmatic (the *objet a*). Again, this does not foreclose the possibility of two human beings experiencing pleasure in their physical contact and emotional connections. It does, however, indicate how difficult that project might be. For our purposes, it shows us where anxiety can be found in this relationship and why it occurs.

In his discussion of sexuality in *Seminar X: Anxiety*, Lacan turns from the Möbius strip to another non-orientable object: the Klein bottle. Like the Möbius strip, one can crawl along the outer surface to the inner surface of the Klein bottle and back without changing "sides." But unlike the Möbius strip, the Klein bottle also constructs an inner void. A simple vase or pot also has a void, and this void is a figure of the lack that constitutes the subject. But the Klein bottle figures this emptiness not only as "inside" the subject but also "outside" at the same time. For Lacan, this image points to the way the *objet a* "only has meaning for men when it has been poured back into the emptiness of primordial castration." For Lacan, this means that anxiety is not provoked by this "primordial" castration because it was this "emptiness" that allowed for desire to emerge. But anxiety comes from the way that the masculine subject's encounter meets up with the object it is seeking. The way this happens, figured by the strange shape of the Klein bottle, provokes anxiety because it "allows neither inside nor outside to be distinguished."[17] To borrow again the language from Mladen Dolar's essay on the uncanny, anxiety is the truth of sexuality because of the coincidence of the intimate kernel with the external object. *Castration* itself produces desire, not anxiety. The *sexual relationship* produces anxiety because it is where we can no longer distinguish between the "inside" and the "outside." In sexuality, the subject's interiority is externalized and the external object becomes intimate. While fantasy tells us that sexuality is the source of our ultimate fulfillment, anxiety signals to us this extimacy that figures for us the truth of sexuality, which is what we are seeking is the fulfillment promised in the fantasy of a sexual relationship, but my entry into this relationship depends on having something I don't have (masculine subjectivity) or being something I am not (feminine subjectivity).

THE ANXIETIES OF SEX/GENDER

The central place sexuality plays in the constitution of subjects explains the importance of issues related to sexuality in the "culture wars." As Rothenberg has pointed out:

> The desire to stabilize meaning (which . . . is desire plain and simple) implies that the space in which meaning merges is under threat: when we note a need to protect the social space, we are actually acknowledging that it is (always) in the process of being both dissolved and re-generated.[18]

The centrality of sexuality to our identities and its relatedness to social roles makes it a contested space. The meanings associated with sexuality affect both individual and community, and their extimate quality makes them always unstable. This leads to another level of anxiety, the one that expresses itself in the desire to stabilize the meanings associated with sexuality by policing expressions of sexuality.

Alenka Zupančič has concisely described the way this can be anxiety-producing at the level of personal identity. Her basic claim is that *masculinity is a matter of belief, while femininity is a matter of pretense.* The person who believes he is a man is a man, but that belief means simply that his identity is "sustained by the repression of castration." This repression does not eliminate anxiety because the person who believes he is a man still must worry about "how much of a man" he is. Conversely, as Zupančič explains, when people who believe they are men confront women who excel in "male" professions, they ask if they are "really women" and if they can conclude that such women are "not really women but 'men' ('mannish' or homosexual)," it relieves them of the "anxiety . . . that behind these accomplishments there is no substantial subjectivity and that this . . . could be a general state of things, with masculinity being but a simulacrum of substantial subjectivity." Such women are threatening to men not because of a "threat of castration" but because "their presence makes it harder for men to sustain the repression of castration; it weakens the defense wall of anxiety."[19]

What she is suggesting is that because being a man is about belief, the presence of women in roles where men traditionally function—that is, in roles that seem to require the phallus—creates a kind of crisis. This is a crisis of meaning that must be stabilized not by denying that the phallus is required for this function, but, ironically, that the women performing these functions must somehow actually have the phallus. What is striking about this analysis is the way it explains the reaction of these men in a way that they could never themselves consciously avow. Rather than concede that these "male roles" do not require the "phallus," which would mean that the performance of these roles by men is not proof that they have the phallus, they would rather believe that somehow these women have the phallus. The performance of traditional male roles by women is castrating because it deprives men of the "proof" that sustains their belief in (their possession of) the phallus.

Jack Halberstam makes a similar point, arguing that not only can females be masculine, but that female masculinity might give us a clearer understanding both of what masculinity is and of what is at stake in gender conformity. For example, Halberstam argues that in the James Bond film, *Goldeneye*, it is M, not Bond, who "most convincingly performs masculinity, and she does so partly by exposing the sham of Bond's own performance."[20] Such masculinity, appearing in the "butch" and the "tomboy" as well as in images of female competence, is all legible as masculinity, even when expressed by an obviously female body. It is precisely the possibility of masculinity being expressed in this way that generates anxiety. In fact, Halberstam says that "the culture generally evinces considerable anxiety about even the prospect of a manly woman" and that in most cultural situations, there is a demand that one's gender be "readable at a glance." These expressions of masculinity in relation to female bodies provoke this kind of anxiety for the way they demonstrate precisely the lack of biological determinism inherent in it.[21]

One would think that in such a situation the gender binary would disappear, but as Halberstam argues, this anxiety-driven commitment to the gender binary seems to be as much a product of its failure as it is of any prior social commitment. Halberstam says it is "the failure of 'male' and 'female' to exhaust the field of gender variation [that] actually ensures the continued dominance of these terms." It is because "virtually nobody fits the definitions of male and female" that the gender binary persists. The categories of man and woman "gain power and currency from their impossibility. In other words, the very flexibility and elasticity of the terms 'man' and 'woman' ensures their longevity."[22] The anxiety associated with being a man or a woman is fueled precisely because of the impossibility of anyone ever truly being either a man or a woman. This anxiety manifests itself in a determination to stabilize meanings by trying to disavow the ways that the paradigm fails.

However, as the stories of trans* men and women have become more widely available and their experience is becoming more rigorously theorized, it is becoming increasingly clear that the trans* experience, rather than being seen as marginal or aberrational, *should be seen as, in some sense, paradigmatic of human sexuality*. The anxiety experienced around trans* issues, both by trans* people and by those who denounce, attack, and persecute them, makes clear the relationship between sexuality, fantasy, and anxiety. In this light, trans* narratives make clear that the tendency to divide our theorization of sexuality along a sex-gender divide is inadequate. To think of sex as somehow biological and gender as somehow cultural would be to fail to account for the existence of trans* people (and a denial of the extimacy of the subject). Certainly, to understand the sex-gender relationship along the traditional lines of what Judith Butler calls the "expressive" view is completely destroyed not only by the trans* experience but also by the endlessly repeated admonitions by traditionalists to "be men" and to constantly drone on about "real women." If biology determined gender expressions, there would be no need to exhort us to follow them. At the same time, if we see gender as a cultural construct that is imposed on us, it is hard to explain why we do not all simply conform to these demands. If it is only cultural, then why would someone put themselves through the struggle, opposition, even violence one experiences as a trans* person? What the trans* experience demonstrates is that subjects are unavoidably sexual beings, but being a sexual being is not a matter of biology. Sex is intersubjective, not biological nor culturally constructed. It is a feature of the Möbius subject and with an extimate causality.

For this reason, anxiety is the truth of sexuality, and the trans* experience generates anxiety, especially among cis-gendered people, for the way that it threatens to expose the illusory and phantasmatic nature of sexuality.

In her novel *Detransition, Baby*, Torrey Peters goes beyond characterizations of gender and sex as fluid and multifaceted to explore the ways in which the trans* experience serves as foundational for our understanding of sex in general. The novel, described by Peters as "a story of trans feminine culture in the new millennium," focuses on the stories of Aimes/Amy, a M-F trans* woman who detransitions, Reese, a M-F trans* woman who was in a relationship with Amy until she detransitioned (to Aimes), and Katrina, a mixed-race cis-gendered woman who is dating Aimes and becomes pregnant.[23] The brilliance of the novel is the way it depicts the universal experience of sex and sexual difference as both illusory and somehow stubbornly persistent.

The universal nature of Peters' project is apparent in the novel's dedication:

> *To divorced cis women who, like me*
> *had to face starting their life over without either*
> *reinvesting in the illusions from the past,*
> *or growing bitter about the future.*[24]

Her dedication to divorced women points to the failure of cultural discourses to adequately make sense of the world and to meet the disruptions, challenges, and failures we might encounter within it. At the same time, the emphasis on cis-gendered women in the dedication is a gesture of solidarity with other woman who regardless of their status as cis or trans* nevertheless have much in common. But what they have in common is not the success of their identification with culturally approved models of femininity, but rather the failure of those very narratives to make sense of the experience of women in general.

Reese makes the same point in the novel when she tells Katrina that "the only people who have anything worthwhile to say about gender are divorced cis women who have given up on heterosexuality but are still attracted to men." It is the disillusionment she associates with divorce that gives divorced women something worthwhile to say about sexual difference. "Giving up on heterosexuality" while still "being attracted to men" points to the role of cultural narratives and demands (heterosexuality) while paradoxically being contrasted with "attraction to men" which we can understand as referring to an experience that neither supports nor is supported by the cultural narrative, but nevertheless somehow comes into conflict with it. Attraction to men and heterosexuality thus become two different things. Heterosexuality is the cultural demand supported by a fantasy of fulfillment that is linked to marriage, while attraction seems to lie elsewhere. Reese goes on to explain that it is not necessarily all divorced women who experience this revelation, but only those who "felt their divorces as a fall, or as a total reframing of their lives." These are women who see "how the narratives given to them since girlhood have failed them, and who know there is nothing to replace it all" but who still move forward "without investing in new illusions or turning bitter—all with no plan to guide them. That's as close to a trans woman as you can get."[25] The lack of narratives to support both divorced women and trans* women is part of the failure. Thus, for Reese, the trans* woman's experience is not understood in terms of a dysphoria that emanates from distortion on her part as an individual—something malfunctioning at the level of the individual—but rather as a failure of cultural understandings to adequately frame one's life. In this way, we see the extimacy of sexed subjectivity, which registers, as we would predict, in failure. This implies that the real failure is the narratives that attempt to structure the experience of cis-gendered women. To put it in our terms, the reality of womanhood is supported by a fantasy structure whose limits are marked by both the experience of the divorced cis-gendered woman and the trans* woman, both of whom have had to confront the anxious experience of finding no place for oneself within the Other's desire. Thus, the trans* woman (and the divorced woman) is "more true," to borrow a phrase from Lacan, because she sees the illusory nature of womanhood itself, as the *objet a* itself is illusory. At the same time, the novel's narrative itself shows just how much Reese is invested in precisely those narratives.

The pregnant, cis-gendered Katrina responds in a similar way when discussing pregnancy and miscarriages. Katrina had been pregnant before with her ex-husband, and they had become "attached to the idea" of having a baby, only for Katrina to have a miscarriage. At this point in the novel, Katrina, Aimes, and Reese are contemplating the possibility of raising Katrina's baby together. She tells Reese both about the miscarriage and about the fact that she had flushed the fetus down the toilet afterward, only to later wonder why she hadn't felt the more pronounced sense of loss some women feel when they have had miscarriages. This raises concerns for Katrina regarding her suitability as a mother and her fear that her body may not be able to support a pregnancy. This triggers something in Reese, who, as a trans* woman, has a body that for sure cannot support a pregnancy, and she says to Katrina, "I feel the same. Like, if you feel unmotherly—I'm a tranny who just asked about flushing babies." To this Katrina replies, "That's what I mean! It's not about who you are! As far as I can tell, at least from the outside, motherhood is just some vague test designed to ensure that everyone feels inadequate."[26] Again, the universal nature of the experience is what Peters stresses in this novel. What is universal is the experience of both failing to meet the demands of our culture regarding sexuality and gender roles while at the same time finding that cultural fantasies around sex and gender are perpetually failing. Yes, perhaps there a different ways one can fail the "mother test," but the universal experience is of failing that test and, at the same time, finding that fantasies of motherhood do not provide the plenitude they promise.

Another way these maternal narratives fail is in their relationship to "reproductive rights." Katrina points out that these narratives tend to emphasize the rights of women *not to have* children, but for women of color, they should also include the right *to have* children. "Black women, poor women, immigrant women" are often described in terms of being "welfare queens" or of having "anchor babies" in ways that suggest their reproductive practices are suspect. Or she points out that her Vermont neighbors saw her mother as illegitimate because she was Chinese and her father was Jewish. All of this, for Katrina, leads to the conclusion that "the right and naturalness of motherhood" is not "presumptive."[27] The traditional expressive view of motherhood that sees it as natural (i.e., produced by biology) and the historicist view that sees it as discursive (i.e., produced by culture) fail to account for the ways in which motherhood is always located somewhere else, neither in biology nor in discourse, but in the extimacy of the subject.

Earlier in the novel, Reese explains the nature of her early investment in the illusory and demanding narratives of womanhood and mothering. When she was in a lesbian relationship with Amy, "a trans woman with a good job in tech," living together in a bright, airy apartment in Prospect Park, she felt that their bourgeois lifestyle had "finally granted [her] the womanhood that she suspected the goddesses of her childhood," the "nice white Wisconsin moms" who represented for her the "pinnacle of womanhood," had. But even here she recognizes that motherhood, for her, was in part because she felt (wrongly) that if you were a mother "you were never truly alone," and she hated being alone and desperately wanted to flee her own loneliness and neediness. She also reflected that this ideal vision of motherhood was somewhat undermined by the fact that her "trans friends' actual experiences of unconditional parental love always turned out to be awfully conditional." Then when Amy detransitioned, it "all fell apart."[28] Again, Peters aims to universalize the experience of the trans* woman by linking it to a specific bourgeois historical narrative to which women are typically subjected. At the same time, her sense of identity as a woman is not linked to body dysmorphia but to boring, conventional understandings of bourgeois sexuality. On the one hand, we could see Peters' novel as simply constructing a conservative narrative in which trans* women simply aspire to become bourgeois subjects. But the narrative actually subverts this simplistic reading in two ways. First, by showing how Reese is cut off from ever fully embodying that narrative, it forces her to see new ways of imagining family, kinship, and life as a woman. In the end, the novel leads to a new vision of family as Reese, Aimes, and Katrina come together to imagine a life that includes a child. Second, the universalizing of this narrative is by way of showing how all women fail both to live up to its demands and to find the fulfillment it promises; the novel subverts this narrative by demonstrating its phantasmatic quality.

That this holds true for men as well is only hinted at in the novel, since its focus is on the lives of trans* women, but Peters makes sure to point out that the same dynamic is at work in the experiences of men, both trans* and cis. Similar to Halberstam's view of female masculinity, Peters affirms the way trans* masculinity seems not only more legible but also *more authentic* than cis-gendered masculinity. One of the characters, Iris, at one point says that "if you want a manly man . . . find yourself a trans man. They're the only ones you can be sure want to be that way, instead of compensating their way into it." It is unlikely that trans* men are compensating any less than cis men, but the key point is that masculinity is all compensation. Perhaps what Iris means is that trans* men are not embracing masculinity in order to conform to something imposed on them culturally, but to find something that seems to more authentically register with them at the level of their own desire. Here, too, there is something universal about the understanding of the problem that transcends whatever difference we might see between cis and trans* men. I would suggest that many cis men do not feel any ambiguity about their being men, but at the same time, because of their own experience of symbolic castration, they unconsciously need to constantly compensate for the loss of the phallus. Peters links this to trans* womanhood in an interesting way when Reese wonders why people accuse her, a trans* woman, of "trying too hard" when she "delights in dolling up," but the idea of "New York men wearing flannel and slamming whiskey in a cabin is seen as a sorely needed release of their barely tamed and authentic manliness."[29] Of course, while this undermines the "expressive" model of gender, it fails to account for the difference between "dolling up," which is masquerade, and "slamming whiskey in a cabin," which is imposture. Similarly, toward the end of the novel, when Aimes has concerns about his ability to be a father because, even though he has detransitioned, his feelings about masculinity and assuming male identities are more than a little ambivalent (he still thinks of himself as a woman), he brings it up with a cis father, Jon. Jon's counsel addresses not Aimes' trans* identity but his desire. Jon does this by showing the problematic nature of fatherhood in general in terms of one's own disavowed castration. "At some point," he says, "I have to realize that my kid is his own person, he doesn't make me who I am." This hints at the way (narcissistic) desire shapes parenting, pointing to the ways that parents derive an identity for themselves from their children. Just as becoming a mother does not end one's neediness and loneliness, becoming a father does not establish one's secure identity as a man (which seems to be what Aimes is recoiling from). Jon points out that if you try to get a sense of yourself through your child, you will "end up being one of those dads who ends up in a brawl with the referee and a bunch of other dads at his Little League hockey games."[30] Again, what is universal is not that all men are the same in that they act, think, and talk the same, but that they all fail to find a sense of identity that would cover over their castration. "Brawling with a referee" is an attempt to disavow castration just as much as using one's children to verify one's manliness is. Our attachment to the external object of sexual identities and the roles assigned to them by our culture immerses us in a fantasy of wholeness in our attempt to overcome the anxiety around sexuality.

In one of the novel's clearest statements of this position, Reese "decides for the ten thousandth time" that

> heterosexual cis people, while willfully ignoring it, have staked their whole sexuality on a bet that each other's genders are real. If only cis heterosexuals would realize that, like trans women, the activity in which they are indulging is a big self-pleasuring lie that has little to do with their actual personhood, they'd be free to indulge in a whole new flexible suite of hot ways to lie to each other.[31]

This clear acknowledgment of both the failure of sexual identity—cis or trans*, gay or straight—is at the core of the novel's story, but one that does not foreclose possibilities for pleasure, even for "hot ways to lie to each other."

Rather than flee from the anxiety of sex into the illusory narratives of sexual fulfillment, Peters' central characters find a path that recognizes the fantastic nature of the sexual narratives without becoming cynical. Cynicism can also be a flight from anxiety. To be cynical is to pretend to give up on the satisfaction and fulfillment we are seeking. It is to find satisfaction in refusing to seek satisfaction. On the other hand, sexuality is a powerful site for fantasies of fulfillment. By tracing the pathways of sexuality through the lives of *trans men and women, the novel makes clear Lacan's claim that anxiety is the truth of sexuality while, at the same time, showing a kind of life that can work in the face of those anxieties, finding pleasure and connections along the way.

EROTIC TRUTH AND THE TROUBLING GAP

At this point, it should be clear that analyzing sexual difference in terms of the categories of sex and gender fails to helpfully account for our experience. To see sex as biological and gender as cultural is to misunderstand the human situation as always taking shape within the intersubjective field of culture in ways that inevitably produce failure. We can also see not only why anxiety is present in our experience of ourselves as sexed beings, but why anxiety is the truth of sexuality.

Alison Bechdel's graphic memoir, *Fun Home*, addresses these issues by problematizing what are often called "gender identity" and "sexual orientation" (not terms she uses) by recasting these issues in terms of an ontology of signification under the rubric of what she calls "Erotic Truth."[32] Her graphic memoir opens up a way of thinking about sex that overcomes the problems associated with the sex-gender binary by seeing sex as the site of a "failure of language" out of which subjectivity emerges. This is another way of thinking the thesis: anxiety is the truth of sex.

Probably the most influential contemporary theorization of gender is Judith Butler's. For many people, her conception of gender in terms of performance and compulsory heterosexuality seems to be the key to understanding what it means to be a sexed being.[33] But this formulation has been subjected to a number of critiques, most notably that coming from Joan Copjec.[34] Following Copjec, we might ask if Butler is proposing a sort of discursive ontology in which meaning and being are blurred. For Butler, bodies materialize discourse by way of performance, and this performance bolsters the binary of male-female sexual division as a product of enforced heteronormativity. While there are many intriguing features to this account that have made it almost the standard view in gender studies today, Bechdel's narrative complicates this analysis by questioning what we might call Butler's *ontology of performance*, in favor of something we could call an *ontology of the signifier*, the sign of which is our experience of anxiety.

Bechdel's graphic memoir centers around her relationship with her father, a relationship complicated by her coming out as a lesbian while in college and her father's own secret homoerotic relationships. Amid these stories is a complicated tale about a father-daughter struggle over "gender," one which she describes as her attempt to "compensate for something unmanly in him" just as "he was attempting to express something feminine through [her]."[35] In one sense, what she describes is pure performance, an arrangement of culturally recognizable signifiers meant to convey "masculine" or "feminine." But on the other hand, she does seem to imply the presence of something *that needs expressing, as if there was* some sort of "essence" that forms the basis of this expression. In the case of her father, the "something feminine" he is trying to express is on full display in a photograph she discovers after his death. The photograph is of her father, in college, wearing a woman's swimsuit and swimming cap. It is clearly not a prank or some sort of silly fraternity ritual, but a "lissome, elegant" pose that suggests nothing but sincere aspiration to femininity.[36] There is certainly something expressive about the photograph, but what we might call this "expressive dynamic" seems to point to a disposition that cannot be reduced to simply a retroactive reification of a fictive "essence" affirmed by the repetition of performance. Instead, Bechdel and her father are expressing these gender divisions but not in conformity with their own biologically based designation of gender given to them at birth, nor are they expressing masculinity and femininity in the service of enforced hetero-sexuality. The inadequacy of a discursive ontology, one where discourse can become materialized in the acts and dispositions of subjects, becomes clear in light of this impulse seen in Bechdel's childhood relationship with her father to play with performance not in terms of compliance, but in terms of resistance. Put another way, something is being expressed in the photograph of Bechdel's father in a woman's swimsuit and cap, but it is not a biological essence, but something in the psychic life of her father that "had to get out." This is why Bechdel uses the language of expression: something is being expressed and it comes not from biology, nor from "power" or "discourse" but from the failure of discourse. The demands placed on her father by culture demand a male "performance," but in the photograph recreated in Bechdel's book we see a young person absorbed in femininity as if it expresses some truth of his (her?) subjectivity. Yes, femininity is nothing but masquerade, but for Bechdel's father the mask seemed to fit.

Similarly, when Bechdel describes traces of her own expression of "gender" in ways that imply some internal something or other that seeks expression in masculine forms of cultural signification, she recounts a trip she took with her father, as a young girl, in which she encountered "a most unsettling sight," a woman she later describes as a "truck-driving bull dyke," whom she claims to have "recognize[d] . . . with a surge of joy" as an image of her own semblable, an expression of her own desire.[37] While there is something performative in the "bull-dyke's" mode of being in the world, there seems *to be something ontologically prior to the performance*, especially for Bechdel who recognized what she wanted to be immediately when she saw it. At the same time, it is equally obvious that what is ontologically prior to the performance cannot be biology. It cannot be associated with genitals or chromosomes. But neither can it be accounted for in terms of "gender" if gender must be tied ontologically to performance. It is not the sheer repetition of displays of masculinity that created, in Bechdel, an immediate identification with those images, yet such an identification would not have been possible without the repetition of such performances culturally.

The language she ultimately resorts to in order to describe this dynamic as it emerges in her relationship with her father is drawn from the nineteenth and early twentieth centuries, especially Proust, who relies on the term "invert." The use of the term was generally applied to homosexuals, implying a disconnect between one's body and one's desire. In her case, Bechdel thinks of her father and her as "inversions" of each other.[38] Yet even here she is reluctant to adopt conventional labeling practices. She claims her preference for Proust's term, "inverts," is *because* it is "imprecise and insufficient, defining the homosexual as a person whose gender expression is at odds with his or her sex." We should also point out that "invert" is not the same thing as a mirror image. She and her father are not mirror images of each other, but inversions. She wants to express something masculine; he wants to express something feminine. The difference, as we have been outlining it, is that masculinity is an unconscious belief in the possibility and necessity of possessing the phallus that leads to imposture, while femininity is a more knowing understanding of the reality of castration that leads to masquerade. In a sense, both are performances, but the performance is not what sustains the form. Rather, *the inadequacy of the form sustains the performance.* At one point in her narrative, she explains her desire for masculinity in terms of the lack of masculinity she sensed in her father: "I sensed a chink in my family's armor, an undefended gap in the circle of our wagons which cried out, it seemed to me, for some plain, two-fisted sinew . . . and where he fell short, I stepped in."[39] But the way she draws this scene in her graphic memoir suggests that such images of masculinity did not come out of nowhere. She had observed them on television and in the men she saw outside her home. So there is something cultural here—images gathered from television, magazines, and comparing her father to other men in her small town—but there is also something more pressing, a sense that something is missing. Bechdel does not name the phallus in her account. Her book does not develop these ideas in this way. But her belief in the reality of this missing signifier supports the project of masculinity that made her an "invert" of her father. Such an inversion only makes sense for an extimate, Möbius subject.

Along these lines, in *The Psychic Life of Power*, Butler clarifies her theory of gender performance in relation to psychoanalysis. She argues that "to reduce the psychic workings of gender to the literal performance of gender would be a mistake" and that psychoanalysis is right to insist that "the opacity of the unconscious sets limits to the exteriorization of the psyche" and that "what is exteriorized or performed can only be understood by reference to what is barred from performance, what cannot or will not be performed."[40] She then offers a rereading of her own analysis of drag performance in *Gender Trouble* in relation to this claim. In *Gender Trouble*, she pointed out that when a man is performing drag as a woman, the "imitation" is taken to be an imitation of femininity, but femininity itself is not taken as an imitation. But in *The Psychic Life of Power*, she suggests a possibility that a kind of melancholia may be at the root of such performance in which the performance might be a form of "acting out" in the face of an "unacknowledged loss." In this sense, she wonders if the drag performance might not be a "loss that is refused and incorporated in the performed identification, one which reiterates a gendered idealization and its radical uninhabitability." To understand drag performance this way would be to see it neither as a "territorialization of the feminine by the masculine nor a sign of the essential plasticity of gender," but as a sort of "allegory" of a loss that cannot be grieved.[41]

This opens up an interesting way to account for Butler's gender performance not in terms of enforced heteronormativity, but in terms of loss. To rethink sex and sexual difference in this way is not to deny that culture polices the boundaries of the gender binary and does enforce heteronormativity, but to argue that it is the very "uninhabitability," as Butler puts it, of the heteronormative gender binary that is reflected in such attempts to enforce it. But we could go one step further, arguing that enforced heteronormativity is a sign that sexed identities are, necessarily, uninhabitable. Nevertheless, the subject is sexed because signification itself presents the subject with two options: pretend you have the phallus or make yourself into the location of the *objet a*. Both options say to the Other (or, to the m(O)ther, if you will, but also to "others") the thing you want is right here with me, but they do this in one of two different ways, either by positing "I can get it done," or by appearing to be "the very thing you've been looking for." Since both positions depend upon objects that do not exist (the phallus, the *objet a*), there can be no sexual relation; nevertheless, because culture does try to enforce norms related to these positions, those whose internalization of the desires of the Other have responded in ways that are at odds with the expectations associated with the "gender" assigned to them at birth will find themselves explicitly failing to match that set of expectations. But "gender" is never out of reach *because of its* basis in fantasy. If it were real, it would be out of reach at least for some. This is why Butler's notion of performance seems to fit so well with our experience of "gender." For that very reason, though, it is also a potential site of anxiety. To address that anxiety, one has to see the Real behind the sexed Möbius subject. We are sexed because meaning and Being can never coalesce. We can never be self-identical, which is why we find meaning either in imposture or masquerade. This is why anxiety is the truth of sexuality.

At the end of *Fun Home*, Bechdel wonders about her father's "erotic truth,"[42] something she admits "is a rather sweeping concept," only to tell us she can't "pretend to know" what her father's was. She admits she doesn't know if he was "gay"—in quotes—the way she is "gay," or if he fits some other category, and then provocatively suggests that her attempt to think of him that way might be some sort of "inverted Oedipal complex."[43]

What's on display in this account is a messy configuration of sex and sexuality (Bechdel doesn't use the term "gender") that does not easily fall in line with either the traditional tendency to see sex as a term referring to some brute biological fact that inevitably expresses itself in gender, nor the performative view in which there is nothing to express prior to expression taking place.

Instead, Bechdel's is an account of *sexual difference that makes a difference*, which, though certainly appearing in the forms of clearly identified stylized performances of gender, seems grounded not in biology but in what Butler referred to as "the psychic workings of gender" and what Bechdel refers to as "Erotic Truth." But what are those "psychic workings," and do they apply to gender, or might we rightly be referring here to something better thought simply in terms of "sex?" Might the sex-gender dichotomy be a dead end?

Bechdel's narrative tries to make sense out of all of these issues by way of a recurring theme in her memoir, something she calls "an epistemological crisis." It began when as a child her father gave her a calendar and encouraged her to record what was happening in her life. At first, things seemed easy enough as she proceeded with short, banal descriptions of some of her day's events. But soon, things broke down as she began subjecting her simple declarations, like "we made popcorn," to a compulsive need to interrogate the veracity of her statements. How could she know that what she was writing was "absolutely, objectively true?"[44] As the mature narrator considers the nature of this crisis, she describes it in terms of a "gaping rift between signifier and signified,"[45] "a troubling gap between word and meaning,"[46] a rupture dividing "the symbolic and the real"[47] that ultimately points to a kind of "language failure"[48] in which she recognizes the inability of her words to convey her experience. The more emotionally laden and disturbing the experience, the more obscure her journal entries became.

As she grew older, this kind of obfuscation developed into a strategy. She uses her own algebraic cipher, "N-ing," to substitute first for menstruation and then for masturbation.[49] But she leads us to believe this was not simply a strategy of concealment, but a recognition of the inability of language to fully integrate these experiences. The fact that she can use the same signifier for two different experiences points to a gap between the signifier and the signified. It is only when masturbation exists for her, that is, when it comes into the world of language, into the symbolic order, that it becomes a problem: "Argh!!" she writes in her journal after giving up N-ing for Lent only to do it twice that same day. Like "man" or "woman," "N-ing" gains its power from its ability to represent almost anything.

In a similar way, Lacan characterizes our entrance into language as always accompanied by a kind of loss. Lacan likens this to the ultimatum "your money or your life," which he points out is a forced choice. Confronted with this choice, I can only keep my life by giving up my money, but to give up my life would be to also lose my money. It is not a choice at all. No matter what, I will lose my money. Similarly, he argues, as subjects it is *as if* we had been forced to choose in the same way between being and meaning. By entering into the world of meaning, I lose my contact with the fullness of being, but if I give up meaning, then I give up my capacity for my being to mean anything to me. But of course, we did not choose; rather, by becoming subjects, we acquired meaning but at the loss of the fullness of being. Sex is the place that marks this loss.[50] Sex is the place where we realize ourselves in relationship to the loss that allows this realization to occur. The point here is that while patriarchy deploys the sexual binary in ways that clearly benefit men and oppress and exploit women, this binary itself is the product of this fundamental loss that marks the subject's entrance into language and culture. That this loss is understood in terms of castration is a reflection of the inter-subjective nature of subjectivity. If the subject were a self-enclosed, autonomous monad, it would not be castrated and would therefore not be sexed. We are sexed because we are lacking, and in seeking to fill that lack, we necessarily become embroiled in the desires of others in ways that force us to come to terms with the inability of subjects to meet that lack for themselves and others. Our desire for others makes it seem like we ought to be able to find wholeness through our union with them, but the truth of our circumstances as subjects of the signifier is that we cannot. The psychoanalytic name for this loss is "castration."[51]

Bechdel highlights this loss in a reflection on two different translations of Proust with two distinctly different translations of the title. The older title, *Remembrance of Things Past,* changed in the newer translation to *In Search of Lost Time*. Pointing out that while the newer title is a more literal translation of *À La Recherche du Temps Perdu*, it fails to fully account for the meaning of *perdu*, which she says means "not just lost but ruined, undone, wasted, wrecked, and spoiled."[52] (119) Then she concludes that "what's lost in translation is the complexity of loss itself."[53]

What Bechdel's book illustrates is that what is at stake in "Erotic Truth" is a "Real," in the Lacanian sense, that is, the Real understood as a hole, gap, or contradiction in the Symbolic order itself. When we pass into subjectivity, we do so sexed, but sex is understood as a result of this "gap," "rift," and "failure," and what is lost in this translation is the repression of the primal loss of symbolic castration, the very site of sex, or sexual difference itself. Sex is not a matter of biology, but a failure of the symbolic, a site characterized by the impossibility of identity where the social order is produced by way of identifications.

Thus, Bechdel's narrative avoids a discursive ontology that would imply a kind of voluntarism while refraining from a sexual ontology based on an expressive model of gender. Again, Lacan is clear on this point, not only that biology does not determine sex, but that "there is nothing by which the subject may situate himself as a male or female being."[54] Instead, as Bechdel frames it, because there is a "gaping rift" between the signifier and the signified, there is a fundamental gap between meaning and being. In his later work, Lacan locates this gap on the side of the signifier itself. "Woman,"

"Femme," "Frau," "Mujer" are all signifiers that refer to the same signified, but this signified is not being as such, but a conception of being for which there is no "real" signified. As Simone de Beauvoir pointed out long ago, "man" has falsely assumed the position of "essence" and consigned woman to "existence." But this claim to essence is a form of imposture, even as it consigns woman to masquerade. Contra Irigaray and Kristeva, it's not that psychoanalysis banishes women to obscurity, but that there is something about "woman" that is "Truer, and more Real." [55]

Lacan illustrates this point of the two siblings, a boy and a girl, sitting opposite each other on a train as it pulls into a station. The brother declares, "Look, we're at Ladies," and the sister responds, "Don't you see we're at Gentlemen?" In the case of the restrooms, we have two identical doors, representing two identical restrooms, but with two signifiers representing a binary opposition. In the case of the children on the train, as Alenka Zupančič points out, this illustrates how, for Lacan,

> two topics (the topic of the logic of the signifier and the topic of sexual division) coincide . . . because sexual difference (and all the contrived dialectics of sexuality, desire, love) is the consequence—not simply of the signifying order, but of the fact that something is lacking in it . . . This is the difference that has no ground: it does not spring from two different grounds, which would allow it to settle as difference between two "homelands" . . . their homeland is one and the same: yet this oneness and sameness is the oneness and sameness of pure difference.[56]

This is the same as Bechdel's concept of "inversion" as it relates to her and her father, but as we see here, the inversion is better understood as a parallax, in which the inversion is only apparent because of how each subject has approached the signification process—a process that is cultural but can never be coextensive with the subject. Understood this way, Bechdel is right to conclude that her father is not "gay" in the way she is, but wrong to conclude that his "Erotic Truth" is different from hers.

As in Bechdel's narrative, for Lacan, sex is *the* site of failure. It is the place where the process of signification always leads to an epistemological crisis. All of the discursive, performative identifications produced by culture are a response to, and evasion of, this fundamental failure. Yet, at the same time, this gap itself leaves something to express; we just cannot know what that is.

At the end of Bechdel's memoir, she recounts the publishing history of Joyce's *Ulysses*. She notes that in the early history of the book it was banned in most markets. In this context, many of its first publishers were lesbians—Margaret Anderson, Jane Heap, Sylvia Beach, and Adrienne Monnier—and she acknowledges that this might just be a coincidence. But then she says that she would like to think "they went to the mat for this book because they were lesbians, because they knew a thing or two about erotic truth."[57] Her claim is not that only lesbians have an erotic truth, but rather that *being queer makes one aware of the nature of erotic truth*. When one is heterosexual and cis-gendered, it is *much easier* to assume that sex is just the expression of a biological (or even spiritual?) nature, rather than to see its illusory and phantasmatic nature. At the same time, we must resist theoretical positions that see sexual identity as a social construction; it is not. Sex is the Real. Yes, there are cultural expressions of sexual identity as well as what counts as sexually appealing and healthy when it comes to sexuality, but these expressions exist and persist because they fail. As Lacan so brilliantly put it, "the sexual relationship doesn't stop not being written."[58] Sex and the sexual relationship will always continue to be not being written, so there is no way we can ever definitively inhabit a sexual identity or establish a relationship with another human being grounded on the identities we find there. Nevertheless, we cannot seem to just let them go. This is why anxiety is the truth of sexuality. It all depends on something we do not have (the phallus) and can never be (the *objet a*), yet for this very reason, it keeps us coming back to each other for more.

THE ANXIETY OF *COITUS INTERRUPTUS*

Jamieson Webster has returned to one of Freud's earliest musings on anxiety, his theory of *coitus interruptus* as the cause of anxiety, as a way to unpack the truth of sex. She acknowledges that this is not normally where people look to find insights about sex or anxiety—it is, she says, a theory that is "easily derided" and "a terrible cliché"—but she nevertheless believes it offers important insights on both sex and anxiety. In this early conception of anxiety, Freud claimed that an orgasm is basically the ejection into the "outside" of scraps of libido, while anxiety was the trapping inside of these same scraps. Webster tells us that in *coitus interruptus*, Freud makes "anxiety a half-enjoyed interruption, the stoppage of orgasm, the strange choice of this anxious pain against the pain of uninterrupted or complete enjoyment."[59] But Webster argues that while he abandoned this particular theory of anxiety, the basic contours remain in his later theorizations. According to Webster, for Freud anxiety is a "foolproof argument against any easy Darwinian perspective because it embodies evolution gone haywire, the involuting effects of the civilizing function of society, and, simply, the sheer problem of sex."[60] What she likes about Freud's theorization of sex in terms of anxiety (and of anxiety in terms of sex) is that such explanations are "also diagnoses of culture" in which the "structure of the drive must also be a question of social and historical configurations."[61]

She argues that anxiety arises in "liminal spaces, in the sensation of oneself as a body in relation to something outside, the sense of a foreign edge." Because of this, actions that are based in anxiety tend to aim at controlling the "appearance of Otherness" in oneself or in the other person. This is why she says that "anxiety must be tied to sexuality." In her view, separation is key, but separation does not mean "this is my arm and that is yours, my arm does what I want it to" but rather something more like "who knows whose arms any of these are, all the same, I'm doing just fine, it's not going to come off if my attention lapses." What she is getting at is that separation is not about clear boundaries and achieving autonomy, but about having a relationship with one's own unconscious.[62] To put her conception in the terms we have been using, "separation" is about coming to understand the extimate nature of one's own subjectivity. In seeing oneself as "extimate," one comes to understand that their own subjectivity is grounded in the Other. We could say this is a kind of separation by way of confrontation with alienation. For Webster, this realization allows us to understand that separation is just another way of saying "there is no sexual relationship." We cannot find a common satisfaction because my relationship with others does not depend on my isolation in order to found a unitary and autonomous subjectivity (which is no subjectivity at all), but precisely on my relationship with the Other.

Webster's analysis on sex and anxiety focuses on a case study Lacan recounts in *Seminar X: Anxiety* that illustrates this point:

> This woman, whose sexuality is quite normal, bears witness to what occurs for her if, when she is driving, for example, an alert flashes up for a moving entity that makes her say to herself something along the lines of God, a car! Well, inexplicably she notices the existence of a vaginal swelling. This is what strikes her that day and she notes that, during some periods, the phenomenon will occur when just any old object comes into her visual field, to all appearances utterly foreign to anything of a sexual nature. This state, which she says is not disagreeable, which is rather of an awkward nature, stops of its own accord.[63]

She tells Lacan that when this happens, she notices that the object seems to force her to "evoke" Lacan, her analyst, "as a witness." She says that she is not seeking his approval, but only his "gaze," and then adds that what she really means is that "this gaze helps [her] to make each thing assume meaning." The eye, the sexual organ, the Other. They all seem in this example to come together in a project of meaning-making.[64] She then tells Lacan about her first love—"with whom she remained in correspondence, in the full sense of the term," Lacan tells us—for whom she created a "web of lies" that created a "character, what [she] wanted to be in his eyes." She then tells Lacan that what she does with him (i.e., Lacan) is the opposite of what she does with her first love. Lacan says that what she wants is to replace her gaze with his because she feels her own gaze is "insufficient when it comes to capturing everything that stands to be absorbed from the outside. It's not about watching me do something, it's about doing it for me."[65]

Webster's conclusion regarding this case study is that it is an example not only of transference but also of a way to approach the gaze in the field of sex. The fiction the patient constructs for her first love "props her" up and allows her to exist, but what happens in this transference with Lacan is "something else more desirous." What she gets from her relationship with Lacan is "a support that allows her to see the everything that is there for the taking." Unlike her relationship with the first love, she is not duping anyone, nor is she "taken in by her own ideal," but rather she "allows her gaze to drop by replacing it with her analyst's eyes, and it is through this falling away that the world flares up—God, a car!" By getting this source of assistance from the Other (Lacan as her analyst) she finds that any object can become "a source of desire, a great love to live, a literal swelling in her surroundings." Though Webster is not sure what Lacan concludes about this (and neither am I), she wonders if it might be what it is like to encounter another without castration anxiety. Whether this is possible or not, both Lacan and Webster agree that what we see here is a satisfaction in a (transference) relationship (between Lacan and his patient) which is not based on reciprocity but on exactly the kind of separation Webster emphasizes.[66]

Anxiety is the truth of sex because sex locates us precisely at the point where we enter the intersubjective field most directly in relationship to desire, both as subjects seeking the object of our desire and as objects for the Other/other. In our anxiety, we tend to want to minimize the role of this otherness in our own subjectivity, but such a denial is the very thing that cuts us off from enjoyment. *Coitus interruptus* is a form of birth control, yes, but also a form of control in general. It is an attempt to interrupt, limit, and rein in one's desire in order to facilitate a larger, more civilized project. By contrast, Lacan's patient finds herself, with the support of the gaze of the other, able to let her desire go, to let it move from object to object, to make the other nothing more than a witness to her desiring. But more typically, the other of the sexual relationship is perceived either as an object that can bring total satisfaction to me, or as some version of the giant praying mantis ready to consume me. No wonder anxiety is the truth of sexuality.

NOTES

1. Lacan, *Seminar X: Anxiety*, 269.
2. Jacques Lacan, *Seminaire XVII : L'enverse de psychanalyse*, ed. Jacques-Alain Miller (Paris: Editions du Seuil, 1991), 191.

3. Lacan, *Seminaire X, L'angoisse*, 310. Translation mine. The same passage is found in *Seminar X: Anxiety*, 268.
4. Freud, *Civilization and Its Discontents*, 61–63, n. 7.
5. Lacan, *Seminar XX: Encore*, 78–89.
6. Lacan, *Seminar X: Anxiety*, 190.
7. Lacan, *Seminar X: Anxiety*, 192.
8. Lacan, *Seminar X: Anxiety*, 201.
9. Lacan, *Seminar X: Anxiety*, 201.
10. Lacan, *Seminar X: Anxiety*, 191.
11. Lacan, *Seminar X: Anxiety*, 190.
12. Lacan, *Seminar X: Anxiety*, 190.
13. Lacan, *Seminar X: Anxiety*, 191.
14. Lacan, *Seminar X: Anxiety*, 189.
15. Lacan, *Seminar X: Anxiety*, 189. In later seminars, he will describe this more explicitly in terms of a feminine or "other" jouissance. See Lacan, *Seminar XX: Encore*, 61–77.
16. Lacan, *Seminar X, Anxiety*, 188–189.
17. Lacan, *Seminar X, Anxiety*, 204–205.
18. Rothenberg, *The Excessive Subject*, 204.
19. Alenka Zupančič, *What is Sex*? (Cambridge, MA and London: The MIT Press, 2017), 56–57.
20. Jack Halberstam, *Female Masculinity* (Durham, NC and London: Duke University Press, 1998), 1, 3–4.
21. Halberstam, *Female Masculinity*, xi, 19–21.
22. Halberstam, *Female Masculinity*, 27.
23. Torrey Peters, *Detransition, Baby* (New York: One World, 2020), 339.
24. Peters, *Detransition, Baby,* [Dedication Page].
25. Peters, *Detransition, Baby*, 167.
26. Peters, *Detransition, Baby*, 174.
27. Peters, *Detransition, Baby*, 177.
28. Peters, *Detransition, Baby*, 8.
29. Peters, *Detransition, Baby*, 287.
30. Peters, *Detransition, Baby*, 314.
31. Peters, *Detransition, Baby*, 287.
32. Alison Bechdel, *Fun Home: A Family Tragicomic* (Boston and New York: Houghton Mifflin Company, 2006), 230.
33. Judith Butler, *Gender Trouble: Feminism and the Subversion of Identity* (New York and London: Routledge, 2007, first published 1990), 194–203.
34. Copjec, *Read My Desire*, 201–236.
35. Bechdel, *Fun Home,* 98.
36. Bechdel, *Fun Home,* 120.
37. Bechdel, *Fun Home,* 117–118.
38. Bechdel, *Fun Home,* 98.
39. Bechdel, *Fun Home,* 95–96.

40. Judith Butler, *The Psychic Life of Power: Theories in Subjection* (Stanford, CA: Stanford University Press, 1997), 144–145.
41. Butler, *Psychic Life of Power*, 145–146.
42. Bechdel, *Fun Home,* 228.
43. Bechdel, *Fun Home,* 230.
44. Bechdel, *Fun Home,* 141.
45. Bechdel, *Fun Home,* 142.
46. Bechdel, *Fun Home,* 143.
47. Bechdel, *Fun Home,* 147.
48. Bechdel, *Fun Home,* 144.
49. Bechdel, *Fun Home,* 169.
50. Lacan, *Seminar XI: Four Fundamental Concepts*, 210–215.
51. Lacan, *Seminar XI: Four Fundamental Concepts*, 210–215.
52. Bechdel, *Fun Home*, 119.
53. Bechdel, *Fun Home*, 119–120.
54. Lacan, *Seminar XI: Four Fundamental Concepts*, 204.
55. Lacan, *Seminar X: Anxiety*, 182–196.
56. Zupančič, *What is Sex*?, 60–61. Lacan, "The Instance of the Letter in the Unconscious," in *Ecrits,* 416–417.
57. Bechdel, *Fun Home*, 229.
58. Jacques Lacan, *Seminar XX: Encore, On Feminine Sexuality, The Limits of Love and Knowledge*, trans. Bruce Fink (New York and London: W.W. Norton and Company, 1998), 94. The French phrase is: "*le rapport sexuel ne cesse pas de ne pas s'écrire*" in Lacan, *Séminaire XX: Encore*, , 120.
59. Webster, *Conversion Disorder*, 156.
60. Webster, *Conversion Disorder*, 156.
61. Webster, *Conversion Disorder*, 157.
62. Webster, *Conversion Disorder*, 163–165.
63. Lacan, Seminar X: Anxiety, 188.
64. Lacan, *Seminar X: Anxiety*, 188
65. Lacan, *Seminar X: Anxiety,* 188–189.
66. Webster, *Conversion Disorder,* 172–173.

Chapter 5

Anxiety and the Fantasy of Race

In the last chapter, I argued that to be a cultural being is to be a sexual being, though this required a rethinking of what it means to be both sexual and cultural. Because of the subject's relationship to culture, this makes sex an inevitable site of anxiety. The sexual subject—which I am claiming is a redundant way to phrase it—is inevitably caught up in the dialectic of anxiety-fantasy. The phallus, a signifier that only appears as missing, makes sense of our subjectivity. To be a subject is to be subjected to castration. Masculinity and femininity are not expressions of a biological essence but are two different ways of coming to terms with the anxiety around castration. Neither totalizes the subject, but rather creates different ways of failing in response to the demands of culture. Anxiety is, thus, the truth of sexuality, and this truth is that there is no sexual relationship. Culture not only addresses the ways in which we must sustain ourselves in terms of material production but also provides ways to cope with the very castration that culture has imposed on us all. The sexual relationship fantasy is the most conspicuous and foundational form of this response, but in the modern era, the second-most conspicuous fantastic response would have to be race.

But while the Möbius subject partakes of the same dialectic of anxiety-fantasy in relation to race as it does with sex, they are not analogous. First, while the dynamic of sexuality hinges upon the invisibility of the phallus, race depends on visibility for its confirmation. But it is a visibility of a weird sort where what is seen—marks on the body—is supposed to be the evidence of some unseen reality that is the basis for the meaning of the visible marks themselves. In race, certain physical features serve as markers of a heritage that is supposed to be the key to an indelible essence that does not manifest itself in those bodily markings but only coincides with them. As Seshadri-Crooks has put it, "race is fundamentally a regime of looking, although race cannot be reduced to the look." Despite its emphasis on appearance, "identity is a question of 'heritage,' not skin color," but once the heritage is claimed, it is "ultimately marked on the body." For this reason, "racial passing" points to an "anxious fascination with miniscule but all important differences" because these minuscule differences "shore up one's symbolic position."[1] In the regime of race, our normal ways of marking differences between individuals are deployed to mark members of a group said to share a common heritage. The "markings" on the body *seem* to confirm the idea of a heritage that is prior to history and beyond discourse. As Sheldon George puts it, "by grafting itself onto biology," race can present itself as "pre-dating the system of the Symbolic, masquerading as an inherent component of nature."[2] There is something circular about this mode of apprehension, which is why "passing" can cause so much anxiety. Someone who can "pass" for white but nevertheless is of black heritage is, under this racial regime, considered to be "black," despite their physical features conflicting with this conclusion.

This odd, circular form of reasoning emerges as a result of the new class positions that emerged under capitalism. Non-capitalist modes of class difference are rooted in and maintained by mythological and legal mechanisms. Unlike capitalist class differences, which are assumed to be contingent and permeable, non-capitalist class differences are grounded in mythological tales and find support in legal institutions that govern labor, property ownership, and marriage without any recourse to outward physical differences to justify these claims. In fact, sumptuary laws have often been imposed under such non-capitalist regimes to make class differences visible. But under capitalism, the assumption is that any worker can become a capitalist, and any capitalist can "sink" to the level of the worker. One's class identity is linked to one's place in the system of production (and, to some extent, to their wealth). While actual capitalist societies never live up to this level of permeability, the ideological position of capitalism, mirrored in the Enlightenment discourse around "rights" and rooted in Reformation (and counter-Reformation) notions of a universal calling, proposes that all of us are equal and should be treated the same. This position of equality ran counter to the projects of imperialism and capitalism that emerged in the sixteenth century in Europe and traveled by way of conquest to the Americas, Africa, South Asia, and to some extent East Asia, where a class of European imperialists asserted their right to seize, appropriate, murder, and manage the lands and affairs of other people. In such a context, "whiteness" emerged, for political, economic, and even intellectual reasons, as the marker of civilization and as the identity of the imperialists and colonizers. Over time, notions of privilege and hierarchy based on aristocratic heritage were replaced by the notion of privilege and hierarchy based on "whiteness," but only after a certain level of liberty and mobility could be assumed by the mass of the non-enslaved people. This had the effect of papering over regional, class, and even, to some extent, religious social antagonisms that had been emerging in Europe for centuries by suggesting that Europeans, at least in their roles as imperialists, colonizers, and slavers, were part of a singular identity thought in terms of "whiteness," a concept that came with legal privileges and protections from which non-whites were exempted. Whiteness thus becomes the central concept in race, which is to say, in racism, and thus becomes the source of anxiety for everyone within the racist orbit.

Barbara Fields and Karen Fields have framed this dynamic in terms of a conflict between egalitarian values and the impulse toward exploitation, which found a loophole in the discourse of racism. As Fields and Fields point out, historically, the adoption of chattel slavery in the British colonies in the Americas required just such a solution, and this solution has had a lasting legacy on the history of the United States. As they put it, "Racial ideology supplied the means of explaining slavery to people whose terrain was a republic founded on radical doctrines of liberty and natural rights."[3] The paradox of racism and chattel slavery is that it only takes root in a context where equality and liberty can be taken for granted to some degree.

Along these lines, Seshadri-Crooks has declared that "whiteness" is the master signifier of race. A master signifier is a signifier without a signified that organizes a discursive field. Unlike sexual difference, which depends on the "phallus" as the signifier without a signified, "whiteness" posits a way for the unsignifiable to be marked by way of bodies. First, "whiteness" develops a "knowledge" about race by positing the non-white other as its own limit. While attempts have been made over the years to define "whiteness" in biological and physiognomical ways, none could provide a stable set of criteria by which "every non-white" would be excluded and every "white" person included. This failure, though not always acknowledged, points to the way the physical markings associated with race serve only to identify the supposed racial essence at the subject's core. Furthermore, the emergence of "whiteness" in a particular historical moment—that of the emergence of the bourgeoisie in Europe and the launch of a global imperialist project—and as a signifier that conceals an unlimited difference among those whom it signifies, stations itself as a precarious identity that must be continually reinforced. In this context, the physical markings on the body serve not as the basis for racial distinctions but as a way to rescue the concept of race by appealing to its supposedly natural features.

This dynamic has lingering effects that are not easily countered. Despite the drumbeat coming from anti-racist circles that race is a cultural construct, that we are all basically the same, and that everyone must be treated equally, the "evidence" from our eyes of racial difference *seems* to point to a difference in the Real that cannot be evaded. But as we saw in chapter 3, while "seeing" may be "believing," we do not see things as they are. Our look is always mediated by what Lacan calls the "Other." I am always already in the picture that is painted in my eye. While I see race, my seeing it is only possible because of this mediation. I see race in the other because of the way I am already racialized. Hegel makes the same point when he argues that though in "searching and describing" we

> seem to be concerned only with things . . . what enables things to be intelligently apprehended is more important to it than the rest of the complex of sensuous properties which, of course, the thing itself cannot dispense with, but which consciousness can do without.

He explains that in this "distinction into what is essential and what is unessential, the Notion rises above the dispersion of the sensuous, and cognition thus makes it clear that it is just as essentially concerned with its own self as with things."[4] When we see something, we always see it *as something*. Seeing is an experience not of the immediate but of the mediated encounter with the object. Race is not our immediate apprehension of difference, but a differentiating as a result of prior mediation. But it does not generally appear to us as such.

Of course, the phenomenon of passing already shows the instability and inadequacy of this visibility, but at the same time, "passing" points to the strong sense *we have* (unconsciously) of a racialized subject whose essence precedes its appearance (as "heritage"), though the confirmation of this essence is confirmed in a difference registered at the level of appearance. It is notable that many anti-trans* demagogues mock the reality of the trans* experience by claiming sex is analogous to race. In his Netflix special, *The Closer*, Dave Chappelle mocked the idea that a person might identify with a gender other than the one assigned to them at birth by claiming he, a black man, had decided he was now Chinese. The joke is not only mean-spirited (and not funny), but it also fails to understand the difference between sex and race. They are the same in that neither is a choice, but they are different in terms of the way their signifiers function. In sex, the phallus creates division in terms of how different people, under the sway of unconscious effects (and not biology), come to terms with their own symbolic castration (either by way of imposture or by way of masquerade). This is true for reasons related to the emergence of human beings as subjects. It is this gap in the signifying chain itself that creates sexual difference. But in race, the master signifier "whiteness" emerges from a particular historical-political field as a way to bolster the bourgeois imperialist project that laid claim, against notions of aristocratic privilege, to a universal equality that it nevertheless chose to deny to peoples of non-European descent in most parts of the world. Chappelle's joke invests itself in these visible markers of difference which he analogizes to biological differences. In doing so, he makes two mistakes at the same time. First, he assumes bodily differences are decisive for subjective identities in ways that they clearly are not. Bodily differences serve only to stabilize the meanings associated with various identities. The meanings come first, and then we see the differences. Second, he fails to see that sexual difference is fundamental to subjectivity; the subject is "forced" to respond to the phallic function by entering into the Symbolic order. Race is a project of a particular political economy that justifies forms of exploitation first by claiming an equality for all that "naturally" produces inequality on the basis of individual performance (capitalism), while at the same time arguing that natural differences (race) lead inevitably to hierarchies grounded in racial differences (imperialism and chattel slavery). Similarly, academics who insist that both sex and race are social constructs are following the same logic as Chappelle, but in an inverted form. While Chappelle grounds both racial and sexual difference in biology, this academic approach (there are plenty of academics outside the humanities who follow the logic of biology as well) sees both of them as socially constructed. Both positions fail to see the differences between sexual difference and race.

Furthermore, sexual difference can, conceivably, exist without hierarchies and oppressions. To see sexual difference in the way outlined in the previous chapter is not to necessitate patriarchy. However, to invest in the "truth" of race is to automatically be in the place of racism, because racism is what grounds racial difference. It appears otherwise because, as already mentioned, racism appeals to the "evidence" of our eyes to point to something "real" as the basis for its difference, even though this "evidence" is only the mediation of the Other. Secondly, racial difference has led to a sense of solidarity among those who have been racialized in similar ways. But we should point out that such solidarity is not grounded in the minuscule differences that mark bodies but in a common experience of oppression under a racist regime.

But, like sex, the link between culture and subjectivity makes race a site of the anxiety-fantasy dialectic. Unlike sex, though, the anxieties associated with race do not operate in the same way for people of all races. My position is that whiteness is at the center of the problem of race. The necessity of establishing "whiteness" as a core, but fantastic, identity was crucial to establishing a system of exploitation and imperialism in the wake of egalitarian discourses that renounced natural differences based upon birth (i.e., aristocracy) and replaced them with supposedly more scientific differences based on race. Race was thus conceived as "real" while aristocratic lineage became ideological. Thus, for those who identify, consciously or not, as "white," anxiety is always a problem of borders—a fear that whiteness will lose its advantages or that the racial other will, or has, somehow stolen the enjoyment that makes the white person "white"—while for the racialized other (the non-white person), anxiety is always connected to what W. E. B. Dubois called "double consciousness."[5] This dynamic can easily become violent. Race is all fantasy, but for that very reason it is always haunted by anxiety; however, the anxiety that sustains racial systems is the anxiety of the white person. Even those white people who do not occupy positions of great power or privilege can be invested in the fantasy of whiteness in ways that create great anxiety. This is not to suggest that we must sympathize with them in their anxiety, but rather to argue that the fantasy of whiteness must be undermined at every turn, not simply by mocking it, but by showing its emptiness. In doing so, other racial significations will also show their emptiness. The effect of this is not to be the erasure of non-white racialized groups, but to point out that their solidarity is based on a collective experience of resistance to a regime of racism and not on any biological or even cultural heritage. In pursuing this line of thought, we will center on the ways in which "whiteness" as a master signifier generates a fantasy of wholeness. But whiteness is not simply a fantasy; it is a structure that is crucial to the capitalist imperial order. For this reason, structural changes must be enacted to undermine this harmful fantasy, but these structural changes cannot be changed without subverting the fantasy structures that sustain them through the psychic investment they enlist from subjects in a racist society.

THE MÖBIUS SUBJECT OF RACE

In the preceding brief sketch of race, by positing racism as a feature of a particular political economy, we have run the risk of seeing race as externally caused. While such external causality could account for laws and even certain institutions that enforce a particular racial hierarchy, such a model of causality would fail to account for the psychic investment in race by subjects, some of whom consciously claim to renounce the formulation of race itself. A worse mistake would have been to see race as somehow the result of an internal "essence" that manifests itself in the cultural and social world. Both approaches—locating racism/race in external, institutional causes or essentializing it—fail to account for the way *anxiety* is entangled with race. Throughout this book, unpacking the way anxiety emerges in relationship to various features of culture has depended on the relationship between anxiety and fantasy, a relationship I have been claiming, based on Lacan's assertion that the structure of anxiety and fantasy is the same, is dialectical. In the experience of anxiety, there is always a fantasy structure whose fantastic nature is being repressed. In experiencing fantasy, the subject is fleeing anxiety as the signal of the Real that would disclose the anxiety of the subject's extimate causality. For this reason, centering anxiety in our account of the subject's relationship to the cultural and social world has also depended on the model of subjectivity itself that was so central to Lacan's *Seminar X: Anxiety* and to Rothenberg's *Excessive Subject*: the Möbius subject (with its extimate causality). This relationship between anxiety and fantasy that points to the Möbius quality of subjectivity is crucial for understanding what our experience of anxiety indicates regarding the function of race and the durability of racism.

As Molly Anne Rothenberg has pointed out, the Möbius quality of the social field produces a "parallax view" of every subject in that field, such that the subject's role vacillates between being the "cause of social discord" (i.e., the obstacle to social harmony) and the solution to this discord.[6] This has important implications for understanding the relationship between anxiety and race. The world of others is always a world where others seem to serve as either hoped-for solutions or recalcitrant obstacles to our search for the very thing that would make up for the constitutive lack at the heart of our subjectivity and produce a set of harmonious relationships in the social field. Lacan's *objet a*, as perceived in other people, always manifests this parallax potential that corresponds to the relationship between anxiety and fantasy. Because of our relationship to *objet a* in the founding of our subjectivity, any and every person can be seen as either a solution or an obstacle.

This has profound implications for the way our social reality appears to us. Rothenberg argues that

> social antagonism never appears as such: rather, its effects are always attributed to some specific element in the subject's world . . . conceived as an obstacle to the jouissance of the subject or group. Racism is a good example of this phenomenon.[7]

The Möbius subject encounters this same dynamic in relation to "its own excess with respect to itself—its non-self-coincidence registered as angst, anxiety, and anger," leading the subject to project "the source of its problems onto other people." This dynamic is a "defensive project" such that "every person in the society can be targeted as the source of discord for every other person."[8] From this point of view, the world of others offers the constant possibility of encountering another person who could make things right in the subject's world, or who could be the obstacle, that, if removed, would allow life to become harmonious and complete. Sometimes the same person can be both. We have all probably had the experience of meeting someone we hope will change our lives, save our academic program, or produce the radical change we have been seeking in our society, only to come to think of them as the very obstacle to the thing we wanted. (The dynamic seems to go in the other direction very rarely.) Or, as Todd McGowan has pointed out, in racism, the very fantasy of the racial subject as an obstacle to jouissance sustains our desire; the racial other as an obstacle thus becomes crucial to our fantasy. I would add that this is why the removal of the obstacle would cause anxiety: it would create a "lack of lack" as one seemingly encountered the missing object once the obstacle to it was removed. If there was no racism, we would need some other obstacle to avoid anxiety. Otherwise, one might think that given the potentially volatile nature of such "parallax" encounters that we might feel anxiety all the time. However, racism/race actually provides a way to avoid anxiety. Immersing oneself in what McGowan calls the "racist fantasy" relieves one of anxiety by sustaining lack and avoiding the "lack of lack" at the core of anxiety.[9]

Similarly, Seshadri-Crooks sees the relationship between anxiety and race functioning in terms of the subject's desire for "wholeness," and in that regard, "the order of racial difference is an order that promises access to an absolute wholeness." She argues that it is the failure of the sexual relationship to provide this wholeness that race is trying to accommodate. But her theorization of this is more nuanced than it at first appears. She claims first that "whiteness . . . attempts to install itself in [the] place of linguistic contradiction—of being—where the subject fades from meaning." She thinks this attempt itself—that is, the "attempt to totalize and inflate the subject"—can only produce anxiety. But this anxiety is avoided because "visual difference then rescues the subject from such anxiety by reinstalling difference."[10] This dynamic is governed by the idea that "whiteness represents complete mastery, self-sufficiency, and the jouissance of Oneness."[11] For her, the anxiety comes from the "encounter with the historicity, the purely symbolic origin of the signifier [whiteness]."[12] Here "whiteness" is proposed as the "solution" to the subject's self-contradiction and lack, which is posed in terms of naturally constituted differences, but this "solution" is called into question when one realizes that "whiteness" has a history and is not the effect of a natural difference. However, her critique is still a psychoanalytic one because she believes psychoanalysis is the best way to approach racism/race because it is the best way to account for the "investment we make in appearance . . . beyond simple historical or material explanation." In this sense, though, her account of anxiety in relation to racism tends toward Heidegger's approach. It is the contingency of race that produces anxiety for Seshadri-Crooks, and the "bodily marks" of race serve as a "powerful prophylactic against the anxiety of race as discursive construction."[13] But in a sense, this amounts to claiming that race (in terms of its physical markings) becomes the defense against the anxiety created when one realizes the contingency of the concept itself.

By contrast, we could say that for Rothenberg, it is the subject's own non-self-coincidence, that is, its own excessiveness, that generates anxiety, which is defended against by finding obstacles and solutions in the racialized others we encounter. As long as one can locate such obstacles and/or solutions in others, the basic fantasy structure of the subject's relationship to reality can be sustained. As Rothenberg points out,

> the desire to stabilize meaning (which, I would argue, is desire plain and simple) implies that the space in which meaning emerges is under threat: When we note a need to protect the social space, we are actually acknowledging that it is (always) in the process of being both dissolved and re-generated.[14]

Such an account also ends up seeming like the one offered by Heidegger, for whom anxiety is an experience of the "world as world," but it is not the "world" which is the source of anxiety for Rothenberg, but the subject's own extimate causality.

To bring out the significance of both Seshadri-Crooks' and Rothenberg's positions in more clearly psychoanalytic terms, we need to emphasize the Möbius nature of the subject itself, that appears in racism/race as anxiety related to the "lack of lack." It is not simply a loss of meaning that leads to anxiety, but a loss of the lack in response to which the subject emerges as desiring. To use Lacan's analogy, what causes the child's anxiety is not the "alternating presence and absence" of the mother because the "security of presence is the possibility of absence," but rather "when the mother is on his back all the while."[15] Without the *objet a* structuring our reality (through fantasy), we would encounter a world structured by a totally smothering m(O)-ther that would be intolerable for the subject, which is founded not only on alienation but also on separation. It is not the "loss of meaning" per se that causes anxiety, because the subject confronting lack can always find another fantasy, but rather the apparent lack of the *objet a* that produces anxiety. The ethnic-racialized subject causes anxiety by their very presence because of their being associated with *objet a* in this parallax encounter unless they can, as *objet a*, be put in their "place" relative to the subject's desire for mastery and wholeness.

Antonio Viego, whose approach draws heavily on Seshadri-Crook's *Desiring Whiteness*, makes this functioning of the *objet a* in relationship to the Möbius subject more clear: "the subject is an effect of the signifier, not a substance, not a preexisting essence that could precipitate itself outside the locus of the Other, the Symbolic, outside of language as structure."[16] This subject as "effect of signifier" is meant to counter the view of the "ethnic-racialized subject" as "the sum of 'the perfectly calculated cultural context in which the subject is immersed'" that leads to a "psychologization" of the "ethnic-racialized subject" only in terms of the "ego."[17] Viego's insight suggests that much of the work done in ethnic studies is based on a denial of subjectivity in order to replace it with the ego of ego psychology. From the point of view of psychoanalysis, the ego is a façade, a false image of wholeness, and mastery based on an alien image. Thus, by using Viego's critique of psychological approaches to race, we can extend Seshadri-Crooks' analysis to posit that when one approaches the ethnic-racialized subject as ego (instead of subject), one is only ever encountering an alien image of themselves in relation to this ethnic-racialized subject meant to convey an image of wholeness that covers over the constitutional lack and non-self-coincidence of the subject. The effect of this would be to reduce the ethnic-racialized subject to a non-subject, that is, to an exemplar of an ethnic-racialized type. This refusal of subjectivity locks the ethnic-racialized subject into the realm of Images, which assumes a level of wholeness—that is, it rejects the subject's extimate causality—registered at the level of the very bodily images that supposedly confirm race as a natural effect. By conceiving the ethnic-racialized individual in this way, we are no longer encountering an individual, which is to say, we are no longer dealing with a subject. The price to pay for this supposed wholeness, granted by way of the ethnic-racialized identity, is to obscure the subjectivity of the ethnic-racialized individual. Since they are no longer lacking, they no longer desire. They are assumed to function only as an expression of the ethnic-racialized identity they have been assigned. Rey Chow has conceived this as "coercive mimeticism—a process . . . in which those who are marginal to mainstream Western culture are expected . . . to resemble and replicate the very banal preconceptions that have been appended to them."[18] For this reason, Viego emphasizes the need for us to think of ethnic-racialized subjects in terms of Hortense Spillers' "interior intersubjectivity" because of its ability to "interrupt the moribund lock-step movement between ethnic-racialized resemblance and ethnic-racialized social and cultural intelligibility."[19] This approach contrasts sharply with the intelligibility that is offered by a social-psychology, ego-centered approach to ethnic studies, which fails to see the incompleteness, contradiction, and unintelligibility that mark both the ethnic-racialized subject and the culture in which that subject emerges.

Historicism makes a similar mistake. Viego argues that

> the exhaustive interpretive reduction of ethnic-racialized subjectivity and experience to the "indwelling network of relations of power and knowledge" constitutes a new form of biologism, evolution that is also a species of ethological analysis since the specifically human dimension the effects of language as structure on the human organism—are not taken into consideration when we conceptualize ethnic-racialized subjectivity and experience.[20]

Any emphasis on these "indwelling networks of power and knowledge" ends up again reducing the ethnic-racialized subject to an effect of the very discourse that has aimed at its exploitation and degradation. By contrast,

Viego argues that "Lacan's theory of the incalculable subject in language" is "the only way to challenge any explication of the ethnic-racialized subject as wholly reducible in and exhausted by language."[21] This line of thought works in the same vein as Copjec's claim that

> in language and yet *more than* language, the subject is a cause for which no signifier can account. Not because she transcends the signifier but because she inhabits it as limit. The subject, radically unknowable, radically, incalculable, is the only guarantee we have against racism.[22]

She goes on to say that this guarantee slips away from us whenever we fail to account for the non-transparency of the subject, or when we think that the subject coincides with the signifier rather than seeing it as always failing to correspond to it.

What we can take from this line of thought is that all racial identities are signifiers, but these signifiers do not correspond to any particular subject. It is precisely this failure of the subject to coincide with itself, that is, to coincide with its own signification, that makes the subject a subject. So how does anxiety relate to this dynamic?

Anxiety is a signal of the Real.[23] Racism is an attempt to avoid the Real, and thus avoid anxiety. Racism avoids the Real by constituting the subject in terms of race, an identity that appears to be rooted in something natural because it relies on visible markings on the body for its support. But race is a matter of signifiers. Following Seshadri-Crooks, I argue that "whiteness" is the master signifier of race. Linked as it is to a historical project of imperialistic exploitation, genocide, and enslavement, we would expect that "whiteness" would work to justify that exploitation. But justify to whom? The answer, from a psychoanalytic point of view, can only be the Other. The anxiety of "whiteness" boils down to a failure of the fantasy associated with it to frame it as its own justification. "whiteness" works as a justification only when it can maintain its status as the Other's understanding of what counts as civilized, rational, beautiful, lawful, and so on. This factor explains why, in an era where racism has been called into question, people will avoid claims to "whiteness" instead laying claim to "western culture," "rational ideas," "progress," "lawfulness," et al. The question of what the Other wants finds an answer, an answer that can forestall anxiety precisely because "whiteness" is a signifier without a signified, thus allowing the subject to endlessly engage in the production of knowledge, a knowledge based on the Other's presumed desire. When one encounters "whiteness" as a historical contingency, the project of whiteness does not disappear because the knowledge this master signifier generates subsists in a chain of signifiers—civilization, order, lawfulness, cleanliness, and so forth—that sustain the fantasy of whiteness in the face of historical evidence. Rather than the confrontation with the historical contingency of whiteness leading to anxiety, what we see is a response of re-signification that maintains the racism that it found while disavowing it. Anxiety comes not from the realization of the historicity of "whiteness" but rather from encountering the Real of the subject's own non-self-coincidence and excess in the form of the realization that one does not coincide with the signifier, that is, that one is not "white," all evidence to the contrary. It is not the historicity of "whiteness" that is its weakness, but its failure to provide what it promises by way of wholeness, satisfaction, and harmony. This failure removes "race" as a potential site of desire and fantasy, converting it into anxiety. This failure is registered not only in lack but also in the lack of lack created by the excess produced by its signification.

Because anxiety and fantasy have the same structure, that is, because they both involve the way the (Möbius) subject relates to the *objet a*, they are in a dialectic relationship with each other. In a world where our reality as subjects is constituted by our racial identities, we are living in a reality supported by a particular fantasy. We are allowing the signifier to coincide with the subject, applied both to ourselves and to others. Lacan's analysis of the Master's discourse figures the repressed truth of the master signifier as the subject's own self-division.[24] The painful truth behind all this is that we will not be able to marshal a truly anti-racist movement without experiencing a significant amount of anxiety. We might go so far as to say that if one is not feeling anxiety, one is not being anti-racist. At the same time, this anxiety can be liberating as one comes to grips with the way everyone fails to coincide with the (racial) signifiers that provide them with meaning and to find new paths of desire that support a universal project of emancipation.

THE PARALLAX EXPERIENCE OF RACE

My claim that a truly anti-racist position will entail experiencing anxiety finds an instructive parallel in Sara Ahmed's claim that anxiety can explain the conversion of the ethnic-racialized subject into a phobic object. Ahmed engages with anxiety in order to analyze the origins of racism by drawing on Freud's understanding of the sorts of displacements and condensations that constitute the unconscious (though she does not frame this in terms of the Freudian unconscious itself). Her understanding of the relationship between anxiety and racism is an effect of the way she understands the relationship between fear and anxiety. For her, fear is linked to the "passing by" of an object. Fear is an "anticipation of fear and injury" that can overwhelm us. For Ahmed, fear is always "not quite present," while anxiety has the quality of being "not present at all."[25] She points out that, according to Freud, fear is a symptom that can be put in place of another fear. She argues that repression is not so much the repression of an affect as the repression of *the idea* to which the affect is attached. She uses Freud's own example of the case of Little Hans to make this point. Freud wrote that Little Hans's symptom—his inability to go out into the street because of his fear of horses—was an "inhibition which his ego had imposed on itself so as not to arouse the anxiety-symptom."[26] Little Hans's fear of his father—his anxiety-symptom—was transferred to his fear of horses. He could not avoid his father or the fear he associated with him, so his anxiety transferred that fear to horses, which he could avoid by staying out of the streets. Ahmed describes this phenomenon as a "sliding" between fear and anxiety in relation to the passing of the object, such that objects can be linked together by way of this displacement, especially when such links "may already be in place in the social imaginary." She suggests that "the sideways movement between objects, which works to stick objects together as signs of threat, is shaped by multiple histories" such that this "movement between signs" does "not have its origin in the psyche" but instead in a "trace of how such histories remain alive in the present."[27] Here, her contrast between what is "in the psyche" and "histories" seems to mirror the extimate causality of the Möbius subject, but she does not commit to that model of subjectivity. Her sense of affect tends toward external causality rather than the sort of extimacy we have been developing. Because of this, for her, things simply "stick together" in ways we might better describe in terms of the displacement and condensation that were central to Freud's understanding of the unconscious (and Lacan's assertion that the unconscious is structured like a language). For Ahmed, there is a sort of affective "sliding" rather than the symptomatic focus of Freud's account. For Freud, Little Hans's fear of horses was a symptom requiring interpretation, but for Ahmed, there is a shifting of anxiety (which is unavoidable) to a fear of the racial other (who can be avoided). For her, anxiety is a cause of racism, but only by way of the fact that the ethnic-racialized other can be avoided (hence a "passing" object of fear) in ways that the anxiety around the loss of maternal love (and social belonging) cannot.

This framing has obvious implications for her analysis of the affective experience of racism, where anxieties in one area of experience can be converted into fears of the racial other. For this, she turns to another psychoanalytic thinker, Frantz Fanon, who wrote about his experiences of "passing by" white people as an example of the "production of the black man as the object of fear" that depends on "past histories of association" linking such terms as "Negro, animal, bad, mean, ugly." It is, she says, this "movement of fear between signs" (we would say "signifiers") that "allows the object of fear to be generated in the present (the Negro *is* an animal, bad, mean, ugly)."[28] According to Ahmed, in the racist encounter, the fear is aroused in the racist by the "passing by of the object," which is contained in the black body so that the black man becomes more fearsome by passing by: "the economy of fear works to contain the bodies of others, a containment whose 'success' relies on its failure, as it must keep open the very grounds of fear."[29] The logic of her reading of Fanon depends upon seeing fear as something that is approaching and passing, while anxiety is not present at all. Fearful objects can be avoided in ways the sources of our anxiety cannot. In this way, she sees fear not as defending borders that already exist but rather as *making the borders* by establishing objects that can be fled. Finally, in terms that are analogous to some degree with McGowan's "obstacle," the need to "keep open the very grounds of fear" in Ahmed's theory shows the necessity of this regime of avoidance failing. However, she means failing to rid the racist observer of their fearful objects in order to continue to defend against anxiety by displacing anxiety about the loss of maternal love and social belonging onto the ethnic-racialized phobic object. But, for McGowan, the ethnic-racialized subject is the obstacle that supposedly leads to the failure of the subject to attain its desire and thus sustains the fantasy so central to the racist's reality. This is not a minor difference.

Ahmed's understanding of the cause of anxiety is helpful for figuring out the underlying role of anxiety in the subject's sense of social belonging. She sees the sliding of racism from fear to anxiety occurring as, in part, a result of love. She speculates that the "love of the (m)other" appears as "a love that can be taken away, as the taking away of that which secures the subject's relation to the world." This leads her to conclude that "anxiety is then an effect of the impossibility of love; an impossibility that returns in the diminishment of *what is possible to be*" (emphasis mine). Here she is linking the recognition (love) of the other to the subject's own possibilities for being in ways that suggest an extimate causality for the subject's being as the source of anxiety. This is the most psychoanalytic feature of her theorization of the relationship between anxiety and race. Following the pattern developed by Freud in his analysis of Little Hans, she analyzes racism as originating in "the anxiety about the possibility of loss" that becomes "displaced onto objects of fear, which seem to present themselves from the outside as dangers that could be avoided and as obstacles to the fulfillment of love itself."[30] Here again, she seems to circle back to a position close to McGowan's. As a reminder, for McGowan, the ethnic-racialized subject is a necessary obstacle in terms of the racist's desiring. The obstacle explains why the satisfaction figured in the racist's fantasy has not been attained and maintains the status of the fantasy object as desirable; the ethnic-racialized subject has blocked the racist from attaining it either as a spoiler or as a thief of what rightly belongs to the racist. For McGowan the obstacle is crucial. Something similar happens with Ahmed for whom the mother's love, which can always be lost, creates the motivation to figure a phobic object that lies elsewhere, but for her, there is no logical connection between this phobic object any more than there is a logical connection between Little Hans's father and horses. Ahmed does help us think about how the fear we express toward racialized others is grounded in anxiety about a loss of love and social belonging. The important thing for Ahmed is that social and even legal barriers can be put in place between the individual who fears the loss of the mother's love and the racial other; but nothing can secure the mother's love.

Ahmed's account has the advantage for us of linking racism with anxiety. But in making this move, she has shifted the focus away from "whiteness" as the central concern of racism and placed it on the "histories" that allow for the "sticking" of negative associations to various people of color. It is possible to read her argument as implying that anxiety about the loss of maternal love is tantamount to the originary trauma figured in psychoanalysis. We could link it to the function of wholeness in Seshadri-Crooks' argument. But for Ahmed, there is something arbitrary about the response that seems difficult to align with the ubiquity and persistence of racism. In the case of Little Hans, no other children developed similar phobias around horses. We might ask: what would be the basis for an anti-racist position in Ahmed's account of such racism? Certainly, it could not be to assure the fearful racist of the mother's love, since such an assurance can never be granted. This leaves us with trying to "unstick" the associations of "histories" from the flesh-and-blood people walking the streets who can be identified as "black" or "Asian" or whatever. Though Ahmed relies on Freud's Little Hans case study to work out how such transferences and "slippages" can occur, this account fails for not developing this in terms of the unconscious. As Ahmed certainly knows, terms like "black" work not because they have a fixed signification, but precisely because they don't, and they "work" to label people not because all people who are labeled "black" actually look the same (and they aren't even black), but because the signifier allows such an association to be made. What happens unconsciously from there is, to some extent, up for grabs, but in the case of racism, something pervasive seems to dominate the social field.

Ahmed's analysis follows Fanon's closely, but she does not fully embrace the psychoanalytic aspects of his theory. She follows Fanon closely when he cites Charles Odier's claim that "all anxiety derives from a certain subjective insecurity linked to the absence of the mother" to make his own claim that "the phobic object is . . . *overdetermined*."[31] But the question is how, and in what way, the ethnic-racialized subject is overdetermined? Fanon's psychoanalytic reading of the object of racism insists upon the presence of an underlying psychic structure that "defies all rational thinking" but nevertheless follows an inner logic ("prelogical rationality" in Fanon's terms) that is rooted in the "accident that made [the subject] insecure."[32] It is this inner psychic process that makes the black man "a 'phobogenic' object, provoking anxiety."[33] Fanon goes further than Ahmed, noting the ways in which the black man is sexualized and this fear of him seems to correspond to anxieties, not about sex, but about civilization itself. Fanon argues that "every intellectual gain calls for a loss of sexual potential."[34] It is this association of the black man with the primitive, with biology, and with the sexual organ itself that leads to his being a phobic object as well. It is not simply, for Fanon, a matter of history, though he does not exclude that, but of what Freud and Lacan both describe in terms of "castration." Culture itself has castrated us. The anxiety that Fanon locates, while linked to the loss of maternal love, is expressed in an anxiety about castration. What is being displaced onto the black man is the white man's own anxieties about his loss of sexual potency as a result of becoming civilized. He thinks of the black man as not being castrated, which is to say, he is not civilized (in Freud's sense), or that he has access to an undiluted jouissance (in Lacan's sense). "Rodin's *Thinker* in erection—now there's a shocking image," Fanon says, to underscore the point.[35] The black man is not simply an avoidable object; he also, at the same time, seems to occupy the place of the solution, but a threatening solution that is framed in terms of a lack of (symbolic) castration. In Lacanian terms, in the figure of the black man the phallus "appears" and this is what causes anxiety. In psychoanalysis, the phallus is what could secure the m(o)ther's love. This is anxiety and not simply a fear that relies on historic associations that "stick" to the ethnic-racialized subject.

Furthermore, though Fanon died before Lacan had been able to more fully develop his thinking regarding the role of the signifier in the emergence of the subject and before Lacan published his *Écrits*, Fanon developed a version of this problematic in relation to his attempt to critique any psychopathological approach which tends to universalize an experience that seems grounded in specific historical and cultural contexts. He somewhat approvingly quotes Gabriel d'Arbousier's critique of Sartre's tendency to lump together black people from various countries and situations, but he nevertheless confesses that in his own analysis "dialectics, at all costs, got the upper hand" and has forced him to see that at the heart of the issue is that a black man, regardless of where he comes from, will still be a black man. (This supports my claim that "whiteness" is at the core of the race problem.) Fanon claims that world culture has become infused with representations of blackness that always frame the black man so that "*wherever he goes, a black man remains a black man.*"[36] Fanon knows full well that "blackness" is not an innate feature and that its deployment effaces not only differences between different (black) cultures but also between individuals; nevertheless, blackness is that thing that follows a man because it is not about the man at all, or the culture he comes from, but his place within a structure of displacement that figures him as a phobic object. The meaning of this object does not reside in the object itself (i.e., in the human person who has been identified as "black"), but in the psychic workings of the racist. If we think about how this sexualized version of the black man in relation to the black man as "animal," we can see that the real issue is the tendency to associate "whiteness" with civilization, beauty, sexual control, and goodness. The "black" man is part of the knowledge production related to "whiteness."

In response to this relation, at the beginning of *Black Skin, White Masks*, Fanon responds to various researchers who seem to want to get human beings to think of themselves as just like other animals or to turn humans into machines. Instead, he insists on approaching the topic of race/racism at the "psychoanalytical level: in other words, the 'misfires' just as we talk about an engine misfiring."[37] Fanon thinks that we can *only* analyze race/racism in terms of the way it misfires. These racist ideas always reveal themselves in their contradictions since the emptiness of fantasies related to whiteness will inevitably involve exactly these kinds of contradictions. By contrast, Ahmed's understanding seems to see things working smoothly: anxiety can be avoided when negative histories stick to ethnic-racialized individuals who become fearful, so we can avoid them. One of Fanon's more striking examples is the way the colonial black subject is understood in France in relationship to language. He tells us that the black man "proves himself through language."[38] But the response to this "proof" from white people in France manifests itself in contradictory ways. On the one hand, he notes how André Breton could approvingly refer to Aimé Césaire as "a black man who handles the French language unlike any white man today" and how Charles-André Julien introduced Césaire as a "black poet with a university *agrégation*" or simply as a "great black poet."[39] Césaire was Martinican. French was his native language. He had an advanced university education in France, studying at the *École Normale Supérieure*, yet his command of the French language created surprise and wonder in his white counterparts. Furthermore, despite this facility with the French language, he was constantly referred to as a "black man." What is "sticking" to him is the signifier "black," which is what creates the surprise at his use of language. Breton and Julien were admirers of Césaire; he was not a phobic object they were trying to avoid, yet he was still marked by his race as "other" because he was not conceived as "white." Ahmed is right that this anxiety around social belonging can express itself in racism, but it is not necessarily by converting someone into a phobic object. Breton and Julien's investment in "whiteness" as the signifier of "culture" (along with the ability to speak an elevated form of French serving as a mark of civilization, and thus, "Whiteness") creates an instability in them around their own social belonging, which is linked to "whiteness." This is why they responded to Césaire as they did. They were trying to fend off anxiety not by creating a phobic object, but by stabilizing the signification of "whiteness" that had been disrupted by the fact that this Black man laid a stronger claim to "whiteness" (understood in terms of "civilization," "culture," etc.) than many white people. At the same time, Fanon tells us that for some white people in France (he says not academics) "a black man who quotes Montesquieu must be watched." What makes the Montesquieu-quoting black suspect is not the negative "histories" associated with blackness, but precisely his failure to correspond to the significations associated with his identity as a black man.

Ultimately, Fanon thinks it all comes back to the way his being recognized as black intervenes in his encounters with white people. He complains, "I'm not given a second chance. I am overdetermined from outside. I am a slave not to the 'idea' others have of me, but to my appearance." The "appearance" here is shaped by the gaze of the Other, to put it in Lacanian terms, which centers "whiteness" as the marker of humanity. He says that "the white gaze, the only valid one, is already dissecting me. I am *fixed*."[40] Being fixed is the problem *because he is not allowed, as a black man, to be non-identical with the signifier attached to him*. "I did not create a meaning for myself: the meaning was already there, waiting,"[41] he complains. But this meaning is not simple. "There is a quest for the black man," Fanon explains, "he is yearned for: white men can't get along without him. He is in demand, but they want him seasoned a certain way. Unfortunately, the black man demolishes the system and violates the agreements."[42] It is this demolishing of the agreements, the phallus "appearing," that generates anxiety for those who believe themselves to be "white."

SEEING THROUGH RACE

Jennifer Friedlander has argued against the idea that the post-racist position is an anti-racist position. But she also opposes any attempt to think that simply adopting a "cynical" view of race can be an effective anti-racist position either. Instead, she says we should think of race as something we can "see through" in both senses of the phrase. We can "see through" race in the sense of seeing its constructed, false, and mistaken nature, but we must also recognize that we are always "seeing through" race in the sense of race being a frame, or even a lens, through which we view reality. She follows Sheldon George's conviction that the way to destabilize race is by identifying with the incomplete nature of the Symbolic order, which implies the impossibility of grounding any subjective identity, including racial ones. To understand this is to "see through race" in the sense of not being duped by its claims. But unlike George, she does not believe a cynical distance is possible, nor would it be effective in opposing racism. In doing so, Friedlander insists that because race involves "seeing through" in both senses, the pressure necessary to combat the effects of racism must come "from entering into the meaninglessness of the Other's signifiers and desire, rather than, as George claims, distancing ourselves from them."[43] It is this "entering into" these "meaningless signifiers" associated with race that we can begin to develop an effective anti-racist position.

Frielander's approach is helpful because it maintains the contradictory nature of racism itself. This contradiction is rooted in and corresponds to the contradictory nature of the Möbius subject with its extimate causality. What is tricky about race is that it seems to register itself in the visual field. Here, our analysis of anxiety in the visual field is crucial. That differences in melanin content should be definitive for understanding the nature of any group of individuals, let alone those individuals themselves, is absurd on its face. If we understand the visual field as operating in terms of a binary like the one we associated with Sartre's gaze, then such visual associations, like the ones described by Ahmed, seem not only arbitrary but individual. One way to read Ahmed's account would be to suggest that since every individual experiences anxiety around the potential loss of maternal love, they forestall that anxiety by transferring it to a phobic object in the form of another person they can then avoid. For "historical reasons," various ethnic racialized persons will become phobic objects to keep anxiety at bay. But why should this transference fall on the ethnically racialized other? Why not make horses the phobic object, just like Little Hans? It also does not explain why we "see through race," even when we "see through race." In other words, why do we still see race as a feature of the natural world, even when we know it is "culturally constructed?"

The answer lies in the Lacanian conception of the gaze. First, we are all already in the picture in ways that Ahmed's account implies but does not make explicit. For Ahmed, the racialized other becomes a phobic object because the gaze of the racist subject is avoiding the anxiety around the potential loss of maternal love. But this view of the gaze empowers the looking subject, whose psychic issues result directly in the marginalization of the other. But in the Lacanian view of the gaze, however, the racist "looker" is not empowered but *complicit*. The world we see always appears to us in relation to our own desires, and our desire is the desire of the Other, but we each invest in the Other's desire in our own way. We see race because the Other sees it. We see race because the desire of the Other is somehow invested in it. But the Other's gaze is not a panoptical one, nor does it install itself in us as an "indwelling network of relations of power and knowledge."[44] Instead, our racial seeing, if we can think of it that way, has an extimate causality. It is not simply that the Other sees race and thus compels me to see it, but that I am also invested in the idea of race in ways that are obscure to me. Race is unconscious. Because of that, it is incredibly difficult to dislodge. The racist is neither all-powerful nor innocent, but *complicit*, because the racist subject is neither entirely the cause nor the effect of racist discourse, but the very place where such cause and effect meet.

For this reason, we do well not to analyze racism/race in terms of power, knowledge, and *dispositifs*, which all already come too late, already infused with our unconscious investments in race and what it signifies. Instead, we must analyze race in terms of the Möbius subject and its situatedness in relationship to discourse. Here, Lacan's elaboration of the four discourses can be particularly useful for the way it understands discourse as the relationship between four elements: a master signifier (S_1), knowledge (S_2), the *objet a* (a), and the (divided, castrated) subject ($\not{S}$). The paradigmatic form of discourse for Lacan is the "Master's discourse," which is based, structurally, on a reading of Hegel's master-slave dialectic. The master signifier relates to knowledge in the same way the master relates to the slave in Hegel's master-slave dialectic, where the master depends on the slave's work for his survival and the slave chooses survival/life over death at the cost of serving the master. In Hegel's dialectic as well as in the common experience many of us have of being employees, the servants, slaves, and employees have all the knowledge of how things get done, and they use this knowledge to serve the master's interest. In the same way, the master signifier (S_1), which has no signified (like the Hegelian master who is master only because of the slave), both requires and makes possible knowledge, which attempts to fill in the master signifier's constitutional void. If the master signifier had a signified, then there would be no need for this knowledge (just like if the master were self-sustaining, he would not need the slave/servant). But because the master signifier has no signified, there is no end to the proliferation of this knowledge beyond the experience of the master signifier as a master signifier itself. The (repressed) "truth" of the master (i.e., the master signifier) is the master's (i.e., the subject of the discourse's) own self-division as a subject ($\not{S}$). The product produced by this discourse is nothing other than the *objet a*. Lacan thus creates a fourfold structure that identifies the role each element plays in the functioning of a given discourse. There is the agent who is the one who governs the discourse. Lacan says the "agent" is "not at all necessarily someone who does but someone who is caused to act" such that in the case of the Master's discourse, it is "not at all clear that the master functions."[45] This suggests the agent is less the active participant in the process as much as something like a "force" that causes the various reactions in the discourse to take place. Thus, the "other," which is the partner or addressee of the agent's discourse, is actually where the production of the discourse occurs. Or to be more precise, in the relationship between the agent and the other that sets the terms for the discourse. The product of the discourse is a matter, then, of the (repressed) truth driving the agent into a relationship with the other. This is true of all four of Lacan's basic discourses. In the case of the Master's discourse, "knowledge" (S_2) provides signification for the master signifier (which has no signified). The product of the Master's discourse, what the knowledge produces, is the *objet a*. The truth of the Master's discourse is the non-self-identical subject. The reason the master signifier engages knowledge in pursuit of the *objet a* is because of its own unacknowledged self-division, its own lack. We could simplify by saying the Master's discourse functions to cover over the lack in the master. Or, to put it in terms of discourse, the Master's discourse functions to make sure that the master signifier seems to be real. This is how the master's discourse is configured, according to Lacan (see figure 5.1).

If we applied this configuration to race, we would get something as shown in figure 5.2):

$$\frac{\text{agent}}{\text{truth}} \rightarrow \frac{\text{other}}{\text{product}} \qquad \frac{S_1}{\$} \rightarrow \frac{S_2}{a}$$

Figure 5.1 Basic Formula for Lacan's Model of Discourse: the Master's Discourse.

"Whiteness" →	civilization, goodness, beauty, lawful, hardworking, etc.
Möbius Subject	ethnic racialized subject as obstacle or solution

Figure 5.2 Adaptation of the Master's Discourse to Race/Racism.

The normal functioning of racism/race occurs within the master's discourse. Following Seshadri-Crooks, the master signifier, i.e., the signifier without a signified, is "whiteness." While it *sounds as if* it symbolizes something in the visual field that refers to a heritage, as a master signifier, "whiteness" has no signified. This lack of a signified requires a chain of signifiers, S_2, to provide knowledge for the S_1 by filling in what is missing. But because this knowledge, this infinite chain of signifiers aiming to make up for what is missing by way of signification, produces an excess—its product is the *objet a*. The physical markers associated with "whiteness" never emerge in the master's discourse since the fact of "whiteness" is assumed as self-evident, while the meaning of "whiteness" is deferred to the field of knowledge. But this knowledge can never account for the lack of signification in the master signifier "whiteness." This is why it produces this excess, which I have associated here, somewhat heavy-handedly, with the ethnic-racialized subject. The ethnic-racialized subject is the excess of "whiteness," which is why it appears in this parallax fashion as either solution or obstacle to the longed-for satisfaction proposed by "whiteness." This is why the "other" of "whiteness" is not simply "non-white." In its most generic terms, the other of "whiteness" could be labeled as "people of color," but even this generic designation indicates a plurality of responses—an excess. There is not one way to be non-white. The knowledge of "whiteness" is necessarily excessive because there is no signified of "whiteness," meaning the limit of "whiteness" is only experienced as the master signifier itself, which has no signified. Thus, the other of "whiteness" never stops being written. This excess—as *objet a*—means that the ethnic-racialized other is always potentially either solution or obstacle to the satisfaction the subject of "whiteness" seeks, a satisfaction that can never be found in "whiteness" but that is also not consciously realized because the truth that "whiteness" represses is the subject's own castration (i.e., its extimacy). The truth that is repressed in this discourse is the truth of the subject's own self-division, excess, and extimate causality that results from the subject's entrance into language, culture, and the Symbolic order. The ethnic-racialized subject then becomes an object meant to secure the integrity of "whiteness" by serving as its other.

For Lacan, all signifiers "are in some sense equivalent," and for that reason, "each is able to come to the position of the master signifier"[46] so that being a master signifier depends on the function of a particular signifier in a particular discourse. So, for comparison's sake, we might imagine the way "whiteness" might function as S_2 for the master signifier "American." Here we designate "American" as the signifier with no signified. There is, therefore, no correct definition of an American, but from the white nationalist perspective, "American" would certainly include "whiteness" among its qualities. (Not to mention that on a global level, "America" refers to an entire hemisphere.) Even for Americans (here to be taken as "citizens of the United States") who consciously renounce the project of white nationalism, they betray this unconscious "knowledge" of "American" when they ask natural-born Americans of non-white descent, "Where are you from?" This unconscious knowledge operates even for non-white Americans whenever they understand "American" to be primarily a designation that necessarily involves "whiteness." In such a scheme, the non-white American emerges in the place of the *objet a* and functions in a similar way to how the ethnic-racialized subject functions for the signifier "whiteness."

Obviously, the Master's discourse cannot be an anti-racist discourse given its functioning in our current racialized situation relative to the master signifier "whiteness." Therefore, we must look to the other three discourses in Lacan's schema for possible anti-racist discourses. One of the dominant approaches to anti-racism, especially in many institutional settings, might be the one that corresponds to Lacan's University discourse (see figure 5.3):

This discourse makes knowledge the agent with the *objet a* as its other. In Lacan's description of the *objet a* in the University discourse, he once claimed it stood for the "exploited in the university discourse, who are easy to

agent → other		S_2 → a	
---------	---------	----	----
truth	product	S_1	$\$$

Figure 5.3 Basic Formula for Lacan's University Discourse.

recognize—they are students."[47] In making that connection, he pointed to the way he thought the university's function had "become clogged up, blocked, maintained" in ways that make it a "masking discourse" that obscures the master's role. This can be seen in the formula itself, where the (repressed) truth of the university discourse is the master signifier. In this discourse, Lacan says, the student as "other" of the agent of knowledge is the *objet a* in order to produce a certain kind of (divided) subject, namely one whose castration corresponds to the repressed master signifier(s) of the institution. The students, always potentially recalcitrant, are both obstacle and solution to the knowledge project as conceived in the institutional setting of the university. From the point of view of the students, their position in the university is defined by the lost object, the object-cause of their desire, which looks to the agent, knowledge, for its satisfaction and fulfillment in the form of knowledge. It is the students' lack, their sense of loss, that does the work of this discourse. We often hear it said that the reason we (the faculty) are here (the university) is because of the students, and yet the students function as a strange causality for the knowledge the university produces. Is the knowledge really produced for them? But the product is also the students, but in a different way than in their association with the *objet a*. As "product" of the university, the students experience a special kind of division/castration around the university's master signifiers. While they may come to the university for knowledge, what they come to value are the credentials and status conferred by the institution itself. In the University discourse, the knowledge acts as the agent for the institutional discourse based on the institution's master signifier(s). What such institutions produce are (symbolically) castrated individuals ($\$$) who identify with the institution's master signifiers. In the United States, at least, this factor is almost never even thinly veiled, let alone disavowed; we are "training" students to be productive (castrated) laborers, which is very different from what would happen if knowledge were the (repressed) truth of the University discourse instead of its agent. This is not necessarily an indictment of academic research, or of teaching, per se, but of the institutionalization of knowledge with the ultimate, but disavowed, goal of aligning students with the master signifiers of the institution.

If we analyze how the University discourse might handle race, it would look something like this (see figure 5.4):

Here, the very knowledge that is supposed to signify "Whiteness" in the Master's discourse becomes redeployed as the agent of discourse in the

civilization, etc.	→	ethnic racialized subject as obstacle or solution
--------------		--
"Whiteness"		the subject castrated by "Whiteness"

Figure 5.4 Adaptation of Lacan's University Discourse to Race/Racism.

University discourse. In this knowledge-centered approach, the knowledge itself, as the agent, is not called into question (i.e., the very categories of what defines "whiteness"). Furthermore, what this knowledge disavows is the "whiteness" that still serves as its master signifier. Such a knowledge-based approach to race/racism, while formally disavowing whiteness, nevertheless fails to comprehend the way it still engages, unconsciously, with "whiteness" as its master signifier. "Whiteness" remains in the discourse as a repressed "truth," that cannot be acknowledged. The other of this knowledge (*objet a*) is the ethnic-racialized subject as an obstacle or solution. Here, it is not only the students of color but the faculty of color as well (or employees in non-university institutions) who must serve knowledge by adhering to their own identities. Viego puts this strikingly when he points out that in the university setting, "'faculty of color' are required by the university to reduce their function to their difference."[48] These students and faculty are constantly addressed as the bearers, dare we say, the "embodiment" of this knowledge. They are both problem and solution. Increasing enrollments for students of color and hiring more faculty of color are seen as something like the solution that masks the way the institution views them as a problem. Here we can start to see the difficulty of the knowledge-based institutional approach. In structure, it is the same as the nineteenth-century phrenologists and physiognomists who studied the skulls and bodies of people of color, not to better understand the human condition in general but to better understand the difference of "whiteness." What is produced by this discourse are subjects who are castrated by the signifier of "whiteness," meaning that they are unconsciously invested in racial difference, but with a knowledge-centered approach that disavows its real foundation by repressing its own master signifier, "whiteness." The University discourse on race is therefore haunted by the master signifier, "whiteness," which it disavows. This results in the endless production of knowledge on race, racism, ethnicity, and so on because the disavowal of its master signifier remains in place.

What Lacan calls the "Hysteric's discourse" seems much more promising as a potentially anti-racist discourse. For the hysteric, the divided subject itself is the agent of the discourse. But it represses the truth of its own subjectivity, namely, that it is caused by the impossible missing object, the *objet a*. Having disavowed this truth, it engages with its other, the master signifier itself, in order to produce new knowledge (see 5.5 and 5.6)

agent →	other		$\$ \rightarrow$	S_1
---------	---------		----	----
truth	product		a	S_2

Figure 5.5 Basic formula for Lacan's Hysteric's Discourse.

Möbius Subject →	"Whiteness"
--------------	----------------------
objet a	[new] knowledge

Figure 5.6 Adaptation of Lacan's Hysteric's Discourse to Race/Racism.

The hysteric questions the master signifier, and this is the strength of this discourse. It does not assume the substantiality of "whiteness" as the Master's discourse does, nor does it disavow it as the University discourse does, but it interrogates the master signifier, questioning its account of the subject. It does this with the aim of producing new knowledge. This quest for new knowledge is both its strength and its weakness. For example, as Viego has pointed out, Latinx studies is hysterical.[49] This makes a lot of sense because the subject of Latinx studies is itself a liminal figure. Even a superficial encounter with the subject of Latinx studies can see that there is no signifier that could easily account for the figure of the Latinx subject, emerging as it does from a colonial context founded in an avowedly *mestiza* context. The signifier of Latinx is already something like "mestiza." There is also something exciting about operating within the Hysteric's discourse. One of the reasons Viego situates Latinx studies in relation to the Hysteric's discourse is that they both "get off" on knowledge and on undermining the master.[50] It is fun to question cherished truths, and there is a certain excitement about keeping things open, not to mention the *jouissance* that comes from undermining the master. The usefulness of the Hysteric's discourse is not confined, though, to Latinx studies. It can always be used to call into question the designations and proclamations that come from the master (i.e., that come from "whiteness"). But in the Hysteric's discourse, knowledge becomes an end in itself. If this S_2 cannot ever be foreclosed, one can never stop writing what it is to be Latinx, or Asian-American, or Muslim, or . . . Thus, the weakness of the hysteric's approach to race/racism is that it makes the master signifier, "whiteness," its other. The discourse proceeds from this master signifier, even in the process of its interrogation. It also disavows the loss that has grounded its own subjectivity. This critique might certainly seem strange given how many discourses in the fields that study race and ethnicity foreground loss, but the key in considering these approaches to ethnic studies and race is to analyze what a given discourse does with this loss and how it accounts for it. Is it possible to talk about loss only to disavow it? I would argue that it is when that loss is conceived in relationship to "whiteness." Instead of seeing loss as a constitutional and necessary feature of subjectivity itself, it is possible to account for loss as a product of "whiteness." Certainly, white supremacy has done unspeakable and irremediable harm to innumerable people. But here we are talking about the logic that sustains white supremacy and not simply its effects. To conceive "loss" as an effect of "whiteness" and not as an effect of the universal process of signification that founds the subject is to deny the subjectivity of the ethnic-racialized subject by seeing it only as the result of the onslaught of "whiteness," which is a return to the same master signifier. Put differently, it is to concede one's self-identity within the knowledge of which "whiteness" is the master signifier. Because with racism/race, "whiteness" is the master signifier; producing more knowledge does not undermine "Whiteness," which remains in place as what we experience as the limit of race. Put another way, to develop anti-racism within the Hysteric's discourse is to see oneself not as a subject but as an object coinciding with a signification of otherness.

While both the University and Hysteric's discourses are discourses from which anti-racist approaches have been developed, only the Analyst discourse undermines the master signifier, "whiteness," and confronts the subject with its own self-division and castration (figures 5.7 and 5.8):

The *objet a* itself is the agent in the Analyst's discourse. But how can this be? In an actual psychoanalytic session, one can see how the analyst must occupy this position. The analyst must appear to the analysand as the lost object. The analyst must cause the subject's desire to emerge. The analysand must also believe that facing her is someone who has what they have been seeking. They have come to this place precisely *for that*. At the same time, there is knowledge involved, both the preparation attributed to the analyst and, more importantly, the analyst's knowledge of the extimate causality of subjectivity, but also the knowledge that is assumed to be "in" the unconscious of the analysand. But this knowledge is not articulated, but rather assumed, so it is in the position of the "repressed" truth beneath the *objet a*. In this position, knowledge does not produce the same excess generated by

agent	→	other		a	→	$
---------		---------		----		----
truth		product		S_2		S_1

Figure 5.7 Basic Formula for Lacan's Analyst's Discourse.

objet a	→	castrated subject
--------------		---------------------
knowledge		new master signifier(s).

Figure 5.8 Adaptation of Lacan's Analyst's Discourse to Race/Racism.

the Master's discourse. In this position, knowledge is no longer disavowing the master signifier in order to produce a castrated subject who will simply identify with the master signifier in this disavowed manner (as in the University discourse). Nor does knowledge function here the way it functions for the hysteric, producing new knowledge in relation to the same master signifier. Instead, this non-articulated knowledge, this knowledge that is assumed, is the truth that the *objet a* mobilizes in addressing the castrated subject in order to produce new master signifiers.

In terms of race, we can see that this is the only truly anti-racist position. In the first place, the very fact that its product is a new master signifier changes the terms of our understanding. "Whiteness" does not haunt this discourse. Instead of assuming "whiteness" (Master's discourse), repressing "whiteness" (University discourse), or interrogating "whiteness" (Hysteric's discourse), the Analyst's discourse replaces "whiteness" with a new master signifier. What this new signifier would be is up for grabs. It would still be a master signifier, which would mean it would have no signified, but it would alter the terms of the discourse entirely. It must be admitted that there is no guarantee that what would emerge as the new master signifier would be less onerous, but it opens up the possibility for "racial" difference becoming a difference without a difference in the way society is organized. Such a change would no doubt also entail radically changing the economic, social, and political conditions governed by "whiteness." But for this very reason, the anti-racism of the Analyst's discourse does not reject changing economic, social, and political conditions in advance of changing the master signifier, that is, it doesn't endorse a view that claims we must never take race into account when making political and social decisions about the distribution of goods and privileges, but it does require that we begin with the *objet a* as the impossible object that causes our desire. In doing this, we come to terms with the foundational lack of our own castration and the impossibility of ever bringing our lack to an end. Only this confrontation with the loss that characterizes the subject can liberate us from the solution to loss proposed by "whiteness." In the Analyst's discourse, the agent is the lost object itself that causes desire. By placing the objet a in the position of the agent, we find a new form of universality, what Todd McGowan calls universal "non-belonging."[51] This universal non-belonging is mirrored in the other of the *objet a*, the Möbius subject. This encounter between the objet a and the subject is what makes clear the emptiness of all racial significations. One can never truly belong to any identity, and no signifier can account for the subject's being. Only the Analyst's discourse makes this clear. Finally, only this discourse addresses the subject itself. It is the subject addressed in relationship to its own desire that can make room for the experience of universal non-belonging that can form a truly anti-racist discourse.

It is not clear what the new master signifier might be that would emerge from an anti-racist approach developed within the Analyst's discourse, but McGowan's "non-belonging" seems like a good and likely candidate. "Whiteness" functions as a signifier of a certain kind of belonging, though it is a belonging that can never be realized because, as a master signifier, it has no signified. This is why McGowan believes the only true basis of a universality that can be discovered (as opposed to constructed) is the universality of non-belonging. Our solidarity with others would become a function of our realization of the Möbius quality of our own subjectivity, which renders any complete and successful identification with any identity, racial or otherwise, impossible. This is something we understand but rebel against. We all know that we do not truly belong to any group, which is why we cling so tenaciously to these fictive identities. Ahmed's linking of anxiety to the potential loss of maternal love, which she associated with social belonging, makes the same point. If non-belonging were to become the new master signifier of identity for human beings, it would undermine all social orders based on such fictive identifications because it would undermine all identifications. This is the aim of the Analyst's discourse: to stage a confrontation between the subject and the *objet a*. It is no coincidence that this relationship in the Analyst's discourse figures the same relationship that Lacan associates with the structure of anxiety/fantasy: S/◇a. So where is anxiety in these discourses, and how does it relate to our attempts to conceive an effective anti-racism?

In *Seminar X: Anxiety*, Lacan teaches us to look for anxiety in relation to the *objet a*. He tells us that anxiety is "not without object" and that this object is the *objet a*. In fact, he says that the *objet a* takes "center stage" in the entire year-long seminar on anxiety because "anxiety is the sole subjective translation" of the *objet a*.[52] Anxiety, Lacan tells us, is a signal that the "*objet a*" is "intervening," and it signals a certain relationship between the *objet a* and the divided subject.[53] That anxiety marks, signals, and intervenes in the relationship between the castrated/divided subject and the *objet a* makes clear the rationale for my claim that anti-racism will necessarily involve anxiety. McGowan makes a similar claim relative to his project of universal non-belonging when he states that "freedom leaves subjects in anxiety before the other, which is why we don't choose it."[54] The Analyst's discourse is based precisely on this relationship between the subject and this lost object, the *objet a*. The other discourses find ways to avoid anxiety by refusing this relationship. The Master's discourse represses the divided, castrated nature of the subject in order to produce the *objet a* as its product. In this configuration, the *objet a* is as far structurally from the divided subject as it could be. In the University discourse, the relationship is closer, the other of the discourse being the objet a and the product being the subject, that is, the castrated subject's investment in knowledge founded on the master signifier provides a way of limiting the destabilizing effects of the loss associated with the *objet a*. In the Hysteric's discourse, the subject and the *objet a* are closer to each other, but the *objet a*, this signifier of loss, though the truth of the subject, is repressed. Only in the Analyst's discourse is the relationship between the divided, castrated subject and the *objet a* centered in a productive way at a level where it can be addressed. Only here do we find a discourse that centers the extimate causality of the subject and all of the excess and loss associated with it. Only this discourse confronts the subject with non-belonging. This process will involve anxiety because it exposes the extimate causality of the subject and thus undermines the "reality" that sustains this subjectivity. It demonstrates the fantastic nature of all racial identities in a way that does not produce more knowledge grounded in the master signifier of "whiteness" but requires a re-signification that alters the subject's relationship to all the identities produced by "whiteness." This confrontation leaves the subject without the reliable, if destructive and painful at times, fantasies of wholeness that are sustained by racial identities. But this anxiety is liberating and therapeutic. It confronts the subject both with the foundational nature of loss in relationship to subjectivity and the inability of any identity to heal that subjective wound or to suture the social field. But in this confrontation, the subject finds a freedom to choose, act, and feel that does not depend on any sort of coercive mimeticism that is ultimately doomed to fail but can, instead, find a new solidarity precisely in the non-belonging of symbolic castration itself.

THE SIGNIFIER BETWEEN THE WORLD AND ME

Ta Nehisi Coates' *Between the World and Me* develops an analysis of race/racism in America that works in the realm of the Analyst's discourse. He focuses on what he calls "the Dream" in relation to a group of people who "believe they are white." This relationship between "people who believe they are white" and "the Dream" mirrors the relationship between Lacan's divided subject and the *objet a*, undermining both "whiteness" and the "Dream" in the process. Following Lacan's typology, we can say that it mirrors the structure of fantasy in this way, and thus can also become a site of anxiety.

Coates' "The Dream," a term no doubt chosen for its valence with the "American Dream" and with Martin Luther King Jr.'s "I Have a Dream," maintains an important opacity while linking it to specific mediated images of what counts for a good life in the modern United States. Coates tells us "The Dream" is the

> pinnacle . . . to grow rich and live in one of those disconnected houses out in the country, in one of those small communities, one of those cul-de-sacs with

its gently curving ways, where they staged teen movies and children built treehouses, and in that last lost year before college, teenagers made love in cars parked at the lake. The Dream seemed to be the end of the world for me, the height of American ambition.[55]

Similarly, he characterizes it as "perfect houses with nice lawns. It is Memorial Day cookouts, block associations, and driveways. The Dream is treehouses and the Cub Scouts. The Dream smells like peppermint but tastes like strawberry shortcake."[56] The specificity of this image of The Dream helps to link it to a particularly American ideological project. It is the vision of the good life that American movies and television shows have laid out for us. However, his reference to The Dream "smell[ing] like peppermint" but "tast[ing] like strawberry shortcake" underscores its phantasmatic nature. Yes, all the specific features of The Dream exist somewhere for someone, but it does not, for all that, offer the satisfactions suggested by the fantasy that sustains it. Despite the power of these images to stir the imaginations of many Americans, they do not offer the happiness they promise. These idyllic scenes from television and film are, in reality, also places where desperation, depression, anxiety, and domestic violence flourish, and we should not forget that one of the founding ideas behind the suburb in the United States was a commitment to white-only neighborhoods, supported by covenants, red-lining, and discriminatory real estate practices. The hidden logic of the suburban dream is the fantasy of life made possible only when the non-white person is excluded from it. The Dream was not simply one of positive associations like the ones Coates mentions but the negative aim of avoiding non-white people, seen as the obstacle to that enjoyment. Put another way, there is nothing inherently satisfying about living in a suburb. What makes it appear satisfying is what McGowan calls the "racist fantasy" and what Coates calls "the Dream." In *Between the World and Me* Coates wants to paint a picture of the Dream that both suggests its broad ideological appeal and the emptiness of its promises while highlighting the necessary exclusion of black people from this idyllic vision (as what makes it idyllic).

Despite its obvious emptiness, the Dream serves as a powerful motivation for the ongoing oppression of minorities in the United States. Coates acknowledges that he has for long periods of time wanted to "escape into The Dream," but as a black man he recognizes that the Dream "rests on our backs, the bedding made from our bodies" and that the "Dream persists by warring with the known world."[57] Drawing on Solzhenitsyn's claim that to do evil people have to first believe it is good, Coates argues that the Dream rests on just such a foundation whose "adherents must not just believe in it but believe that it is just, believe that their possession of the dream is the natural result of grit, honor, and good works."[58] The result is that "living among

Dreamers" brings with it a burden brought on by their constant need to insist that the "Dream is just, noble, and real."[59] He observes how difficult it is for Americans to turn away from this Dream and to question it. In fact, he says the Dream is "the enemy of all art, courageous thinking, and honest writing." It "thrives on generalization, on limiting the number of possible questions, on privileging immediate answers."[60] We would say that the Dream, like any good fantasy, avoids anxiety by constructing a reality that papers over the Real.

But for Coates, this Dream exists by way of a hidden necessity (that we would elaborate in terms of the *objet a*), and that necessity is that there must always be a racialized underclass in the United States, where a group of people must always serve as "the essential below" of their country. (This is the Master's discourse at work in the service of "whiteness.") Despite this, Coates makes "whiteness" the center of his analysis. He does not refer to white people in his book; instead, he refers to "people who believe they are white." This formula allows him both to constantly center this belief as crucial to understanding racism (in the United States at least) and to undermine the validity of race as a category. He argues that though Americans believe in the "reality of 'race' as a defined, indubitable feature of the natural world," this belief is demonstrably false. Race is the "child of racism, not the father," he tells us. Our normal, common sense understanding of racism is that it is a lamentable byproduct of natural differences. But Coates points out that though natural shades of difference in the hues of skin color, the shape of noses, and the texture of hair have existed for a long time, the belief that those differences point to some essential difference in the essence of a human being that can be the basis for the social organization of a society makes no sense at all. We see race as natural because of racism, not the other way around. If we did not have racism, we would not have race. But then he makes it clear that the primary project of racism has been the construction of whiteness, and "the process of washing the disparate tribes white" and that "the elevation of the belief in being white was not achieved through wine tastings and ice cream socials, but rather through the pillaging of life, liberty, labor, and land; through the flaying of backs; the chaining of limbs; the strangling of dissidents; the destruction of families; the rape of mothers; the sale of children; and various other acts meant, first and foremost, to deny [Black people] the right to secure and govern our own bodies."[61] His graphic description of the practices of white supremacy points to the fact that even though he calls these people who believe they are white "Dreamers," this is not a mental exercise, but a violent social practice. But this violent social practice accounts for itself through discourse, and only a discourse like Coates', that is, one that foregrounds the role of loss and fantasy in the construction of race, can call the Dream into question in terms that actually undermine its causal relationship, which, though rooted in historical-material conditions, is sustained by the ideological commitments that have understood subjects of all races in terms of the master signifier "whiteness."

Therefore, developing a truly anti-racist position will involve anxiety because it will involve disrupting the identity-focused fantasies that sustain, in part, our reality. Adopting something like the Analyst's discourse to undermine "whiteness" will involve a confrontation with our own non-belongingness, which is another way of saying, we will have to avow our own castration, which will cause anxiety. This will be a common experience for both of those signified as "white" and those signified as "people of color." But this experience of anxiety can be liberating because it frees us from our attachments to the identities, dreams, and projects of the capitalist order in which we live. Liberating ourselves from our sense of racial belonging may also support our attempts to liberate ourselves from the capitalist world order by allowing us to come to terms with the emptiness of the dreams it offers us, dreams which, at their core, depend on the racist fantasies that have caused so much pain and trauma.

NOTES

1. Seshadri-Crooks, *Desiring : A Lacanian Analysis of Race* (London and New York: Routledge, 2000), 2.
2. Sheldon George, *Trauma and Race: A Lacanian Study of African American Racial Identity* (Waco, TX: Baylor University Press, 2001), 40.
3. Karen E. Fields and Barbara J. Fields, *Racecraft: The Soul of Inequality in American Life* (London and New York: Verso, 2012, 2014), 141.
4. Hegel, *Phenomenology of Spirit*, 148–149 (sec. 246).
5. W.E.B. Du Bois, *The Souls of Black Folk* (New York, London, Toronto, Sydney: Simon & Schuster Paperbacks, 2009).
6. Rothenberg, *The Excessive Subject*, 191.
7. Rothenberg, *The Excessive Subject,* 141.
8. Rothenberg, *The Excessive Subject,* 49.
9. Todd McGowan, *The Racist Fantasy* (New York, London, Oxford, New Delhi, and Sydney: Bloomsbury Academic, 2022), 1, 4, 8–9, *passim.*
10. Seshadri-Crooks, *Desiring* , 5–6.
11. Seshadri-Crooks, *Desiring* , 7.
12. Seshadri-Crooks, *Desiring* , 7–8.
13. Seshadri-Crooks, *Desiring* , 8.
14. Rothenberg, *The Excessive Subject*, 208.
15. Lacan, *Seminar X: Anxiety*, 53–54.
16. Antonio Viego, *Dead Subjects: Toward a Politics of Loss in Latino Studies* (Durham, NC and London: Duke University Press, 2007), 15.

17. Viego, *Dead Subjects*, 28.
18. Rey Chow, *The Protestant Ethnic and the Spirit of Capitalism* (New York: Columbia University Press, 2002), 107.
19. Viego, *Dead Subjects*, 29. See Hortense Spillers, "'All the Things You Could be by Now, If Sigmund Freud's Wife Was your Mother': Psychoanalysis and Race," *boundary,* 23, no. 3 (1996), 83–85.
20. Viego, *Dead Subjects*, 45–46. The phrase he quotes "indwelling network of relations of power and knowledge" comes from Copjec, *Read My Desire*, 6.
21. Viego, *Dead Subjects*, 48.
22. Copjec, *Read My Desire,* 209.
23. Lacan, *Seminar X: Anxiety*, 132, 185.
24. Lacan, *Seminar XVII: The Other Side of Psychoanalysis*, 92–93.
25. Ahmed, *The Cultural Politics of Emotion*, 65.
26. Freud, *Inhibitions, Symptoms, and Anxiety*, 22–23.
27. Ahmed, *The Cultural Politics of Emotion*, 66.
28. Ahmed, *The Cultural Politics of Emotion,* 66–67.
29. Sara Ahmed, *The Cultural Politics of Emotion,* 67.
30. Sara Ahmed, *The Cultural Politics of Emotion,* 67.
31. Frantz Fanon, *Black Skin, White Masks*, trans. Richard Philcox (New York: Grove Press, 2008), 133.
32. Fanon, *Black Skin, White Masks*, 133.
33. Fanon, *Black Skin, White Masks*, 129
34. Fanon, *Black Skin, White Masks*, 142.
35. Fanon, *Black Skin, White Masks*, 143.
36. Fanon, *Black Skin, White Masks*, 150.
37. Fanon, *Black Skin, White Masks*, 6–7. In French Fanon says "Je consens à le mener sur celui de la psychanalyse, c'est-à-dire de l'exigence fondamentale de la réalité humaine, je consens à le mener sur celui de la psychanalyse, c'est-à-dire des « ratés », au sense où l'on dit qu'un moteur a des ratés." The reference to the misfiring of the car justifies the translation of "ratés" (failures) as "misfires." Frantz Fanon, *Peau Noire, Masques Blancs* (Las Vegas: Kiyikaat Editions, 2022), 61.
38. Fanon, *Black Skin, White Masks*, 8.
39. Fanon, *Black Skin, White Masks*, 22.
40. Fanon, *Black Skin, White Masks,* 95.
41. Fanon, *Black Skin, White Masks,* 113.
42. Fanon, *Black Skin, White Masks,* 153.
43. Jennifer Friedlander, "In Medium Race: Traversing the Fantasy of Post-Race Discourse," in *Lacan and Race: Racism, Identity, and Psychoanalytic Theory,* ed. Sheldon George and Derek Hook (New York: Routledge, 2022), 105–120. .
44. This phrase refers to Joan Copjec's definition of historicism in *Read My Desire,* 6.
45. Jacques Lacan, *Seminar XVII: The Other Side of Pscyhoanalysis*, trans. Russell Grigg (New York and London: W.W. Norton and Company, 2007), 169.
46. Lacan, *Seminar XVII: The Other Side of Psychoanalysis*, 89.
47. Lacan, *Seminar XVII: The Other Side of Psychoanalysis*, 147–148.

48. Viego, *Dead Subjects*, 112.
49. Viego, *Dead Subjects*, 113.
50. Viego, *Dead Subjects*, 113.
51. Todd McGowan, *Universality and Identity Politics* (New York: Columbia University Press, 2020), 50, 60–69, 73–80.
52. Lacan, *Seminar X: Anxiety*, 100.
53. Lacan, *Seminar X: Anxiety*, 86.
54. McGowan, *Universality,* 87.
55. Ta-Nehisi Coates, *Between the World and Me* (New York: Spiegel & Grau, 2015), 116.
56. Coates, *Between the World and Me,* 11.
57. Coates, *Between the World and Me,* 11.
58. Coates, *Between the World and Me,* 98.
59. Coates, *Between the World and Me,* 106.
60. Coates, *Between the World and Me,* 50.
61. Coates, *Between the World and Me,* 8.

Conclusion

In Defense of Anxiety or, How to Get Cancer without Becoming Wise

In August of 2017, I was hiking near Mammoth Lakes, California, with my partner, Corinne, her parents, and our dog, Oliver. As we were coming back down from the mountain, Oliver wanted to go off the trail down to Cold Creek, fifty yards or so below. Just before we got to the creek, Oliver and I hopped onto a small boulder, just a couple feet off the ground, and then when Oliver jumped down, his leash tugged me slightly, and I fell. I could not get up. Immediately, Oliver seemed very worried. I was disturbed that I could not get up, and as my father-in-law and Corinne made their way toward me, all I could think of was those medical alert commercials: "Help, I've fallen, and I can't get up." I remember as a child, my father would often warn us not to be too rowdy around elderly people, lest we knock them over and they "break a hip." Despite the pain, my first thoughts were anxious ones, rooted in a kind of vanity: if I had broken my hip, would that mean I was an old man? Is that how Corinne would now see me? I hoped it was something else. "Broken femur" sounds like something that happens to young active men; "broken hip" sounds like something that happens to old women. You could call all those thoughts "vanity" or "ageism" or maybe even "misogyny," but we know it was anxiety, a fear that I had suddenly become less lovable, maybe even unlovable.

Corrine, who is a registered nurse, could see from the angle of my leg that my hip was broken. Her training and experience also suggested to her that a man my age would not just break his hip; something more serious had to be wrong. But she kept those thoughts to herself. I insisted that they help me get up so we could see if I could get down the rest of the trail to my car. Corrine suggested we call 9-1-1, but, because I am an American, my first thoughts were to wonder what portion of such a rescue and ambulance ride would be covered by my insurance—more anxious thoughts, these stimulated by the precarity of life in a place where people go bankrupt when they get sick. The proximate cause of this anxiety is the precarity of our economic situation in the United States. But this precarity draws on deeper anxieties. What if I "lost" all of our money to the ambulances, doctors, and hospitals? What if I could no longer work and the loss of my income made it impossible for us to continue living in a comfortable house in a safe neighborhood, with a good school district, reliable cars to drive, fees and equipment for sports teams, dance lessons, musical instruments, and all the other things parents "must" now provide their offspring? This anxiety, perhaps dressed up in love, was really asking, "if I can no longer contribute financially will these people I love still love me?" After all, what exactly is it about me they loved in the first place? *Che vuoi?* This anxiety is also, unfortunately, rooted in an understanding of masculinity that I have not been able to shake, despite all my theoretical engagement with it as a problem. "Suck it up, deal with the pain, get yourself down this mountain and *drive yourself* to the hospital." What was not verbalized but was certainly there, was the thought that if I was injured, weak, and incapable—if I could no longer provide for everyone—then no one would love me anymore. Castration anxiety.

It turns out, we did not pay a dime for my rescue: three doses of fentanyl, an ambulance trip to Mammoth Hospital, two surgeries, dozens of X-rays, and four days in the hospital. I am part of a labor union that has fought for and won excellent insurance for its members. But it turned out that the reason for the hip fracture—which probably was the cause of my fall and not the effect—occurred because I have a type of cancer called Multiple Myeloma. One of the effects of this blood cancer is that it stuffs junk immune cells into the bones, weakening them and making them more susceptible to fracture. X-rays revealed that these lesions were in my left hip and femur, my spine, and my skull (et al). The excellent orthopedic staff at Mammoth Hospital was able to replace the hip and quite a bit of my femur. Later, my oncologist would give me a treatment that leached calcium from my blood and put it back in my bones, providing them with the strength that has prevented subsequent fractures. But then there was the cancer to deal with.

"Cancer" is a word that strikes fear. It often goes undetected. No one knows how long the cancer had been spreading in me before it was discovered. A secret, malevolent force emerging from within, my own cells mutating, going awry, running amok. As soon as the diagnosis was made, we did what everyone does now: we Googled it. The Internet said I had at the most three years to live. The shock of this was hard to wrap my head around. It was not anxiety; it was mourning. I spent several days thinking about all the years with Corinne and my children that I would not have. All the things I would never get to do with them. But in between two surgeries in Mammoth, we called an oncologist in San Diego, Dr. Caitlin Costello, who specialized in Multiple Myeloma. When I called the scheduler to make an appointment, he allayed our fears by immediately telling us not to seek advice from "Dr. Google." Without making any promises, he let us know that Dr. Costello was an expert in this particular cancer, and we should not jump to any conclusions until we contacted her. It helped.

People fear cancer not just because they know it can kill them; they often fear the treatment: the chemotherapy, with its side effects, the needles, the tests, and so on. Most of us do not like to suffer. But I came to realize it is also possible to be afraid of being afraid. Fearing death is its own kind of suffering, and it is very possible to be afraid of being afraid of dying. I think I fear that more than death itself. What will it be like at the end when I know the end is near? Will that make me afraid? But maybe we mostly do not know the end is near when it is near. We just keep going like there is no end. You can see why the fantasy of a "better place," of "reincarnation," of "heaven," might help someone cope with this anxiety. I used to have that fantasy myself, long before I really needed it, but now I can no longer allow myself that luxury. When it is over it will be over. As Philip Larkin put it:

The sure extinction that we travel to
And shall be lost in always . . .[1]

So, without the fantasy of an eternal life for the subject—which is kind of a nightmare when you think about it—the nothingness of death is the total dissolution of the subject. The whole project crashing to an end.

Unlike other animals, when we are sick and injured, we do not bleakly wander around alone, like a bear with a wounded paw, struggling to find calories a month before the first snow, a solitary struggle against the harsh realities of the natural struggle for survival. We are subjects, forever connected to the Other. All the thoughts in our heads, all the things we see with the Other's gaze for support, and the desires that are the base of our subjectivity are always right there, too. Freud so clearly and pedantically returned again and again to "infantile helplessness" and the "fear of the loss of love," and in my battle with cancer, these primal feelings return again and again in the form of anxiety. Anxiety about being a burden to others (which I most certainly was). Anxiety about losing hair and muscle mass (which I certainly did—more castration anxiety). Anxiety about how we would afford to stay in our home once I had used up all my sick days (castration anxiety again, but also precarity). All of these anxieties are explained well by Freud and Lacan.

But after months of chemotherapy twice a week, a stem-cell transplant which included an extended hospital stay and months of home confinement, and then another year of chemotherapy, tests showed no trace of the blood disease. But I am told I am not cured. We are just waiting for when it returns. (Maybe it won't!) I still take a pill (that costs $16,000 a month!) every day. I go in for a blood test every three months—waiting for the results is always an anxiety-producing event—and so far, the tests still show no sign of the disease's return. Treatments have advanced and are always advancing, they tell me. I am eating better. I try to avoid carcinogens in the environment (not possible). But still, whether Multiple Myeloma kills me or not, sooner or later, something will. The possibility that I might have decades less than I had expected has left me with a shock. If I do not have much time left, what should I be doing with myself? In the movies, when someone gets cancer, they often struggle, lash out, and so forth, until they come to a moment of revelation. They now know what is important. They have "figured it out." They have "become wise." On their death bed, they impart pearls of wisdom; at their funeral, everyone weeps tears at the sheer beauty of this candle that burned out much too soon, and so on, and the audience leaves the theater assured that everything is really quite simple and good.

One version of this has captured the public's imagination and entered into our everyday vocabulary (including in cancer wards): *The Bucket List*.[2] In the film, differences in class and race are overcome by two terminally ill patients who escape their hospital room to do all the things they had wanted to do but never did: the list of everything you want to do before you "kick the bucket." What follows is a heart-warming version of the road trip buddy film where emotional healing occurs, real human connection is formed, and joy is found at the end of life. Sounds great! This does not seem to be what has happened to me.

My oncologist is typically very optimistic. But at one point I was confronted with some paperwork regarding my retirement. I have a defined benefit pension (thank you, union!) that requires me to bet on my own life. I had to sign a form recently on how I wanted my pension to be disbursed. Essentially, if I want to leave as much money as possible to Corinne when I die, it means we will have less money to retire with while I am living. My question for my oncologist. Do you think I am going to live long enough to need my pension? She was reluctant to answer this question given both her optimistic nature and her reluctance to give financial advice based on her ability to predict the future, but in the end, she reluctantly suggested that it was likely Multiple Myeloma would kill me. She then suggested that while I should not be pessimistic, I should perhaps consider checking off some items on my "bucket list." But what should go on that list?

I am convinced that Lacan's account of the subject is the correct one and that there is no better reading of anxiety than his. The connection of anxiety to the mystery of the Other's desire seems to get us through most of our issues with anxiety. But here, with the question of the "bucket list," my anxiety takes a different form. Confronted with death, seeing that my time is running out, what should I do with the time I have left? Of course, this question could have been posed on the first day of my life. That was when time started to run out. Given that we do not have eternal life, and this is our only chance, how should we live? This sounds more like a job for Kierkegaard.

Faced with a terminal illness, what should I do? My first thought was: I have always wanted to go to Paris. I should do that now! But then I thought, so what? I make all these memories, and then I will die, and they will disappear forever. Or should I devote myself to spending time with my family? After I am gone, they will still be here, and what I will want is for them to have memories of me. That sounds noble, but maybe they do not want to spend the next decade or two under the weight of my need to be remembered. Maybe the point is to just do things that I enjoy—surfing, watching movies, reading books, hiking—so that I fill my days with fun. Maybe that is the point. But maybe that would feel like I wasted the last years of my life accomplishing nothing. Maybe I should spend all my time fighting fascism or climate change. At least then I would be making a real difference for millions of people. Or maybe I should just keep doing what I am doing, immersing myself in the mundane concerns that in the end always seem to add up to a life.

It all reminds me of the existential dilemma at the heart of Milan Kundera's *The Unbearable Lightness of Being*. The protagonist, Tomas, an inveterate womanizer, becomes coincidentally and incomprehensibly attached to a young woman, Tereza. He does not know if he should stay with her or return to his carefree, womanizing ways. In so doing, he becomes annoyed with himself until "he realized that not knowing what he wanted was actually quite natural. We can never know what to want, because, living only one life, we can neither compare it with our previous lives nor perfect it in our lives to come."[3] Natural or not, it is hard for us to live with such uncertainty. The higher the stakes, the greater the anxiety, and what stakes could be higher than what one does with their one and only life? As the novel makes clear, it is not even obvious if we should opt for a life of "weight"—held to earth by our commitments—or "lightness," free and refusing the appeal of all ideologies and kitsch.

This cancer patient has not grown wise. Anxiety remains. But the latent argument of this book has been that anxiety, while not something to be cultivated (it needs no cultivation), is something we avoid at our peril. Flights from anxiety lead to flights of fancy. The Lacanian understanding of anxiety and fantasy, linked as both of them are to the enigma of the Other's desire, should not dupe us into believing that the Other exists. In Lacanian terms, only the Real is real, and the Real is nothing but the gaps, inconsistencies, and contradictions in the Other. Heidegger's point is basically the same. Only in anxiety is one able to free oneself from the life of Das Man—of what "one does"—and act with any sense of agency that might be authentic.

Similarly, Mari Ruti, weeks before her tragic death from causes related to her own struggle with cancer, gave a talk defending anxiety for its crucial connection to creativity.[4] For Ruti, sublimation, understood as elevating an ordinary object to the sublime status of the Thing (*Das Ding*) was crucial to living a meaningful life beyond ideological interpellation. She argued that by "curating the objects that bring us genuine satisfaction," we reveal something about ourselves. We let some objects go. We elevate others. This, Ruti tells us, reveals a great deal about our desire, and "this truth . . . cannot be dissociated from the possibility of anxiety." This act of sublimation is creativity, not only in the modes we associate with artistic expression, but in our everyday "capacity to generate new forms of meaning" in the course of living our lives. This meaning-generating activity takes place "between the promise of aliveness and the terror of anxiety." In this creative, meaning-generating activity, anxiety cannot be avoided: "trepidation—anxiety—as a component of our aliveness cannot be conjured away without conjuring away our aliveness."[5] For Ruti, sublimation is central to this experience of aliveness because of the way it brings us into contact with our own singularity. This singularity cannot be realized apart from the experience of anxiety.[6] What I have been arguing is that this relationship between anxiety and "aliveness" can only make sense when we understand Lacan's claim that the structure of fantasy and anxiety are the same. Fantasy supports us in our desire by proposing a solution to the problem of the Other's desire and thus defines for the subject a role in the intersubjective, cultural field. But anxiety points to the failure of this project to adequately solve that problem or to fully establish the subject in relationship to the Other's desire.

We cannot escape anxiety, but neither can we escape fantasy. We require fantasy to avoid falling into melancholy. We require fantasy in order to know what to do with ourselves. We require fantasy for anything to matter to us. This is not to say we live in a dream or that the world is in our heads because, as anxiety shows us, the world is definitely in objects. However, the object of our anxiety is the *objet a*—the things we are missing, what we need if we are to be okay—which we look for everywhere but never find. Fantasy covers certain objects in the world with an alluring veil and thus lures us into pursuing them. Nevertheless, we cannot be cynical. We should not fool ourselves into thinking we alone see through it all, and even if we could, what would life be like without it? As Lacan said, "*Les non-dupes errant.*" Leaving the fantasy is a mistake. But this cannot mean that we just believe anything, can it?

Because the Other does not exist, there can never be an ultimate verification of my reality, but for that reason, because the Real always comes back, anxiety should not be immediately refused. Anxiety can remind us that, after all, I never had the lost object and never will. I will never be fully satisfied. Nevertheless, I desire. I also love. We have seen the way love and anxiety come close together. They both threaten to disrupt things, destabilize the status quo. I was recently discussing Chrétien de Troyes' *Knight of the Cart* and the *Letters of Abelard and Heloise* with an undergraduate student majoring in economics. He was convinced that the kind of love described in these texts ought to be avoided. I asked him if he was interested in being in a relationship and, if so, what place he wanted desire to have in it. He told me what he wanted was to be part of a "power couple" and he did not care at all if there was any desire for each other beyond what they could do for the other's future. Is there anything wrong with this position? There is no Other, so we cannot really settle the question in those terms, but I think we can see behind his thinking an anxiety about the confrontation with otherness that desiring might involve. Paradoxically, this position does not avoid anxiety by fleeing desire, but by fleeing the enigma of the Other's desire. The desire to be a "power couple" is based on a certainty about what the Other wants from me in order to avoid a confrontation with the other's desire. To make being in a "power couple" the object of the Other's desire is to disavow castration and propose the possibility of a non-sexual sexual relationship. The "power couple" model he is proposing is one where everyone gets what they want. No trauma. No lack. No castration. But to relate to others requires, ironically, an understanding that there is no sexual relationship. The only way to establish a relationship with another is through lack. If I am truly complete, lacking nothing, then there is no place for you. Similarly, if you are complete, lacking nothing, there is no place for me. The fantasy of the sexual relationship posits that someone with a phallus encounters someone with a hidden treasure (Lacan's *objet a*, Plato's *agalma*) and everyone leaves getting exactly what they came for. But since there is no phallus or *objet a,* the relation fantasized in this way does not exist. Both the fantasy of the sexual relationship and the non-sexual sexual fantasy of the "power couple" posit subjects without lack. "No lack. Only desiring machines." The power of these fantasies and the theories that support them lies in their power to keep anxiety at bay. But the price to pay for this move is to cut us off from the creativity and aliveness that come only with anxiety.

This student is an earnest, lovely, and generous person, but it is hard not to see the same anxiety about anxiety at the root of nationalism, white supremacy, and misogyny. These are all fantasies that solve the problem of the enigma of the Other's desire by finding in themselves—as members of a particular nationality, as white, as men—a non-lacking subject who can keep anxiety at bay. These positions are perverse, displaying a certainty about what the Other desires—for example, European culture, Christianity, "real men"—and cannot imagine a world in which the desire of the Other remains enigmatic. From such a position, the other becomes a phobic object in order to convert the anxiety around the Other's desire into an object that can be avoided and attacked. The nonexistence of the Other with the necessarily enigmatic expression of the Other's desire makes anxiety inevitable. We cannot avoid it.

This does not mean that we should not work tirelessly to reduce the actual precarity in the world. The kind of anxiety that comes from the disruptions created by war, famine, climate disaster, and other forms of violence cannot be adequately addressed by telling those suffering in these circumstances that there is no Other and they should learn to live with the enigma of the Other's desire. Addressing the structures that make such precarity a central feature of the lives of billions of people is intolerable and must be addressed. But to the extent that this precarity is propped up by the bigotry, misogyny, and nationalism stemming from the attempt to avoid anxiety, we must change the way we think about anxiety.

To do so, to live with anxiety, would be to keep open the question, "What do you want from me?" While this will mean living with anxiety, it can also be therapeutic. This can be seen in Greta Gerwig's 2023 film, *Barbie*. We can read the film as a journey from fantasy to anxiety. In this journey, patriarchy is obviously the main target, but even here we see, in Ken's journey, which for most of the film goes in the opposite direction of Barbie's, that is, from anxiety to fantasy, that patriarchy is based on a fantasy of non-castration that aims to avoid castration anxiety. It is not just the inequality in Barbie land that disturbs Ken; he is bothered by his own anxiety over what Barbie wants and where he fits into her desire. The problem is that Barbie lacks nothing. Her lack of lack causes anxiety in Ken. But he finds a path to addressing that anxiety in patriarchy.

For her part, we could say that at the beginning of the film, Barbie lacks nothing. She is happy. She is not anxious. Until thoughts of death intrude, and she begins to wonder about the point of it all; she wonders about why she is here. Her journey out of Barbieland is a journey of discovery in which she comes to realize the role of the Other in her life in causing her desire and anxiety. The part of the plot that involves the attempt to overthrow the patriarchy is perhaps its weakest point. The anti-patriarchal movement depends on the tactic of voter suppression. They take advantage of the Kens' castration anxiety to distract them so that they miss the vote. I would have preferred an anti-patriarchal movement that demonstrated to the Kens the negative effects the patriarchy was having on them, forcing them into a joyless display of over-compensation for the loss of the phallus that prevented them from experiencing the creativity and aliveness Ruti associates with anxiety.

But at the end, the film returns, brilliantly, to its core idea regarding the overthrow not of patriarchy, per se, but the undermining of the fantasies we have about the Other's desire. The final scene builds in the audience an expectation that Barbie is on her way to a powerful corporate job, only to reveal that she is going to her first visit with a gynecologist. She has become a sexual being, which is to say, she has become a lacking subject. Then the film ends with Billie Eilish's song, "What Was I Made for?" The song has become an unlikely anthem, moving audiences to tears at Eilish's concerts and spawning millions of TikTok videos in which women (and some men) create videos pointing to both the traumas and joys of life as women. It is not a cry of defiance against patriarchy, though, but an expression of anxiety that, expressed through Eilish's moody, soulful voice, becomes cathartic. The song says everything this book has been trying to express:

I used to float, now I just fall down
I used to know but I'm not sure now[7]

The song expresses the phantasmatic nature of life when this anxiety is disavowed, as it is at the beginning of the film when Barbie is living in her fantasy not lacking: ". . . I was an ideal/Looked so alive, turns out I'm not real/ Just something you paid for . . ." It touches on the nonexistence of the sexual relationship, too: "When did it end? All the enjoyment/I'm sad again, don't tell my boyfriend/It's not what he's made for . . ." In the fantasy world of Barbieland, Barbie and Ken are not sexual beings. They have no genitals. They have no lack. Barbie's aliveness only begins with lack and anxiety (which is when we first hear this song).[8]

To write in defense of anxiety is not to write in defense of precarity, nor to make light of the debilitating forms of anxiety that keep people from functioning in their daily lives. Rather, it is to, like Barbie, find a way to interrogate the fantasies that shape our lives and dominate our subjective experience and intersubjective relationships. It is to ask, as Eilish does in her song, "What was I made for?" while also thinking that "happy" is "Something I'm not, but something I can be/Something I wait for/Something I'm made for . . ."

NOTES

1. Philip Larkin, "Aubade," available from the Poetry Foundation: https://www.poetryfoundation.org/poems/48422/aubade-56d229a6e2f07.

2. Rob Reiner, Director, *The Bucket List* (Warner Brothers, 2008).

3. Milan Kundera, *The Unbearable Lightness of Being*, trans. Michael Henry Heim (New York: Harper Collins, 1984), 8.

4. This paper, Mari Ruti, "Creativity Between Anxiety and Aliveness" was presented on April 21, 2023 at the Lack Conference at the University of Vermont. It was posthumously published in *Sublation*, June 17, 2023. Available here: https://www.sublationmag.com/post/creativity-between-anxiety-and-aliveness.

5. Ruti, "Creativity Between Anxiety and Aliveness."

6. Mari Ruti, *The Singularity of Being: Lacan and the Immortal Within* (New York: Fordham University Press, 2012), 162–164.

7. Billie Eilish, "What Was I Made for?" *Barbie: The Album*, July 13, 2023.

8. Greta Gerwig, *Barbie* (Warner Brother, 2023). Eilish, "What Was I Made For?".

Bibliography

Ahmed, Sara. *The Cultural Politics of Emotion*. Edinburgh: Edinburgh University Press, 2004, Second Edition, 2014.

Ahmed, Sara. *The Promise of Happiness*. Durham and London: Duke University Press, 2010.

Bechdel, Alison. *Fun Home: A Family Tragicomic*. Boston and New York: Houghton Mifflin Company, 2006.

Butler, Judith. *Gender Trouble: Feminism and the Subversion of Identity*. New York and London: Routledge, 2007, first published 1990.

Butler, Judith. *The Psychic Life of Power: Theories in Subjection*. Stanford, CA: Stanford University Press, 1997.

Camus, Albert. *The Plague*. Translated by Stuart Gilbert. New York: Vintage Books, 1991.

Chow, Rey. *The Protestant Ethnic and The Spirit of Capitalism*. New York: Columbia University Press, 2002.

Coates, Ta-Nehisi. *Between the World and Me*. New York: Spiegel & Grau, 2015.

Copjec, Joan. *Read My Desire: Lacan against the Historicists*. London and New York: Verso, 1994, 2015.

Dawkins, Richard. *The Blind Watchmaker: Why the Evidence of Evolution Reveals a Universe Without Design*. New York and London: W.W. Norton & Company, 1996.

Dolar, Mladan. "'I Shall Be with You on Your Wedding-Night': Lacan and the Uncanny." *October*, 58 (Autumn, 1991), 5–23.

Du Bois, W.E.B. *The Souls of Black Folk*. New York, London, Toronto, and Sydney: Simon & Schuster Paperbacks, 2009.

Eilish, Billie. "What Was I Made For?" *Barbie: The Album*, July 13, 2023.

Fanon, Frantz. *Black Skin, White Masks*. Translated by Richard Philcox. New York: Grove Press, 2008.

Fanon, Frantz. *Peau Noire, Masques Blancs*. Las Vegas: Kiyikaat Editions, 2022.

Felder, Stephen. "Screening Neoliberalism in *Nightcrawler* and *The Wolf of Wall Street*." In *Screening the Crisis: U.S. Cinema and Social Change in the Wake of the 2008 Crash*. Edited by Juan A. Tarancón and Hilaria Loyo, 83–96. New York, London, and Dublin: Bloomsbury Academic, 2022.

Fields, Karen E. and Barbara J. Fields. *Racecraft: The Soul of Inequality in American Life*. London and New York: Verso, 2012, 2014.

Fleetwood, Nicole. *Troubling Vision: Performance, Visuality, and Blackness*. Chicago, IL: University of Chicao Press, 2011.

Foucault, Michel. *Discipline and Punish: The Birth of the Prison*. Translated by Alan Sheridan. New York: Vintage Books, 1995, Second Vintage edition, 1997.

Foucault, Michel. *The Hermeneutics of the Subject: Lectures at the Collège de France 1981-1982*. New York: Picador, 2001.

Freud, Sigmund. *Civilization and Its Discontents*. Translated by James Strachey. New York and London: W.W. Norton & Company, 1961.

Freud, Sigmund. *Das Unbehagen in der Kultur*. Berlin: Dearbooks, 2016. Originally published in 1930.

Freud, Sigmund. *Inhibitions, Symptoms, and Anxiety*. Translated by Alix Strachey. New York and London: W.W. Norton & Company, 1959.

Freud, Sigmund. *On Sexuality: Three Essays on the Theory of Sexuality and Other Works*. Edited by Angela Richards and translated by James Strachey. London and New York: Penguin, 1991.

Freud, Sigmund. *The Uncanny*. Translated by David McLintock. London and New York: Penguin, 2003. The German text of this essay can be found at the Internet Archive: https://www.gutenberg.org/files/34222/34222-h/34222-h.htm. Originally published in Imago. *Zeitschrift für Anwendung der Psychoanalyse auf die Geisteswissenschaften* V (1919). S. 297–324.

Freud, Sigmund. *The Wolfman and Other Cases*. Translated by Louise Adey Huish. New York: Penguin Books, 2003.

Friedlander, Jennifer. "In Medium Race: Traversing the Fantasy of Post-Race Discourse." In *Lacan and Race: Racism, Identity, and Psychoanalytic Theory*. Edited by Sheldon George and Derek Hook, 105–120. New York: Routledge, 2022.

George, Sheldon. *Trauma and Race: A Lacanian Study of African American Racial Identity*. Waco, TX: Baylor University Press, 2001.

Gerwig, Greta, Director. *Barbie*. Warner Brothers, 2023.

Grant, Annetta and Jay M. Handelman. "Dysplacement and the Professionalization of the Home." *The Journal of Consumer Research*, 49 (2023), 882–903.

Halberstam, Jack. *Female Masculinity*. Durham, NC and London: Duke University Press, 1998.

Halberstam, Jack. Trans*: *a Quick and Quirky Account of Gender Variability*. Oakland, CA: University of California Press, 2018.

Hall, Stuart. *Cultural Studies 1983. A Theoretical History*. Edited by Jennifer Daryl Slack and Lawrence Grossberg. Durham, NC and London: Duke University Press, 2016.

Hegel, G.W.F. *Phenomenology of Spirit*. Translated by A.V. Miller. Oxford, New York, Toronto, and Melbourne: Oxford University Press, 1977.

Heidegger, Martin. *Being and Time*. Translated by John Macquarrie and Edward Robinson. New York, London, Toronto, Sydney, New Delhi, and Auckland: Harper & Row, 1962, reprint 2007.

Heidegger, Martin. *Sein und Zeit.* Elfte, unveränderte Auflage. Tübingen: Max Niemery Verlag, 1967.

Heidegger, Martin. “The Origin of the Work of Art.” In *Poetry, Language, Thought.* Translated by Albert Hofstadter, 17–76. New York: Harper & Row, 1972.

Heidegger, Martin. “What is Metaphysics?” In *Basic Writings.* Edited by David Farrell Krell, 93–110. London, Toronto, Sydney, New Delhi, and Auckland: Harper Perennial, 2008.

Hoffman, E.T.A. “Sandman.” In *Tales of Hoffman.* Edited and translated by R.J. Hollingdale. London and New York: Penguin, 1982.

Holder, Alex. “A Historical-Critical Edition.” In *Translating Freud.* Edited by Darius Gray Ornston, Jr., 75–96. New Haven, CT and London: Yale University Press, 1992.

hooks, bell. “The Oppositional Gaze: Black Female Spectatorship.” In *Movies and Mass Culture.* Edited by John Belton, 247–265. New Brunswick, NJ: Rutgers University Press, 1996.

Horwitz, Allan V. *Anxiety: A Short History.* Baltimore: Johns Hopkins University Press, 2013.

Huh, Jinny. *The Arresting Eye: Race and the Anxiety of Detection.* Charlottesville and London: University of Virginia Press, 2015.

Hyppolite, Jean. *Genesis and Structure of Hegel’s Phenomenology.* Translated by Samuel Cherniak and John Heckman. Evanston, IL: Northwestern University Press, 1974.

Jameson, Fredric. *Postmodernism: Or, the Cultural Logic of Late Capitalism.* Durham, NC: Duke University Press, 1991.

Kierkegaard, Soren. *The Concept of Anxiety.* Edited and translated by Reidar Thomte and Albert B. Anderson. Princeton, NJ: Princeton University Press, 1980.

Kundera, Milan. *The Unbearable Lightness of Being.* Translated by Michael Henry Heim. New York: Harper Collins, 1984.

Lacan, Jacques. *Le Séminaire Livre X, L’angoisse.* Edited by Jacques-Alain Miller. Paris: Editions du Seuil, 2004.

Lacan, Jacques. “Remarks on Daniel Lagache’s Presentation: ‘Psychoanalysis and Personality Structure.” In *Écrits.* Edited and translated by Bruce Fink, 543–574. New York and London: W.W. Norton & Company, 2006.

Lacan, Jacques. *Seminar VII: The Ethics of Psychoanalysis.* Edited by Jacques-Alain Miller. Translated by Dennis Porter. New York and London: W.W. Norton & Company, 1992.

Lacan, Jacques. *Seminar X: Anxiety.* Edited by Jacques Alain Miller. Translated by A.R. Price. Cambridge and Malden, MA: Polity Press, 2014.

Lacan, Jacques. *Seminar XI: The Four Fundamental Concepts of Psychoanalysis.* Edited by Jacques-Alain Miller. Translated by Alan Sheridan. New York and London: W.W. Norton & Company, 1998.

Lacan, Jacques. *Seminaire XVII: L’enverse de psychanalyse.* Edited by Jacques-Alain Miller. Paris: Editions du Seuil, 1991.

Lacan, Jacques. *Seminar XVII: The Other Side of Psychoanalysis.* Edited by Jacques-Alain Miller. Translated by Russell Grigg. New York and London: W.W. Norton and Company, 2007.

Lacan, Jacques. *Séminaire XX: Encore.* Edited by Jacques-Alain Miller. Paris: Éditions du Seuil, 1975.

Lacan, Jacques. *Seminar XX: Encore, On Feminine Sexuality, The Limits of Love and Knowledge.* Edited by Jacques-Alain Miller. Translated by Bruce Fink. New York and London: W.W. Norton and Company, 1998.

Lacan, Jacques. "The Mirror Stage as Formative of the *I* Function." In *Écrits.* Translated by Bruce Fink, 75–81. New York and London: W.W. Norton & Company, 2006.

Lacan, Jacques. "The Instance of the Letter in the Unconscious." In *Écrits.* Translated by Bruce Fink, 412–441. New York and London: W.W. Norton & Company, 2006.

Lacan, Jacques. "The Subversion of the Subject and the Dialectic of Desire." In *Écrits.* Translated by Bruce Fink, 671–702. New York and London: W.W. Norton & Company, 2006.

Larkin, Philip. "Aubade." Available from the Poetry Foundation: https://www.poetryfoundation.org/poems/48422/aubade-56d229a6e2f07.

May, Rollo. *The Meaning of Anxiety.* New York: The Ronald Press Company, 1950.

McGowan, Todd. *Psychoanalytic Film Theory and The Rules of the Game.* New York, London, Delhi, and Sydney: Bloomsbury Academic, 2015.

McGowan, Todd. *The Racist Fantasy.* New York, London, Oxford, New Delhi, and Sydney: Bloomsbury Academic, 2022.

McGowan, Todd. *Universality and Identity Politics.* New York: Columbia University Press, 2020.

Merleau-Ponty, Maurice. *Phenomenology of Perception.* Translated by Donald A. Landes. London and New York: Routledge, 2012.

Mulvey, Laura. "Visual Pleasure and Narrative Cinema." Reproduced in Laura Mulvey, *Visual and Other Pleasures.* Bloomington and Indianapolis: Indiana University Press, 1989.

Musser, Amber Jamilla. *Sensual Excess: Queer Femininity and Brown Jouissance.* New York: New York University Press, 2018.

Ornston, Darius Gray, Jr. "Improving Strachey's Freud." In *Translating Freud.* Edited by Darius Gray Ornston, Jr., 1–23. New Haven, CT and London: Yale University Press, 1992.

Peters, Torrey. *Detransition, Baby.* New York: One World, 2020.

Plato. *Symposium*, Greek text dited by John Burnet. Oxford: Oxford University Press, 1905.

Plato. *The Republic.* Greek text edited by S.R. Slings. Oxford: Oxford University Press, 2003.

Reed, T.V. *Digitized Lives: Culture, Power and Social Change in the Internet Era.* New York and London: Routledge, Second edition, 2019.

Reiner, Rob, Director. *The Bucket List.* Warner Brothers, 2008.

Rilke, Rainer Maria. *Duino Elegies: Bilingual Edition.* Translated by Edward Snow. New York: North Point Press, 2000.

Rivera, Miguel. "'[D]ifferent Even from our 'Own' Differences': Racial Signification and the Legacy of Lacanian Sexuation." *Word and Text: A Journal of Literary Studies and Linguistics*, VII (2017), 168–184.

Rose, Jacqueline. *Sexuality in the Field of Vision.* London and New York: Verso, 1986, 2005.

Rothenberg, Molly Anne. *The Excessive Subject: A New Theory of Social Change.* Cambridge and Malden, MA: Polity Press, 2010.

Roudinesco, Elisabeth. *Jacques Lacan.* Cambridge: Polity Press, 1999.

Ruti, Mari. "Creativity Between Anxiety and Aliveness." Presented on April 21, 2023 at the Lack Conference at the University of Vermont. It was posthumously published in *Sublation*, June 17, 2023. Available here: https://www.sublationmag.com/post/creativity-between-anxiety-and-aliveness.

Ruti, Mari. *Penis Envy and Other Bad Feelings.* New York: Columbia University Press, 2018.

Ruti, Mari. *The Singularity of Being: Lacan and the Immortal Within.* New York: Fordham University Press, 2012.

Salecl, Renata. *On Anxiety.* London and New York: Routledge, 2004.

Sartre, Jean-Paul. *Being and Nothingness.* Translated by Hazel E. Barnes. New York, London, Toronto, and Sydney: Washington Square Press, 1956.

Seshadri-Crooks, Kalpana. *Desiring Whiteness.* London: Routledge, 2000.

Soler, Collette. *Lacanian Affects: The Function of Affect in Lacan's Work.* Translated by Bruce Fink. London and New York: Routledge, 2016.

Sontag, Susan. *On Photography.* New York: Picador, 1973.

Spillers, Hortense. "'All the Things You Could be by Now, If Sigmund Freud's Wife Was your Mother': Psychoanalysis and Race." *boundary,* 23, no. 3 (1996), 74–141.

Terada, Rei. *Feeling in Theory.* Cambridge, MA: Harvard University Press, 2001.

Tone, Andrea. *The Age of Anxiety: A History of America's Turbulent Affair with Tranquilizers.* New York: Basic Books, 2008.

Trigg, Dylan. *Topophobia: A Phenomenology of Anxiety.* London, Oxford, New York, Sydney, and New Delhi: Bloomsbury Academic, 2017.

Tyburazy, Jennifer. *Sex Museums: The Politics and Performance of Display.* Chicago, IL and London: University of Chicago Press, 2016.

Viego, Antonio. Dead Subjects: *Toward a Politics of Loss in Latino Studies.* Durham, NC and London: Duke University Press, 2007.

Weber, Max. *The Protestant Ethic and the Spirit of Capitalism.* Translated by Talcott Parsons. London and New York: Routledge, 1992.

Webster, Jamieson. *Conversion Disorder: Listening to the Body in Psychoanalysis.* New York: Columbia University Press, 2019.

Yerushalmy, Jonathan. "'I Want to Destroy Whatever I Want': Bing's AI Chatbot Unsettles US Reporter." *The Guardian*, February 17, 2023, (online) https://www.theguardian.com/technology/2023/feb/17/i-want-to-destroy-whatever-i-want-bings-ai-chatbot-unsettles-us-reporter.

Žižek, Slavoj. *Sublime Object of Ideology.* London and New York: Verso, 1989.

Žižek, Slavoj. *The Metastases of Enjoyment.* London and New York: Verso, 1994, 2005.

Žižek, Slavoj. *The Plague of Fantasies.* London and New York: Verso, 1997, 2008.

Zupančič, Alenka. *What is Sex*? Cambridge, MA and London: The MIT Press, 2017.

Index

About the Author

Stephen Felder is Professor of Humanities at Irvine Valley College. He received his PhD from the University of California, Irvine, and has taught at UC Irvine, UC Riverside, and Scripps College. His recent research and writing have focused on Cultural Studies and Critical Theory with a focus on the work of Lacan, Heidegger, Merleau-Ponty, and Žižek in relation to television, film, and twenty-first-century culture.

www.ingramcontent.com/pod-product-compliance
Ingram Content Group UK Ltd.
Pitfield, Milton Keynes, MK11 3LW, UK
UKHW041837031026
15587UKWH00002B/834

9 781666 947212